AAT

INTERMEDIATE

(NVQ AND DIPLOMA PATHWAY)

REVISION **COMPANION**   Unit 5

Maintaining Financial
Records and Preparing
Accounts

LEARNING MEDIA

Eighth edition April 2008
First edition 2001

ISBN 9780 7517 4633 4 (previous edition 9780 7517 3229 0)

British Library Cataloguing-in-Publication Data
A catalogue record for this book is available from the British Library

Published by

BPP Learning Media Ltd
BPP House
Aldine Place
London
W12 8AA

www.bpp.com/learningmedia

Printed in Great Britain by
Martins the Printers
Berwick-upon-Tweed

Your learning materials, published by BPP Learning Media Ltd, are printed on paper sourced from sustainable, managed forests.

All our rights reserved. No part of this publication may be reproduced, stored in a retrieval system or transmitted, in any form or by any means, electronic, mechanical, photocopying, recording or otherwise, without the prior written permission of BPP Learning Media Ltd.

We are grateful to the AAT for permission to reproduce specimen assessments and examples from previous assessments. The answers to the specimen exam assessment and sample simulation have been produced by the AAT. All other answers have been prepared by BPP Learning Media Ltd.

©
BPP Learning Media Ltd
2008

CONTENTS

Introduction (v)

Chapter activities		Questions	Answers
1	Revision of how accounting systems work	1	295
2	Revision of double entry bookkeeping	7	299
3	Introduction to financial statements	21	313
4	Value added tax	25	319
5	Capital expenditure	31	323
6	Depreciation of fixed assets	35	327
7	Disposal of fixed assets	37	331
8	Accruals and prepayments	53	345
9	Bad and doubtful debts	59	349
10	Control account reconciliations	65	355
11	Errors and the suspense account	77	363
12	Stock	87	371
13	From trial balance to final accounts – sole trader	91	375
14	The extended trial balance	99	395
15	Partnerships	111	407
16	Incomplete records	123	427
Practice Simulation 1: Candle Contracts		131	437
Practice Simulation 2: Brinton Longhaul Services		155	449
Practice Exam 1: Ammar		205	475
Practice Exam 2: Mark Goss		223	485
Practice Exam 3: Ace Cars		239	495
Practice Exam 4: Ebony Gee		259	507
Practice Exam 5: PL Trading		277	519

INTRODUCTION

This is BPP Learning Media's AAT Revision Companion for Unit 5, Maintaining Financial Records and Preparing Accounts. It is part of an integrated package of AAT materials.

It has been written in conjunction with the BPP Course Companion and has been carefully designed to enable students to practise all aspects of the requirements of the Standards of Competence and performance criteria. It is fully up to date as at April 2008 and reflects the Standards of Competence and the exams and assessments set to date.

This Revision Companion contains these key features:

- graded activities corresponding to each chapter of the Course Companion
- the AAT's practice simulation for Unit 5
- a further practice simulation for the Unit
- a range of tasks from recent AAT exams, up to and including December 2007

The emphasis in all activities and questions is on the practical application of the skills acquired.

Tutors adopting our Companions (minimum of ten Course Companions and ten Revision Companions per Unit, or ten Combined Companions as appropriate) are entitled to free access to the Lecturers' Area resources, including the Tutor Companion. To obtain your log-in, e-mail lecturersvc@bpp.com.

Home Study students are also entitled to access to additional resources. You will have received your log-in details on registration.

If you have any comments about this book, please e-mail helendarch@bpp.com or write to Helen Darch AAT range manager, BPP Learning Media Ltd, BPP House, Aldine Place, London W12 8AA.

Note: Diploma Pathway

This book is suitable for all students preparing for AAT Unit 5, both NVQ and Diploma Pathway. Diploma Pathway students, however, are not required to complete a simulation for this Unit, so they can ignore the two practice simulation that are included. These do, however, provide useful practice for the techniques required for Unit 5, so Diploma students in need of further practice can use them for that purpose, if they so choose.

chapter 1:
REVISION OF HOW ACCOUNTING SYSTEMS WORK

1   **Complete the following sentences:**

a)   When a sale is made today but payment is not to be made for two weeks this is a
.... sale.

b)   When goods are purchased on credit the business will owe money to a ....
.

c)   When a customer returns goods that have been purchased these are known as
....

d)   When a business purchases an item for long term use it is known as ....
expenditure.

e)   If goods are returned to a supplier we would expect to receive a ....
.... from the supplier.

f)   When cheques are received from customers through the post they are initially recorded on a
....

2 **In which primary record would the following documents be recorded?**

Transaction	Primary record

a) Credit note received from a supplier

b) Invoice sent out to a customer

c) Payment by cheque to a supplier

d) Payment by cheque for goods

e) Credit note sent out to a customer

f) Cheque received from a customer

g) Payment of the telephone bill

h) Reimbursement in cash for a business
expense paid by an employee

i) Invoice received from a supplier

3 Picture This is a small firm operating a picture framing workshop. Its business is the framing of items submitted by business clients, mostly retail shops, all of whom are offered credit but many of whom pay by cash or debit/credit card. Its sole proprietor is Harry Gold.

All cash and cheques paid and received are recorded in an analysed cash book. All sales are charged to VAT at the standard rate of 17.5%. When checking the bank statements in previous months, you have found that a number of items of income and expenditure have appeared on the statement for which you can find no information, and have had to seek clarification from Harry Gold by means of a formal memo.

The cash book balance at 1 October 2007 was £2,190.87 overdrawn.

a) Refer to the paying in slip and the BACS list below.

Write up the receipts and payments sides of the cash book for these items and extract totals. Note that no discount was allowed against any of the receipts from debtors.

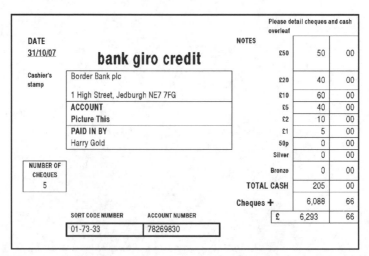

Tutorial note. Cash received is cash sales, whereas cheques received are from debtors. The BACS payment is for salaries.

Border Bank plc

1 High Street, Jedburgh NE7 7FG

Sort code 01-73-33

BACS Payment Listing

Payment ref:	BACS
Name of customer:	Picture This Park Street Jedburgh NE 5 7SD
Account number:	78269830
Date:	26 October 2007

Authority is hereby given to Border Bank plc to make the following payments by BACS transfer from the account designated above

Payee	Sort code	Account number	Amount £
Sarah Johnson	72-09-25	87920348	1,239.87
Robert Callaghan	72-87-09	37849220	1,027.67
Yussef Mohammed	65-26-54	87349209	1,110.70
Total			3,378.24

Please make these payments as soon as possible and debit our account with the total shown above

Authorised signature

Harry Gold

Date

26/10/07

CASHBOOK: RECEIPTS

Date	Details	Cash	Discount allowed	Sales Ledger Control	Cash sales	VAT	Capital	Interest
		£	£	£	£	£	£	£
2007								
5 October	Cash/cheques	7,309.83	245.02	6,959.41	298.23	52.19		
9 October	BACS receipt	1,293.94		1,293.94				
12 October	Cash/cheques	2,738.64	67.00	1,212.86	1,298.54	227.24		
17 October	Cash/cheques	800.00		800.00				
24 October	Cash/cheques	5,309.30	278.27	3,663.72	1,400.50	245.08		

CASHBOOK: PAYMENTS

Date	Details	Cheque No	Cash	Discount received	Purchase Ledger Control	Other
2007			£	£	£	£
1 October	Jedburgh County Council	DD	1,092.87			1,092.87
1 October	Society of Picture Framers	DD	250.00			250.00
2 October	Timbmet Wood Ltd	1397	3,298.93	45.00	3,298.93	
3 October	Glass Products Ltd	1398	5,209.36		5,209.36	
7 October	Lamination Ltd	1399	1,376.84	24.50	1,376.84	
10 October	The Contract Cleaning Co	1400	563.37		563.37	
11 October	Just a Minute Courier Company	1401	357.00		357.00	
12 October	Lynn's Caterers	1402	175.00		175.00	
15 October	Thor Stationery	1403	736.83	13.00	736.83	
16 October	Kinetic Electricity Ltd	DD	200.00			200.00
20 October	High Stick Adhesives	1404	245.09		245.09	
21 October	Big Gas Company Ltd	BACS	150.00			150.00
22 October	Quality Paper Company	1405	1,983.09		1,983.09	
24 October	Glass Ceramics Ltd	1406	3,736.94	51.00	3,736.94	
27 October	Chrome Sheeting Ltd	1407	398.65		398.65	
	Analysis:					
	Direct labour					
	Administration					
	Drawings					

b) Using the bank statement below, update the 'cash' columns in the receipts and payments side of the cash book. Do not analyse the receipts or payments. Calculate the balance on the cash book at 31 October 2007.

Note that any items on the bank statement dated before 13 October that are not in the cash book, were in the cash book in September 2007 and should not be entered in the October cash book.

Border Bank plc

1 High Street, Jedburgh NE7 7FG

STATEMENT

Account Name: Picture This

Statement no: 24

Account No: 78269830   Sort code: 01-73-33

Date	Details	Payments	Receipts	Balance	
2007		£	£	£	
1 Oct	Balance brought forward			457.01	OD
2 Oct	DD – Jedburgh County Council	1,092.87		1,549.88	OD
2 Oct	DD – Society of Picture Framers	250.00		1,799.88	OD
6 Oct	CC		7,309.83	5,509.95	
8 Oct	Cheque issued 1395	523.99		4,985.96	
9 Oct	Cheque issued 1398	5,209.36		223.40	OD
9 Oct	BACS receipt		1,293.94	1,070.54	
9 Oct	Cheque issued 1396	1,209.87		139.33	OD
10 Oct	Cheque issued 1399	1,376.84		1,516.17	OD
13 Oct	Cheque issued 1400	563.37		2,079.54	OD
13 Oct	CC		2,738.64	659.10	
15 Oct	Cheque issued 1402	175.00		484.10	
16 Oct	DD – Kinetic Electricity	200.00		284.10	
18 Oct	CC		800.00	1,084.10	
20 Oct	Cheque issued 1403	736.83		347.27	
21 Oct	BACS payment – Big Gas Co	150.00		197.27	
24 Oct	Cheque issued 1404	245.09		47.82	OD
25 Oct	CC		5,309.30	5,261.48	
25 Oct	ATM withdrawal	100.00		5,161.48	
25 Oct	Debit card payment to Siren.com	248.97		4,912.51	
27 Oct	Cheque issued 1405	1,983.09		2,929.42	
27 Oct	BACS receipt from Harry Gold Personal Account		5,000.00	7,929.42	
27 Oct	Interest paid		459.35	8,388.77	
28 Oct	BACS payment – salaries	3,378.24		5,010.53	

Key   DD: Direct Debit   BACS: Bankers automated clearing services
        O/D: Overdrawn   ATM – automated teller machine cash withdrawal

---

c) Draft a memo to Harry Gold seeking clarification of any receipts or payments as necessary.

d) Assuming Harry's response indicates that the queried payments are personal expenditure by him, and that queried receipts other than interest are payments of capital by him, analyse the receipts and payments that you have entered in, and further analyse the 'other' column on the payments side of the cash book.

chapter 2:
REVISION OF DOUBLE ENTRY BOOKKEEPING

1 What are the two effects of each of these transactions for accounting purposes?

Transaction		Two effects
a)	Payment of £15,000 into a business bank account by an individual in order to start up a business	DR Bank 15,000 CR Capital 15,000
b)	Payment by cheque of £2,000 for rent of a business property	DR Rent 2,000 CR Bank 2,000
c)	Payment by cheque of £6,200 for purchase of a delivery van	DR Motor Vehicle 6,200 CR Bank 6,200
d)	Payment by cheque of £150 for vehicle licence for the van	DR Vehicle Licence 150 CR Bank 150
e)	Payment by cheque of £2,100 for goods for resale	DR Purchases 2,100 CR Bank 2,100
f)	Sale of goods for cash and cheques of £870	DR Bank 870 CR Sales 870
g)	Purchase of goods for resale on credit for £2,800	DR Purchases 2,800 CR PLCA 2,800
h)	Payment by cheque for petrol of £80	DR ~~Petrol~~ Van Exp CR Bank 80
i)	Sale of goods on credit for £3,400	DR SLCA CR Sales 3,400
j)	Payment by cheque of £1,500 to creditors	DR PLCA 1,500 CR Bank 1,500
k)	Payment by cheque of electricity bill of £140	DR Electricity 140 CR Bank 140
l)	Receipt of cheque from debtor of £1,600	DR Bank CR SLCA 1,600
m)	Withdrawal of £500 of cash for the owner's personal living costs	DR Drawings 500 CR Bank 500
n)	Payment by cheque for petrol of £70	DR ~~Petrol~~ Van Exp CR Bank 70

2 For each of the transactions in the previous activity enter the amounts into the ledger accounts given below:

Capital account

£		£
	Bank	15,000

Bank account

	£		£
Capital	15,000	Rent	2,000
Sales	870	Van Account	6,200
SLCA	1,600	Van Exp a/c	150
		Purchases	2,100
		Van Exp	80
		PLCA	1,500
		Electricity	140
		Drawings	900
		Van Exp	70

Rent account

	£		£
Bank	2,000		

Van account

	£		£
Bank	6,200		

Van expenses account

	£		£
Bank	150		
Bank	80		
Bank	70		

Purchases account

	£		£
Bank	2,100		
PLCA	2,800		

Sales account

	£		£
		Bank	870
		SLCA	3,400

Creditors account

	£		£
Purchases	2,800		
Bank	1,500		

Debtors account

	£		£
Sales	3,400	Bank	1,600

Electricity account

	£		£
Bank	140		

Drawings account

	£		£
Bank	500		

3 Balance each of the accounts from the previous activity and prepare a trial balance at the end of this initial period of trading.

4   Given below are the sales day book, sales returns day book and cash receipts book for a business for the week ending 28 May.

Sales day book

Date	Details	Total £
28 May	F Simpson T Weller K Finch	240 160 300
	Total	700

Sales returns day book

Date	Details	Total £
28 May	T Weller F Simpson	20 30
	Total	50

Cash receipts book

Date	Details	Total £	Cash sales £	Sales ledger £	Other £	Discounts allowed £
28 May	K Finch	280		280		10
	F Simpson	120		120		4
	Cash sales	210	210			
	T Weller	80		80		2
		690	210	480		16

You are required to:

a)   post the totals of the day books to the main ledger accounts given

b)   post the individual entries to the subsidiary ledger accounts given

c)   balance all of the ledger accounts

Main ledger

Sales account

	£		£
		21 May Balance b/d	12,370

Sales returns account

	£		£
21 May Balance b/d	1,050		

Sales ledger control account

	£		£
21 May Balance b/d	990		

Discounts allowed account

	£		£
21 May Balance b/d	124		

Subsidiary ledger

K Finch

	£		£
21 May Balance b/d	290		

T Weller

	£		£
21 May Balance b/d	220		

F Simpson

	£		£
21 May Balance b/d	480		

5   Touchstone Cycles Ltd is a small chain of cycle shops. Its business is to sell cycles, cycling equipment and repairs to the general public and certain business clients. Its sole proprietor is Mike Cuthbertson.

All cash, cheques and credit/debit card transactions paid and received are recorded in an analysed cash book. All sales are subject to VAT at 17.5%. Occasionally Mike Cuthbertson withdraws cash from the ATM for his own use. All ATM withdrawals are therefore treated as drawings.

a) Use the bank statement below to update the receipts and payments side of the cash book as required, and calculate the totals. You should ensure that both Assignia plc and Handley & Co are credit customers.

Note that any amounts in the cash book that are not on the bank statment will appear on the March bank statement, and any amounts on the bank statement dated before 10 February were in the January cash book and do not have to be entered in the February cash book.

Valley Banking Company plc
36, Jayes Street, Wallingford

STATEMENT

Account Name: Touchstone Cycles Ltd

Statement no: 19

Account No: 17639123   **Sort code:** 80-62-82

Date	Details	Payments	Receipts	Balance
		£	£	£
1 Feb	Balance brought forward			13,540.12
1 Feb	CC		398.00	13,938.12
1 Feb	DD South Oxon Council	231.50		13,706.62
	DD Thanet Pension Fund	500.00		13,206.62
3 Feb	CC		2,244.27	15,450.89
2 Feb	Cheque issued 6294	7,298.02		8,152.87
5 Feb	Interest paid		54.00	8,206.87
6 Feb	Cheque issued 6295	2,638.39		5,568.48
8 Feb	CC		3,160.47	8,728.95
9 Feb	Cheque issued 6296	4,029.38		4,699.57
9 Feb	Cheque issued 6291	719.71		3,979.86
10 Feb	S/O Mike Cuthbertson	3,000.00		979.86
10 Feb	BACS receipt – StraightCall Insurance		200.00	1,179.86
13 Feb	CC		1,584.02	2,763.88
15 Feb	CC		896.28	3,660.16
16 Feb	DD South Oxon Council	35.00		3,625.16
16 Feb	Cheque issued 6299	1,287.35		2,337.81
18 Feb	CC		3,746.95	6,084.76
20 Feb	Cheque issued 6300	1,243.66		4,841.10
22 Feb	CC		4,887.27	9,728.37
24 Feb	CC		582.33	10,310.70
25 Feb	BACS receipts – Assignia plc		6,283.02	16,593.72
22 Feb	DD Heartlands Electric	150.00		16,443.72
24 Feb	DD Midland Gas	90.00		16,353.72
25 Feb	Cheque returned unpaid – refer to Handley & Co	352.50		16,001.22
25 Feb	ATM withdrawal	200.00		15,801.22

Key   DD: Direct Debit   BACS: Bankers automated clearing services
        O/D: Overdrawn   ATM – automated teller machine cash withdrawal
        CC: Counter Credit

CASH BOOK: RECEIPTS

Date	Details	Bank	Discount allowed	Sales ledger control	Cash sales	VAT	Other
		£	£	£	£	£	£
2007							
2 Feb	Cheques etc paid in	2,244.27	25.00	1,928.20	269.00	47.07	
6 Feb	Interest paid	54.00					54.00
7 Feb	Cheques etc paid in	3,160.47	19.00	2,298.02	734.00	128.45	
10 Feb	BACS – StraightCall Insurance	200.00					200.00
12 Feb	Cheques etc paid in	1,584.02	14.50	1,290.27	250.00	43.75	
14 Feb	Cheques etc paid in	896.28		896.28			
17 Feb	Cheques etc paid in	3,746.95	65.00	3,291.29	387.80	67.86	
21 Feb	Cheques etc paid in	4,887.27	32.00	4,182.27	600.00	105.00	
23 Feb	Cheques etc paid in	582.33		582.33			
26 Feb	Cheques etc paid in	8,539.54	15.00	8,209.54	280.86	49.14	
	Sub-total	25,895.13	170.50	22,678.20	2,521.66	441.27	254.00
	Total						
Analysis	Disposals						200.00
	Interest						54.00
							254.00

CASH BOOK: PAYMENTS

Date	Details	Cheque No	Bank £	Discount received £	Purchase ledger control £	Other £
1 Feb	South Oxon Council (rates)	DD	231.50			231.50
1 Feb	Thanet Pension Fund (rent)	DD	500.00			500.00
2 Feb	Drake Bicycles	6295	2,638.39	20.00	2,638.39	
3 Feb	David Lett Shopfitting	6296	4,029.38	55.00	4,029.38	
7 Feb	Sama Newsagents	6297	176.93		176.93	
10 Feb	Mike Cuthbertson – drawings	S/O	3,000.00			3,000.00
11 Feb	Essex Cycles	6298	2,378.49	35.00	2,378.49	
12 Feb	Firebrand Tyres	6299	1,287.35	10.00	1,287.35	
15 Feb	Patrick's Pumps	6300	1,243.66		1,243.66	
16 Feb	South Oxon Council (waste collection)	DD	35.00			35.00
20 Feb	Crutchleys Accountants (fees)	6301	235.00		235.00	
21 Feb	Lurrells & Co (fees)	6302	293.75		293.75	
22 Feb	Heartlands Electric	DD	150.00			150.00
24 Feb	Midland Gas	DD	90.00			90.00
27 Feb	Salaries	BACS	4,622.12			4,622.12
	Sub-total		20,911.57	120.00	12,282.95	8,628.62
	Total					
	Analysis:					
	Sales ledger control					
	Staff costs					
	Administration/ overheads					
	Drawings					

b)   Analyse the 'other' column on the payments side of the cash book.

c) Post from both sides of the cash book to the main ledger accounts below, and calculate the balance on the bank ledger account.

Administration/overheads

Date	Details	Amount £	Date	Details	Amount £

Bank

Date	Details	Amount £	Date	Details	Amount £
1/2	Balance b/d	5,920.39			

Discount allowed and received

Date	Details	Amount £	Date	Details	Amount £

Disposals

Date	Details	Amount £	Date	Details	Amount £

Drawings

Date	Details	Amount £	Date	Details	Amount £

Interest received

Date	Details	Amount £	Date	Details	Amount £

Purchase ledger control

Date	Details	Amount £	Date	Details	Amount £

Sales

Date	Details	Amount £	Date	Details	Amount £

Sales ledger control

Date	Details	Amount £	Date	Details	Amount £

Staff costs

Date	Details	Amount £	Date	Details	Amount £

VAT

Date	Details	Amount £	Date	Details	Amount £

6   You have been given the following list of balances from the accounts of Pooley as at 31 December 2007.

	£
Stock as at 1 January 2007	22,000
Purchases	223,000
Sales	340,700
Discounts allowed	4,600
Discounts received	5,500
Returns in	6,700
Returns out	5,600
Wages and salaries	34,500
Bad debts	3,100
Carriage in	1,400
Carriage out	2,200
Other operating expenses	24,500
Trade debtors	34,000
Trade creditors	21,600
Provision for bad debts	450
Cash on hand	800
Bank overdraft	23,400
Capital	38,550
Property	50,000
Equipment	64,000
Provisions for depreciation at 1 January 2007	
Property	10,000
Equipment	25,000

You are required to lay out the trial balance and add up the debit and credit columns.

7   On 28 February, which is one month before the end of his financial year, the ledger accounts of A Hubble were as follows.

Cash

	£		£
Capital	9,500	Rent	2,750
Bank loan	3,000	Purchase ledger control	700
Sales	11,200	Interest	350
Sales ledger control	400	Electricity	400
		Telephone	180
		Drawings	1,300

Capital

	£		£
		Cash	9,500

Bank loan

	£		£
		Cash	3,000

Sales

	£		£
		Cash	11,200
		Sales ledger control	4,600

Sales ledger control

	£		£
Sales	4,600	Cash	400

Rent

	£		£
Cash	2,750		

Purchases

	£		£
Purchase ledger control	2,100		

Purchase ledger control

	£		£
Cash	700	Purchases	2,100

Interest

	£		£
Cash	350		

Electricity

	£		£
Cash	400		

Telephone

	£		£
Cash	180		

Drawings

	£		£
Cash	1,300		

During the last month of his financial year, A Hubble recorded the following transactions.

1) He bought goods for £2,000, half for credit and half for cash.

2) He paid the following:

    a) interest £20
    b) electricity £25
    c) telephone £12

3) He made sales of £3,500 of which £500 were for cash.

4) He received £220 from debtors.

You are required to:

a) post the transactions for March into the ledger accounts
b) balance off the ledger accounts and draw up a trial balance

chapter 3:
INTRODUCTION TO FINANCIAL STATEMENTS

1   Decide whether each of the following balances would be an asset, a liability, income or an expense.

Balance	Category
a) Salaries	....
b) Bank overdraft	....
c) Carriage inwards	....
d) Bank loan	....
e) Capital	....
f) Debtors	....
g) Purchases	....

2   Given below is a trial balance for a business. You are required to state whether each item in the trial balance falls into the category of asset, liability, income or expense.

Trial balance			**Category**
	£	£	
Rent	11,400		....
Sales		143,000	....
Stock	2,400		....
Creditors		6,000	....
Purchases	86,200		....
Drawings	17,910		....
Telephone	1,250		....
Discount received		80	....
Carriage outwards	400		....
Motor vehicles	32,600		....
Debtors	11,900		....
Discount allowed	120		....
Capital		40,000	....
Wages	20,600		....
Heat and light	1,600		....
Computer	2,400		....
Bank	300		....
	189,080	189,080	

3   A business has made sales during the year of £867,450. The opening stock of goods was £24,578 and the closing stock was £30,574. During the year there were purchases made of £426,489. The selling and distribution costs for the year were £104,366 and the general administration expenses totalled £87,689.

What is the gross profit for the year and the net profit for the year?

4   What are the main categories of items that appear on a balance sheet for a business?

5   Decide whether each of the following balances would be an asset or liability on the balance sheet, or an item of income or expense in a period end profit and loss account. Which would be neither (in which case have a stab at saying what it is)?

		Category
a)	A company car	....
b)	Interest on a bank overdraft	....
c)	A bank loan repayable in five years	....
d)	Petty cash of £25	....
e)	The portion of rent paid covering the period after the balance sheet date	....
f)	Freehold property	....
g)	Payment of wages for a manager with a two year service contract	....
h)	Payments into a pension fund	....
i)	A debtor who will pay in 18 months time	....
j)	A bad debt written off	....
k)	A patent	....

6   a)   What are the main reasons for and purposes behind preparing accounts, for sole traders and partnerships?

b)   Describe the form and function of the balance sheet and the profit and loss account.

7   On 1 January 2007, a business had assets of £10,000 and liabilities of £7,000. By 31 December 2007 it had assets of £15,000, liabilities of £10,000. The owner had contributed capital of £4,000. How much profit had the business made over the year?

8   For each of the following statements determine which accounting concept is being invoked:

a)   Computer software, although for long term use in the business, is charged to the profit and loss account when purchased as its value is small in comparison to the hardware.

Concept – *Materiality*

b)   The fixed assets of the business are valued at their net book value rather than the value for which they might be sold.

Concept – *Going concern*

c)   The expenses that the business incurs during the year are charged as expenses in the profit and loss account even if the amount of the expense has not yet been paid in cash.

Concept – *Accruals*.

9   a)   Explain the two pervasive accounting concepts dealt with in FRS 18 *Accounting Policies*.

b)   Explain each of the four objectives which according to FRS 18 should determine an organisation's choice of accounting policies.

10   What are the functions of SSAPs and FRSs?

chapter 4:
VALUE ADDED TAX

1 **Complete the following sentences:**

a) VAT on purchases is known as .... tax.

b) VAT on sales is known as .... tax.

c) VAT is paid by a VAT registered business to ....

d) Postal costs are an example of a supply which is .... from VAT.

e) If a car is purchased for use within a business the VAT is ....

2 Given below are the sales day book, sales returns day book and cash receipts book for a business for the week ended 30 June.

Date	Details	Gross £	VAT £	Net £
30 June	L Hibbard P Timms S David	493.50 305.50 176.25	73.50 45.50 26.25	420.00 260.00 150.00
	Totals	975.25	145.25	830.00

Sales returns day book

Date	Details	Gross £	VAT £	Net £
30 June	P Timms	28.20	4.20	24.00
	Totals	28.20	4.20	24.00

Cash receipts book

Date	Details	Total £	VAT £	Cash sales £	Sales ledger £	Discounts allowed £
30 June	S David	135.12			135.12	5.75
	Cash sales	399.50	59.50	340.00		
	L Hibbard	336.25			336.25	
	P Timms	157.80			157.80	
		1,028.67	59.50	340.00	629.17	5.75

You are required to:

a) post the day book totals to the main ledger accounts given
b) post the individual entries to the subsidiary sales ledger accounts given
c) balance each of the ledger accounts

Main ledger

Sales account

	£		£
		23 June Balance b/d	14,375.55

Sales returns account

	£		£
23 June Balance b/d	1,552.68		

Sales ledger control account

	£		£
23 June Balance b/d	3,226.50		

VAT account

	£		£
		23 June Balance b/d	1,263.50

Discounts allowed account

	£		£
23 June Balance b/d	235.47		

Sales ledger

S David

	£		£
23 June Balance b/d	662.50		

L Hibbard

	£		£
23 June Balance b/d	307.25		

P Timms

	£		£
23 June Balance b/d	612.80		

3   A business pays £1,410.00 for goods including VAT. What is the double entry for this purchase in the following circumstances:

a)   the business is registered for VAT
b)   the business is not registered for VAT?

4 A business has the following transactions in one week (all figures are exclusive of VAT at 17.5%).

	£
Credit purchases (at list price)	4,500
Sales on credit (at list price)	6,000
Purchase of a van	10,460
Entertaining	360
Purchase of a car	8,600

A settlement discount of £300 is available on the sales. All figures are given exclusive of VAT at 17.5%.

If the balance on the VAT account was £2,165 credit at the beginning of the week, what is the balance at the end of the week?

VAT

PLCA	787.50	Bal b/d	2,165.00
Van	1830.50	SLCA	997.50
Bal c/d	544.50		
	3162.50		3162.50
		Bal b/d	544.50

VAT   DR Purchases
Credit purchase 4,500 + 787.50 = 5287.50 DR VAT
                                           CR PLCA

Sales on Credit 6,000 - 300 = 5,700
                     |
                settlement
                discount   DR SLCA
        5,700 + 997.50 = 6,697.50 CR Sales
                VAT   CR VAT

                         VAT
Purchase of a van 10,460 + 1,830.50 = 12,290.50
                    DR Purchases
                    DR VAT
                    CR Bank

chapter 5:
CAPITAL EXPENDITURE

1   In each of the following circumstances determine how much capital expenditure has been incurred and how much revenue expenditure has been incurred by a company that is registered for VAT:

a)   An SN63 sanding machine has been purchased at a cost of £12,000 plus VAT. The delivery charge was £400 and the cost of training the staff to use it was £250. After its initial run it was cleaned at a cost of £100.

b)   A building has been purchased at a cost of £120,000. The surveyor's fees were an additional £400 and the legal fees £1,200. The building has been re-decorated at a total cost of £13,000.

c)   A new computer has been purchased at a cost of £10,600. In order to house the mainframe a room in the building has had to have a special air conditioning unit fitted at a cost of £2,450. The computer is supplied with software worth £1,000 and CDs with a value of £100.

d)   A salesman's car has been purchased at a cost of £14,000 plus VAT. The invoice also shows delivery costs of £50 and road fund licence of £160.

2   A business has just spent money on two of its machines. The SPK100 has been repaired after a breakdown at a cost of £2,400. The FL11 has had a new engine fitted at a cost of £3,100 which it is anticipated will extend its useful life to the business by four years.

Would these repairs be treated as capital expenditure or revenue expenditure?

SPK100 (repaired) – Revenue expenditure
(maintaining earning capacity)
FL11 (new engine) – Capital expenditure
(improving earning capacity)

3   Draft journal entries for each of the following transactions by a company that is registered for VAT:

a)   Purchase of a salesman's car for £12,000 plus VAT and road fund licence of £150 by cheques.

b)   Purchase of a machine for £15,400 plus VAT, on credit, and the alterations to the factory floor required that used employees' labour with a wage cost of £1,400.

c)   Purchase of a computer for £3,800 plus VAT by cheque which included £100 of printer paper and £50 of CDs.

d)   Redecorating of the room which houses the computer prior to its installation, £800 paid by cheque. Ignore VAT.

e)   Insurance of the new computer was paid by cheque of £200. Ignore VAT.

4   Write up the following transactions in the ledger accounts given:

a)   A machine was purchased for £13,500 plus VAT by cheque and installed using the business's own employees at a wage cost of £400 and own materials at a cost of £850.

b)   A building was purchased for £150,000 plus £20,000 of alterations in order to make it of use to the business. The unaltered parts of the building were then redecorated at a cost of £4,000.

Machinery account

	£		£
Balance b/d	103,400.00		

Buildings account

	£		£
Balance b/d	200,000.00		

VAT account

	£		£
		Balance b/d	13,289.60

Purchases account

	£		£
Balance b/d	56,789.50		

Wages account

	£		£
Balance b/d	113,265.88		

Buildings maintenance account

	£		£
Balance b/d	10,357.00		

Bank account

	£		£
Balance b/d	214,193.60		

5   Explain the differences between the following methods of funding the purchase of fixed assets:

a)   Borrowing
b)   Hire purchase
c)   Leasing

6   According to SSAP 21 *Accounting for Leases and Hire Purchase Contracts,* how does the accounting treatment of a finance lease differ from that of an operating lease?

chapter 6:
DEPRECIATION OF FIXED ASSETS

1   Explain why depreciation is charged on fixed assets, including the accounting concept that underlies this charge.

2   Calculate the depreciation charge on the straight line basis for each of the following fixed assets for the year ended 31 December 2007. Also calculate the net book value of each asset at 31 December 2007:

a)   Machine purchased for £17,400 on 1 January 2005 with an estimated useful economic life of 5 years and a zero scrap value.

b)   Machine purchased for £12,800 on 1 January 2006 with an estimated useful economic life of 4 years and an estimated scrap value of £2,000.

c)   Computer purchased for £4,600 on 1 January 2007 with an estimated useful economic life of 3 years and an estimated resale value of £700.

3   For each of the following fixed assets calculate the depreciation charge for the year ended 31 March 2007 and the net book value at that date:

a)   Machinery costing £24,600 purchased on 1 April 2006 which is to be depreciated at 20% on the reducing balance basis.

b)   Motor vehicle costing £18,700 purchased on 1 April 2004 which is to be depreciated at 25% on the reducing balance basis.

c)   Computer costing £3,800 purchased on 1 April 2005 which is to be depreciated at 30% on the reducing balance basis.

4   Calculate the depreciation charge for the year ended 31 December 2007 for each of the following fixed assets:

a)   Machine purchased on 1 May 2007 for £14,000. This is to be depreciated at the rate of 20% per annum on the straight-line basis.

b)   Office fittings and fixtures purchased on 1 June 2007 for £3,200. These are to be depreciated on the reducing balance basis at a rate of 25% with a full years charge in the year of purchase and no charge in the year of disposal.

c)   Computer purchased on 31 October 2007 for £4,400. This is to be depreciated at the rate of 40% per annum on the straight-line basis.

5   On 1 January of Year 1 Mr Floss purchased a candyfloss-making machine for his fairground stall. The machine cost £2,800 and has an estimated economic life of four years after which it will have no residual value. The financial year of the business ends on 31 December each year.

Calculate the annual depreciation charges on the machine for each of the four years on each of the following bases.

a)   The straight line basis
b)   The reducing balance method at 55% per annum

Note. Your workings should be to the nearest £.

chapter 7:
DISPOSAL OF FIXED ASSETS

1   A fixed asset was purchased on 1 April 2005 for £12,500 and is being depreciated at 30% per annum on the reducing balance basis, with a full year's charge in the year of disposal. On 31 March 2007 the asset was sold for £6,000.

What is the profit or loss on the sale of the fixed asset?

2   A fixed asset was purchased on 1 January 2005 for £25,000. It is being depreciated over its useful economic life of 5 years on the straight line basis with an estimated residual value of £3,000 and a full year's charge in the year of disposal. The asset was sold on 31 December 2007 for £11,000.

Show the accounting entries for this asset from the day of purchase to the day of sale in the following ledger accounts. The business has a balance sheet date of 31 December each year.

Fixed asset at cost account

£		£

Depreciation account

£		£

Provision for depreciation account

£		£

Disposal account

£		£

3 A motor vehicle had been purchased on 1 April 2005 for £13,800 and has been depreciated on the reducing balance basis at a rate of 30% per annum. It was sold on 31 March 2007 for £7,000.

You are required to write up the ledger accounts for the year ended 31 March 2007 to reflect the ownership and sale of this motor vehicle. A full year's charge for depreciation is to be charged in the year of disposal.

Depreciation expense account

£		£

Provision for depreciation account

£		£

Motor vehicle at cost account

£		£

Disposal account

£		£

4 Complete the following sentences:

a) A profit on disposal is sometimes described as .... depreciation.

b) A loss on disposal is sometimes described as .... depreciation.

5 A machine was purchased on 30 June 2005 for £15,600. The depreciation policy is to depreciate this asset at a rate of 25% per annum on a straight line basis, with a proportionate charge in the year of disposal. On 30 November 2007 the machine was sold for £6,000. The business has an accounting year ending 31 December.

Write up the disposal account to reflect the disposal of this asset.

Disposal account

£		£

6   A motor vehicle was purchased on 31 March 2005 for £12,800. This was then sold on 30 September 2007 for £4,000. The depreciation policy for motor vehicles is 25% reducing balance with a full years charge in the year of acquisition and no charge in the year of disposal. The business's year end is 31 July.

Write up the disposal account given to reflect the disposal of this asset.

Disposal account

£		£

7   A car was purchased by a business on 1 January 2005 for £20,000 and was being depreciated at 25% per annum straight line. On 31 December 2007 this car was part-exchanged for a new car with a total cost of £24,000. The part exchange value of the old car was £6,000.

Write up the cars at cost account and the disposal account to reflect the disposal of the old car and the purchase of the new car.

Cars at cost account

£		£

Disposal account

£		£

8 At 30 June 2007 the following balances were extracted from the ledger accounts of Emma & Co in respect of motor vehicles.

	Debit £	Credit £
Motor vehicles: cost	63,500	
Accumulated depreciation at 1 July 2006		38,000
Motor vehicles: disposals		800

During the year to 30 June 2007, the following took place.

1) A delivery van which was fully depreciated and had cost £1,000 was scrapped. No proceeds were received.

2) A car which had cost £2,500 and which had an accumulated depreciation balance of £1,500 was traded in for a new model priced at £4,000. A trade in allowance of £750 was received. Only the net cost of £3,250 has been entered into the books.

3) A car which cost £2,000 and had a written down value of £625 was sold for £800 (already credited to the disposals account).

4) A delivery van was sold for £1,250. It had cost £5,000 and a loss of £375 was made on its sale. The proceeds have been credited to the fixed asset account.

5) The depreciation charge for the year is £12,500.

You are required to:

a) prepare the motor vehicles (cost) account, the motor vehicles accumulated depreciation account and the motor vehicles disposals account, taking into consideration the information above.

b) show the amounts which would appear in the balance sheet as at 30 June 2007 in respect of motor vehicles.

9   Finbar the Butcher is a retail butcher operating in the town of Hexham. It is owned and run by Finbar O'Hanlon.

The firm prepares and sells a range of meat to wholesalers, restaurants and the general public. Its fixed assets comprise freehold buildings, which are not depreciated, in which there is a butchery, an office and a shop, plus Office and Shop Equipment, Butchery Equipment and Delivery Vehicles. There is a manual fixed asset register showing details of capital expenditure (but not revenue expenditure) incurred in acquiring or enhancing fixed assets, as well as details of depreciation or disposals. For each category of fixed asset the main ledger includes accounts for cost and accumulated depreciation (i.e. the balance sheet accounts). There is one depreciation charge ledger account (i.e. the expense recorded in the profit and loss account) for all classes of fixed asset.

Depreciation rates and methods are as follows:

Office and Shop Equipment	20% p.a. on cost (straight line basis)
Butchery Equipment	20% p.a. on net book value (reducing balance basis)
Delivery vehicles	25% p.a. on cost (straight line basis)

■   A full year's depreciation is charged in the year of an asset's acquisition, regardless of the exact date of acquisition.

■   No depreciation is charged in the year of an asset's disposal, regardless of the date of disposal.

■   Residual value is assumed to be nil in all cases.

Finbar O'Hanlon authorises all acquisitions and disposals of fixed assets by signing invoices.

a)   Finbar O'Hanlon has just handed you the suppliers' invoices below. These refer to the purchase of a new freezer for the Butchery, a new desk for the office and a new computerised till for the Shop.

■   Record the acquisitions in the fixed asset register.

■   Prepare journals to record the invoices in the main ledger.

INVOICE			
Quality Butchery Fittings **4 Smithfield** **London E1 5GH**			
VAT registration:	832 3682 34		
Date/tax point:	31 August 2007		
Customer:	Finbar the Butcher, 56 Main Street, Hexham		
Description		Rate	Total
		£	£
1 x 1,200 cubic feet freezer		15,000.00	15,000.00
Delivery and fitting		500.00	500.00
Approved *Finbar 2/9/07*			
Goods total			15,500.00
VAT		17.5%	2,658.25
Invoice total			18,158.25
2%, Net 30 days			

INVOICE			
JBJ Office Fittings **Yard Square** **Newcastle**			
VAT registration:	638 3349 239		
Date/tax point:	31 August 2007		
Customer:	Finbar the Butcher, 56 Main Street, Hexham		
Description		Rate	Total
		£	£
1 x solid beech desk		800.00	800.00
1 x fully computerised till		3,500.00	3,500.00
Approved *Finbar 2/9/07*			
Goods total			4,300.00
VAT		17.5%	752.50
Invoice total			5,052.50
Net 30 days			

FIXED ASSET REGISTER

Description/serial no	Date acquired	Original cost £	Depreciation £	NBV £	Funding method	Disposal proceeds £	Disposal date
Office and shop equipment							
Depreciation: 20% p.a. on cost (straight line basis)							
Computer	1/9/04	3,000.00			Cash		
Year ended 31/8/05			600.00	2,400.00			
Year ended 31/8/06			600.00	1,800.00			
Printer and photocopier	1/9/04	2,000.00			Cash		
Year ended 31/8/05			400.00	1,600.00			
Year ended 31/8/06			400.00	1,200.00			
Fax machine	30/9/04	800.00			Cash		
Year ended 31/8/05			160.00	640.00			
Year ended 31/8/06			160.00	480.00			
Chiller cabinets	1/4/04	7,000.00			Cash		
Year ended 31/8/05			1,400.00	5,600.00			
Year ended 31/8/06			1,400.00	4,200.00			
Till	1/9/05	5,000.00			Cash		
Year ended 31/8/06			1,000.00	4,000.00			
NBV at 31/8/07 c/f							

FIXED ASSET REGISTER

Description/serial no	Date acquired	Original cost £	Depreciation £	NBV £	Funding method	Disposal proceeds £	Disposal date
Office and shop equipment							
Depreciation: 20% p.a. on cost (straight line basis)							
Security shutters	30/9/04	6,000.00			Cash		
Year ended 31/8/05			1,200.00	4,800.00			
Year ended 31/8/06			1,200.00	3,600.00			
NBV at 31/8/07							
NBV at 31/8/07 b/f							
NBV at 31/8/07							

FIXED ASSET REGISTER

Description/serial no	Date acquired	Original cost £	Depreciation £	NBV £	Funding method	Disposal proceeds £	Disposal date
Butchery equipment							
20% p.a. on net book value (reducing balance basis)							
Workbenches (6)	1/9/04	6,000.00			Cash		
Year ended 31/8/05			1,200.00	4,800.00			
Year ended 31/8/06			960.00	3,840.00			
Grinding machine	1/9/04	3,600.00			Cash		
Year ended 31/8/05			720.00	2,880.00			
Year ended 31/8/06			576.00	2,304.00			
Slicer	1/9/04	2,350.00			Cash		
Year ended 31/8/05			470.00	1,880.00			
Year ended 31/8/06			376.00	1,504.00			
Freezer (600 cu ft.)	1/9/05	9,000.00			Cash		
Year ended 31/8/06			1,800.00	7,200.00			
NBV at 31/8/07							

FIXED ASSET REGISTER

Description/serial no	Date acquired	Original cost £	Depreciation £	NBV £	Funding method	Disposal proceeds £	Disposal date
Delivery vehicles							
25% p.a. on cost (straight line basis)							
Van TY61 CVB	1/4/04	15,000.00			Cash		
Year ended 31/8/05			3,750.00	11,250.00			
Year ended 31/8/06			3,750.00	7,500.00			
Van GH62 UYT	1/5/05	12,000.00			Cash		
Year ended 31/8/06			3,000.00	9,000.00			
Van TY72 BNM	1/1/07	11,500.00			Cash		
NBV at 31/8/07							

Journal 1

Date 2007	Account names and narrative	Debit £	Credit £

b) Finbar O'Hanlon tells you that the computerised till that he bought in 2005 has never functioned properly and has been disposed of for only £200.00. The receipt has been recorded in the cash book but no other entries have been made. There is a balance on the suspense account at 31 August of £200.00.

- Write up the fixed asset register for the disposal.

- Prepare a journal to record the disposal in the main ledger.

Journal 2

Date 2007	Account names and narrative	Debit £	Credit £

c) ■ In the fixed asset register, calculate and record the relevant amounts of depreciation for the year to 31 August 2007 on each fixed asset.

■ Prepare a journal to record depreciation in the main ledger.

Journal 3

Date 2007	Account names and narrative	Debit £	Credit £

d) Post the journals you have prepared to the main ledger accounts below, and balance off the fixed asset cost, accumulated depreciation and disposal accounts.

Butchery equipment (accumulated depreciation)

Date 2007	Details	Amount £	Date 2007	Details	Amount £
			31/8	Balance b/d	6,102.00

Butchery equipment (cost)

Date 2007	Details	Amount £	Date 2007	Details	Amount £
31/8	Balance b/d	20,950.00			

Delivery vehicles (accumulated depreciation)

Date 2007	Details	Amount £	Date 2007	Details	Amount £
			31/8	Balance b/d	10,500.00

Delivery vehicles (cost)

Date 2007	Details	Amount £	Date 2007	Details	Amount £
31/8	Balance b/d	38,500.00			

Depreciation charge

Date 2007	Details	Amount £	Date 2007	Details	Amount £

Disposals

Date 2007	Details	Amount £	Date 2007	Details	Amount £

Office and shop equipment (accumulated depreciation)

Date 2007	Details	Amount £	Date 2007	Details	Amount £
			31/8	Balance b/d	8,520.00

Office and shop equipment (cost)

Date 2007	Details	Amount £	Date 2007	Details	Amount £
31/8	Balance b/d	23,800.00			

Sundry creditors

Date 2007	Details	Amount £	Date 2007	Details	Amount £

Suspense

Date 2007	Details	Amount £	Date 2007	Details	Amount £
			31/8	Balance b/d	200.00

VAT

Date 2007	Details	Amount £	Date 2007	Details	Amount £

e) Complete the reconciliation below, to ensure that the fixed asset register agrees with the main ledger.

Balances per main ledger accounts

	Cost £	Accumulated depreciation £	Net book value per fixed asset register £
Butchery equipment			
Office and shop equipment			
Delivery vehicles			

chapter 8:
ACCRUALS AND PREPAYMENTS

1 During the year ended 31 March a business has paid £845 of telephone bills. However the bill for February and March has not been received and is expected to be approximately £170.

You are required to write up the following ledger accounts to reflect the telephone expense for the year showing the charge to the profit and loss account for the year.

<table>
<tr><td colspan="2" align="center">Telephone account</td></tr>
<tr><td align="center">£</td><td align="center">£</td></tr>
<tr><td></td><td></td></tr>
</table>

<table>
<tr><td colspan="2" align="center">Accruals account</td></tr>
<tr><td align="center">£</td><td align="center">£</td></tr>
<tr><td></td><td></td></tr>
</table>

2 Given below is the electricity expense account for the year ended 30 June for a business. At 30 June it is estimated from meter readings that the electricity bill for the final three months of the accounting year will be £900. The bill for £900 is eventually received and paid on 21 July.

You are required to write up the following ledger accounts showing the year end accrual and the subsequent payment of the bill showing the charge to the profit and loss account for the year.

<table>
<tr><td colspan="3" align="center">Electricity account</td></tr>
<tr><td></td><td align="center">£</td><td align="center">£</td></tr>
<tr><td>30 June Balance b/d</td><td align="center">2,300</td><td></td></tr>
</table>

Accruals account

	£		£

---

3 Given below is the heat and light expense account for a business for the year ended 30 April. The bills for March and April have not yet been received but are estimated to be £480.

You are required to write up the heat and light expense account to reflect the accrual as the balance carried down and to show the charge to the profit and loss account for the year.

Heat and light account

	£		£
30 April Balance b/d	2,400		

---

4 The expenditure on advertising for a business for the year ended 31 March from the cash payments book totals £14,600. However invoices are due for £1,200 for advertising in March. The invoice duly arrives in April and is paid on 30 April.

You are required to write up the advertising account showing the year end position and the subsequent payment of the invoice on 30 April showing the charge to the profit and loss account for the year ended 31 March.

Advertising account

	£		£

5 The cash payments book for a business shows that in the year ended 31 May 2007 £2,300 was paid for insurance. However this includes £250 for the year ending 31 May 2008.

You are required to write up the insurance account and the prepayments account given below to reflect this and to show the charge to the profit and loss account for the period and the reversal of the prepayment after the year end.

Insurance account

	£		£

Prepayments account

	£		£

6 A business pays rent for its premises in advance. The rent expense account for the year ending 30 June is given below but of this expense £400 is for the month of July.

You are required to write up the rent account and the prepayment account to reflect this and to show the profit and loss account charge for the year and the reversal of the entry for the prepayment after the year end.

Rent account

	£		£
30 June Balance b/d	4,500		

Prepayment account

	£		£

7   A business sublets some of its premises and the rental for this space is paid in advance. The rental income account for the year to 30 June is given below. Of the amount received during the year £350 is in advance for the following month.

     a)   You are required to show the entries required in the ledger accounts if a separate account is kept for rental income received in advance showing the profit and loss account income figure for the year to 30 June and the reversal of the income in advance after the year end.

Rental income account

£		£
	30 June Bank	5,600

Rental income received in advance account

£		£

     b)   You are now required to show the entries required if no separate income received in advance account is used.

Rental income account

£		£
	30 June Bank	5,600

8 The following balances were extracted from the ledger accounts of Sheba as at 31 March.

	Debit £	Credit £
Insurance	282	
Commission		150
Telephones	586	
Carriage	154	

The following adjustments are required in respect of these items:

Insurance is prepaid by £78
The business is owed £50 commission
There is a telephone bill outstanding of £152
Carriage costs of £30 are owing

You are required to show the ledger account for each item above after the adjustment has been made and the transfer to the profit and loss account.

chapter 9:
BAD AND DOUBTFUL DEBTS

1   A business which is not registered for VAT has debtors at the year end of £5,479. Of these it has been decided that £321 from G Simms & Co will never be received as this business has now gone into liquidation. A further debt for £124 from L Fitzgerald is also viewed as irrecoverable as the debtor cannot be traced and the debt is now 8 months overdue.

You are required to write off these bad debts in the main and subsidiary ledger accounts given below showing any charge to the profit and loss account and the amended year end balances.

Main ledger

Sales ledger control account

	£		£
Balance b/d	5,479		

Bad debt expense account

	£		£

Subsidiary ledger

G Simms & Co

	£		£
Balance b/d	321		

L Fitzgerald

	£		£
Balance b/d	124		

2 A business which is registered for VAT has debtors of £16,475 at its year end of 30 September 2007. The business's normal terms of trade are that payment from debtors is due within 30 days. On the basis of this it has been decided that two debts are to be written off as bad at the year end:

- £1,200 plus VAT due from H Maguire – invoice dated 28 January 2007
- £400 plus VAT due from J Palmer – invoice dated 30 June 2007

You are required to write off these bad debts in the main and subsidiary ledger accounts given below showing any amounts to be charged to the profit and loss account for the year and the amended year end balances.

Main ledger

Sales ledger control account

	£		£
30 Sep Balance b/d	16,475		

VAT account

	£		£
		30 Sep Balance b/d	2,451

Bad debts expense account

	£		£

Subsidiary ledger

H Maguire

	£		£
30 Sep Balance b/d	1,410		

J Palmer

	£		£
30 Sep Balance b/d	470		

3   In the year ended 31 December 2006 a debt from R Trevor for £488 was written off as bad. In the year ended 31 December 2007 a further debt from E Ingham for £669 was written off as bad but the £488 from R Trevor was unexpectedly received.

You are required to write up the main and subsidiary ledger accounts given below for the year ended 31 December 2007 to reflect these facts (ignore VAT).

Main ledger

Sales ledger control account

	£		£
31 Dec Balance b/d	7,264		

Bad debts expense account

	£		£

Subsidiary ledger

R Trevor

	£		£

E Ingham

	£		£
31 Dec 2007 Balance b/d	669		

4 A business has debtors of £12,700 at the end of its first year of trading, 31 December 2005. At this date it is decided to set up a provision for doubtful debts of 5% of the debtors figure. By 31 December 2006 debtors have increased to £15,200 and a provision of 5% is again required for doubtful debts. Debtors at 31 December 2007 total £14,800 and it has been decided to decrease the provision for doubtful debts to 4% of the debtors figure.

You are required to write up the ledger accounts given for each of the three years.

Bad debts expense account

	£		£

Provision for doubtful debts account

	£		£

5 Marcham has debtors as at 30 September 2007 of £218,940. Marcham has identified that Hendrick will not be able to pay his balance of £2,440, and wishes to write this amount off. Of the remaining debtors as at 30 September 2007, Marcham wants to have a provision for doubtful debts of 3% of the balance. At 1 October 2006 Marcham's provision for doubtful debtors was £5,215. Complete the sales ledger control account, the provision for doubtful debts account, the bad and doubtful debts expense account and Hendrick's account, calculating final balances.

Main ledger

Sales ledger control account

		£		£
b/d		218,940		

Provision for doubtful debts account

	£			£
			b/d	5,215

Bad and doubtful debts expense account

	£		£

Subsidiary ledger

Hendrick

		£		£
b/d		2,440		

64

chapter 10:
CONTROL ACCOUNT RECONCILIATIONS

1   Given below are summaries of the transactions with debtors for the month of February for a business. The balance on the sales ledger control account at 1 February was £4,268.

	£
Credit sales	15,487
Sales returns	995
Bad debt written off	210
Cheques from debtors	13,486
Discounts allowed	408
Contra entry	150
Cheque returned 'refer to drawer'	645

You are required to write up the sales ledger control account showing the balance on 28 February.

Sales ledger control account

	£		£
Bal B/D	4,268	Sales returns	995
Credit Sales	15,487	Bad debt	210
cheque rtn'd	645	Chq's from debtors	13,486
		Discounts allowed	408
		Contra entry	150
		Bal c/D	5,151
	20,400		20,400
Bal B/D	5,151		

2   The balance on the purchases ledger control account for a business at 1 February was £3,299. The transactions with creditors for the month of February are summarised below:

	£
Credit purchases	12,376
Cheques to creditors	10,379
Returns to suppliers	1,074
Discounts received	302
Contra entry	230

You are required to write up the purchases ledger control account for the month and to show the closing balance on 28 February.

Purchases ledger control account

	£		£
chqs to Creditors	10,379	Bal B/D	3,299
rtns to suppliers	1,074	Credit purchases	12,376
Discounts received	302		
Contra entry	230		
BalC/D	3690		
	15,675		15,675
		Bal B/D	3,690

3   Given below is a summary of a business's transactions with its debtors and creditors during the month of May. The balances on the sales ledger and purchases ledger control accounts on 1 May were £12,634 and £10,553 respectively.

	£
Credit purchases	40,375
Credit sales	51,376
Cheques from debtors	50,375
Discounts received	1,245
Sales returns	3,173
Cheques to suppliers	35,795
Purchases returns	2,003
Contra entry	630
Discounts allowed	1,569

You are required to write up the sales ledger and purchases ledger control accounts for the month of May showing the balances at the end of the month.

Sales ledger control account

	£		£
Bal B/D	12,634	chqs from debtors	50,375
Credit Sales	51,376	Sales returns	3,173
		Discounts allowed	1,569
		Contra entry	630
		Bal C/D	8,263
	64,010		64,010
Bal B/D	8,263		

Purchases ledger control account

	£		£
Discounts received	1,245	Bal B/D	10,553
chqs to Suppliers	35,795	Credit purchases	40,375
Purchase returns	2,003		
contra entry	630		
Bal C/D	11,255		
	50,928		50,928

Bal B/D

4   At 31 March the balance on a business's sales ledger control account was £6,237 but the total of the list of debtors balances from the subsidiary ledger was £8,210. The following errors were discovered:

a)   the sales day book had been undercast by £1,000

b)   the discounts allowed of £340 had been entered into the main ledger as £430

c)   a contra entry of £123 had been made in the main ledger but not in the subsidiary ledger
      ⌐nominal ledger

d)   a credit note to a customer for £320 had been entered on the wrong side of the customer's account in the subsidiary ledger

e)   a credit balance of £60 had been included in the list of debtors balances as a debit

You are required to prepare the sales ledger control account reconciliation as at 31 March 2006

Sales ledger control account

	£		£
Bal b/d	6,237	Discounts	
Sales	1,000		
Discounts allowed	90		
	7,327		

Reconciliation

8,210   ← Sales ledger
(123)
(640)
(120)
___
7,327

5   The balance on a business's purchases ledger control account at 31 January was £3,105 but the total of the list of creditors balances from the subsidiary ledger was £1,850 at the same date. The following errors were discovered:

a)   the total from the purchases returns day book of £288 was entered on the wrong side of the control account

b)   a contra entry for £169 was entered in the individual creditor's account but not in the main ledger

c)   the total of the cash payments book was overcast by £100

d)   a purchase invoice for £350 was entered on the wrong side of the creditor's account in the subsidiary ledger

e)   a credit note to F Miller for £97 was entered into the account for A Miller

f)   a creditors balance of £780 was incorrectly listed as £870 when the creditors' balances were being totalled

You are required to prepare the purchases ledger control account reconciliation at 31 January.

Purchases ledger control account

	£		£

Reconciliation

6   Truro Audio Visual Supplies is a small business hiring out display and training hardware (screens, VCRs, overhead projectors etc) and providing trainers to the business community in the county of Cornwall. It is owned and run by Julian Jones. All sales are credit sales. Truro Audio Visual Supplies is registered for VAT and all sales are standard rated (17.5%). All purchases are made on credit. Expenditure in the day books is analysed into: administration; warehouse overheads; despatch; and marketing. The cash book and the sales and purchase ledgers are not part of the double entry system, and are written up as necessary during the month. The main ledger is only written up at the end of the month.

a)   You are required to write up the main ledger accounts below as follows for January.

   i)   Post the cash book to the main ledger.

   ii)   Post the January day books to the main ledger.

Cash book: Receipts

Date	Details	Cash £	Discount allowed £	Sales ledger control £	Interest £
1 Jan	Cheques received	3,109.26	45.00	3,109.26	
3 Jan	Cheques received	4,289.20	60.00	4,289.20	
7 Jan	Cheques received	1,901.82		1,901.82	
11 Jan	Cheques received	5,298.20	15.00	5,298.20	
13 Jan	BACS receipt	4,265.26		4,265.26	
17 Jan	Cheques received	2,198.02	11.00	2,198.02	
21 Jan	Cheques received	3,294.11		3,294.11	
25 Jan	BACS receipt	1,278.34	7.00	1,278.34	
30 Jan	Cheques received	7,289.52	65.00	7,289.52	
31 Jan	Interest credited	103.00			103.00
		33,026.73	203.00	32,923.73	103.00

Cash book: Payments

Date	Details	Cheque No	Cash £	Discount received £	Purchase ledger cntrol £	Other £
1 Jan	Mr G Formwell	7421	1,910.26	12.00	1,910.26	
4 Jan	Ms S Parker	7422	2,877.46		2,877.46	
8 Jan	Jensen Ltd	7423	7,209.45	52.50	7,209.45	
12 Jan	Norton Motors Ltd (new car)	7425	15,000.00	100.00		15,000.00
12 Jan	Mr J Jones drawings	DD	2,000.00			2,000.00
18 Jan	Tremayne Holdings plc	7426	263.29		263.29	
20 Jan	Kerrier District Council (rates)	DD	350.00		350.00	
24 Jan	Westworld Computers Ltd	7427	638.23		638.23	
29 Jan	Quest plc	7428	2,190.63	32.00	2,190.63	
31 Jan	Salaries	BACS	7,092.87			7,092.87
			39,532.19	196.50	15,439.32	24,092.87

MONTH ENDED 31 JANUARY

Purchases Day Book

	£
Administration	1,298.02
Warehouse overheads	2,892.19
Despatch	2,817.29
Marketing	3,198.29
VAT	1,786.01
Total value of invoices	11,991.80

Sales Day Book

	£
Sales invoices	20,189.73
VAT	3,533.20
Total value of invoices	23,722.93

Purchases Returns Day Book

	£
Administration	0.00
Warehouse overheads	0.00
Despatch	192.64
Marketing	32.00
VAT	39.31
Total value of credit notes	263.95

Sales Returns Day Book

	£
Sales credit notes	200.00
VAT	35.00
Total value of credit notes	235.00

Administration

Date	Details	Amount £	Date	Details	Amount £

Cash

Date	Details	Amount £	Date	Details	Amount £

Despatch

Date	Details	Amount £	Date	Details	Amount £

Discounts allowed and received

Date	Details	Amount £	Date	Details	Amount £

Drawings

Date	Details	Amount £	Date	Details	Amount £

Interest received

Date	Details	Amount £	Date	Details	Amount £

Marketing

Date	Details	Amount £	Date	Details	Amount £

Motor vehicles

Date	Details	Amount £	Date	Details	Amount £

Purchase ledger control

Date	Details	Amount £	Date	Details	Amount £
			31/1	Balance b/d	19,190.62

Salaries

Date	Details	Amount £	Date	Details	Amount £

Sales

Date	Details	Amount £	Date	Details	Amount £

Sales ledger control

Date	Details	Amount £	Date	Details	Amount £
31/1	Balance b/d	40,563.29			

VAT

Date	Details	Amount £	Date	Details	Amount £

Warehouse overheads

Date	Details	Amount £	Date	Details	Amount £

b)   Refer to the balances on the debtors' and creditors' accounts in the subsidiary ledgers below and the further information provided.

    i)   Balance off the relevant control accounts in the main ledger.

    ii)   Prepare a sales ledger control account reconciliation and a purchase ledger control account reconciliation.

Sales ledger	
	£
Antrobus & Co	2,298.35
Grenfell Brothers	5,238.29
Jeantons	381.11
Land and Field Association	3,182.39
Nelson Ltd	5,178.20
Pristine Engineering Ltd	830.27
Richard Roop Associates	65.00
Tremayne Holdings plc	7,654.02
Varnells Ltd	3,414.41

Purchase ledger	
	£
Jensen Ltd	239.27
Harrier Ltd	3,189.02
Kerrier District Council (rates)	2,187.19
Westworld Computers Ltd	540.82
Quest plc	1,298.37
Tremayne Holdings plc	5,283.00
Flatscreen Technology	730.27
Robust Engineering plc	2,393.09
Warners Ltd	1,073.52

c)   **Further information**

    An investigation reveals the following errors in the ledgers and day books.

    i)   The invoice totals for the sales day book for January was overcast by £900.00.

    ii)   One invoice for £1,440.00 including VAT was duplicated in the sales day book for January.

    iii)   Cash received of £120.00 from Nelson Ltd was posted to the wrong side of its sales ledger account.

    iv)   The despatch column of the purchase day book for January was undercast by £270.00.

    v)   One marketing invoice total for £872.00 including VAT was omitted from the purchase day book in January.

    vi)   An invoice totalling £1,092.35 was posted twice to the purchase ledger account of Harrier Ltd.

    vii)   A contra of £582.45 was made in the sales and purchase ledger accounts of Tremayne Holdings plc.

You are required to prepare a journal to correct the main ledger accounts fully.

d) **Journal**

Date	Account names and narrative	Debit	Credit
		£	£

e) Post the journal to the main ledger, and recalculate the balances on the control accounts.

chapter 11:
ERRORS AND THE SUSPENSE ACCOUNT

1   For each of the following errors determine whether they would mean that there is an imbalance in the trial balance or not.

		Imbalance	No imbalance
a)	The payment of the telephone bill was posted to the cash payments book and then credited to the telephone account	....	....
b)	The depreciation expense was debited to the provision for depreciation account and credited to the depreciation expense account	....	....
c)	The electricity account balance of £750 was taken to the trial balance as £570	....	....
d)	The motor expenses were debited to the motor vehicles at cost account	....	....
e)	The discounts received in the cash payments book were not posted to the main ledger	....	....

2   A trial balance has been prepared for a business and the total of the debit balances is £228,678 and the total of the credits is £220,374.

If a suspense account is set up what would be the balance on it?

3 Draft a journal entry to correct each of the following errors – narratives should be included.

a) The telephone expense of £236 was debited to the electricity account

b) A sales invoice for £645 was entered into the sales day book as £465

c) A credit note received from a supplier for £38 was omitted from the purchases returns day book

d) The increase in doubtful debt provision of £127 was debited to the provision for doubtful debts account and credited to the bad debts expense account

e) A contra entry of £200 was debited to the sales ledger control account and credited to the purchases ledger control account

4 A business has just drafted its trial balance and the debit balances exceed the credit balances by £1,370. A suspense account has been set up to record the difference and the following errors have been noted:

a) The discounts allowed from the cash receipts book of £240 have not been posted to the main ledger – *Not posted to main ledger.*

b) The sales ledger column in the cash receipts book totalling £2,700 were not posted to the sales ledger control account *did DR cash   DR SUS*
CR SLLS   CR SLCA

c) The wages account balance of £74,275 was included in the trial balance as £72,475

did:
DR BD
DR SLCA
d) A bad debt written off for £235 was debited to the sales ledger control account and debited to the bad debts expense account

CR sus e) . A purchase invoice for £480 was entered into the purchases day book as £580
will not affect suspense.
You are required to set up the suspense account balance and then to clear the suspense account.

Suspense account

£		£

5   When drawing up the trial balance at the end of the accounting year a suspense account debit balance of £3,100 was set up to account for the difference in the trial balance. The following errors were discovered:

a)   The payment of insurance premiums of £1,585 was correctly entered into the cash payments book and then credited to the insurance account. *DR Insurance CR Sus.*

b)   A payment for postage costs of £26 was posted from the petty cash book to the postage account as £62.   *DR Suspense CR Postage*

c) ✗ The total of the discounts allowed column in the cash receipts book was undercast by £100.
no affected

d)   The balance of £34 on the bank interest received account was omitted from the trial balance.
DR Suspence   CR Insurance

e) ✗ One page of the purchases returns day book totalling £130 was not posted to the main ledger.
no affected

You are required to set up the suspense account and then show how it is cleared.

Suspense account

£		£

6   Shortly before the year end a business sold a fixed asset for £4,000. The bookkeeper entered the receipt in the cash receipts book but did not know what else to do and therefore credited a suspense account with the amount. The fixed asset sold had originally cost £15,000 and had accumulated depreciation charged to it at the date of sale of £10,500.

You are to draft a journal entry to correctly account for this disposal and to show how the suspense account is cleared.

Suspense account

£		£

7   Green's Bottles Ltd is a business which manufactures bottles for the soft drinks industry. It is owned and run by Hana Paritova. All sales are credit sales. Green's Bottles is registered for VAT and all sales are standard rated (17.5%). All purchases are made on credit. Expenditure in the day books is analysed into: administration and marketing; factory overheads; raw materials. The cash book and the sales and purchase ledgers are not part of the double entry system, and are written up as necessary during the month. The main ledger is only written up at the end of the month.

   a)   Write up the main ledger accounts below as follows for April.

         i)   Post the cash book to the main ledger.
         ii)   Post the April day books to the main ledger.

Cash book: Receipts

Date	Details	Cash	Discount allowed	Sales ledger control	Other
		£	£	£	£
2/4	Cheques received	5,290.38	15.00	5,290.38	
4/4	Cheques received	6,209.37	23.00	6,209.37	
5/4	BACS receipt	3,350.00		3,350.00	
7/4	Cheques received	2,182.34	31.00	2,182.34	
10/4	Cheques received	1,192.27		1,192.27	
12/4	Cheques received	7,203.27	154.00	7,203.27	
14/4	BACS receipt	8,023.92		8,023.92	
15/4	BACS receipt	6,390.29	85.00	6,390.29	
19/4	Cresswell Gas Co – refund of factory overheads	123.95			123.95
22/4	Cheques received	2,379.27		2,379.27	
23/4	BACS receipt	10,290.23	300.00	10,290.23	
29/4	Cheques received	9,312.39	45.00	9,312.39	
		61,947.68	653.00	61,823.73	123.95

Cash book: Payments

Date	Details	Cheque No	Cash	Discount received	Purchase ledger control	Other
			£	£	£	£
2 April	Raw Sand Ltd	0816	8,290.38	223.00	8,290.38	
	Metal Fasteners plc	0817	5,353.20	120.00	5,353.20	
	Brundells Lubricants	0818	2,392.39		2,392.39	
	Hana Paritova – drawings	DD	3,000.00			3,000.00
	The Repair Shop	0819	560.28		560.28	
	Pharmco Chemicals Ltd	0820	8,234.20	241.00	8,234.20	
	Cresswell Gas Co	0821	4,209.30	52.00	4,209.30	
	Interest on loan and overdraft	0822	230.00			230.00
	Wages (factory labour)	BACS	7,209.86			7,209.86
	Salaries (admin & marketing)	BACS	5,982.38			5,982.38
			45,461.99	636.00	29,039.75	16,422.24

MONTH ENDED 30 APRIL

Purchases Day Book

	£
Administration and marketing	2,109.28
Factory overheads	1,290.38
Raw materials	9,365.47
VAT	2,183.08
Total value of invoices	14,948.21

Sales Day Book

	£
Sales invoices	35,864.86
VAT	6,276.35
Total value of invoices	42,141.21

Purchases Returns Day Book

	£
Administration and marketing	0.00
Factory overheads	139.25
Raw materials	984.22
VAT	196.60
Total value of credit notes	1,320.07

Sales Returns Day Book

	£
Sales credit notes	2,673.36
VAT	467.83
Total value of credit notes	3,141.19

Administration and marketing

Date	Details	Amount £	Date	Details	Amount £
1/4	Balance b/d	32,290.29			

Capital

Date	Details	Amount £	Date	Details	Amount £
			1/4	Balance b/d	50,000.00

Cash

Date	Details	Amount £	Date	Details	Amount £
			1/4	Balance	2,398.20

Discounts allowed and received

Date	Details	Amount £	Date	Details	Amount £
1/4	Balance b/d	375.29			

Drawings

Date	Details	Amount £	Date	Details	Amount £
1/4	Balance b/d	15,000.00			

Factory labour

Date	Details	Amount £	Date	Details	Amount £
1/4	Balance b/d	43,529.18			

Factory overheads

Date	Details	Amount £	Date	Details	Amount £
1/4	Balance b/d	28,254.38			

Fixed assets (NBV)

Date	Details	Amount £	Date	Details	Amount £
1/4	Balance b/d	32,100.10			

Interest paid

Date	Details	Amount £	Date	Details	Amount £
1/4	Balance b/d	1,920.27			

Loan

Date	Details	Amount £	Date	Details	Amount £
			1/4	Balance b/d	15,000.00

Purchase ledger control

Date	Details	Amount £	Date	Details	Amount £
			1/4	Balance b/d	25,131.14

Raw materials

Date	Details	Amount £	Date	Details	Amount £
1/4	Balance b/d	80,265.35			

Sales

Date	Details	Amount £	Date	Details	Amount £
			1/4	Balance b/d	215,189.19

Sales ledger control

Date	Details	Amount £	Date	Details	Amount £
1/4	Balance b/d	67,585.12			

Stock

Date	Details	Amount £	Date	Details	Amount £
1/4	Balance b/d	10,198.19			

Suspense

Date	Details	Amount £	Date	Details	Amount £
		———			———
		═══			═══

VAT

Date	Details	Amount £	Date	Details	Amount £
			1/4	Balance b/d	2,158.26
		———			———
		═══			═══

b) Calculate balances on all the main ledger accounts and draw up an initial trial balance. Enter any imbalance on the initial TB into the suspense ledger account.

c) Refer to the information provided below, and prepare a journal to clear the suspense account.

An investigation reveals the following errors in the ledgers and day books:

i) The balance brought down on the factory labour ledger account was miscast. The correct balance is £43,259.18.

ii) The balance brought down on the purchase ledger control account was miscast. The correct balance is £25,311.14.

iii) Cash received of £891.20 from Lewis & Co was posted to the wrong side of its sales ledger account.

iv) One receipt for £1,191.38 was included in the cash book in March but was omitted from the total posted to the sales ledger control account.

d) Post the journal to the main ledger, and recalculate the balances on any accounts affected.

e) Draw up a final TB and prove that it balances.

chapter 12:
STOCK

1   A business has just completed its year end stock count on 30 June. For most lines of stock the actual count figures agree with the stock records however there are problems with three lines of stock.

	Stock No. 0434	Stock No. 0711	Stock No. 0963
Quantity counted	246	118	93
Quantity per stock record	266	78	118

The following information has subsequently been discovered:

a)   On 28 June 2006 20 units of Stock No 0434 were returned to the supplier due to faults and on 29 June 30 units of Stock No. 0711 were received. However neither the despatch note nor the goods received note had been recorded.

b)   On 29 June 10 units of Stock No. 0711 were returned from the factory floor but the materials returned note had not been recorded.

c)   On 28 June a materials requisition for 20 units of Stock No. 0963 had been despatched to the factory but had not been recorded in the stock records.

Prepare a closing stock reconciliation for each stock line and if there are any outstanding discrepancies suggest possible reasons for them.

2   A business has 125 units of a product in stock which cost £24.60 per unit plus £0.50 per unit of delivery costs. These goods can be sold for £25.80 per unit although in order to do this selling costs of £1.00 per unit must be incurred.

a)   What is the cost of these units and what is their net realisable value?

b)   What would be the value of the 125 units of the product that will be included in the financial statements?

2) $24.60 + 0.5 = 25.10$ Cost

$25.80 - 1 = 24.80$ NRV

b) $125 \times 24.80 = 3,100.00$

3 A business has five lines of stock with the following details:

Stock line	Quantity – units	Cost £	Selling price £	Selling costs £	Value per unit £	Total value £
A	180	12.50	20.40	0.50		
B	240	10.90	12.60	1.80		
C	300	15.40	22.70	1.20		
D	80	16.50	17.80	1.50		
E	130	10.60	18.00	1.00		

You are required to complete the table showing the value per unit for each line of the stock and the total value to appear in the financial statements for this stock.

4 Given below are the movements on a line of stock for the month of March:

1 Mar	Opening balance	80 units @ £8.20
7 Mar	Purchases	100 units @ £8.50
10 Mar	Sales	140 units
15 Mar	Purchases	180 units @ £8.70
26 Mar	Sales	100 units
31 Mar	Sales	70 units

You are required to determine the value of the closing stock at 31 March under each of the following methods:

a) FIFO
b) LIFO
c) AVCO

5 Included in Jason Brown's stock are some standard office swivel chairs. At the beginning of October ten chairs each costing £30 were in stock. Stock movements during the month were as follows.

Stock at		1 October	10 at £30
Purchases		10 October	12 at £32
Sales		13 October	2
Sales		18 October	4
Purchases		23 October	10 at £31
Sales		30 October	6

Chairs are sold at £50 each.

Stock is valued on a FIFO basis.

Calculate the value of the following.

a) Sales for October
b) Cost of goods sold for October
c) Closing stock at the end of October

6 Given below are details of the movements in one line of stock for the month of May:

1 May	Opening stock	200 units @ £3.00
5 May	Purchases	200 units @ £3.20
8 May	Sales	140 units
15 May	Sales	130 units
18 May	Purchases	200 units @ £3.40
24 May	Sales	180 units
28 May	Sales	120 units
29 May	Purchases	200 units @ £3.50
30 May	Sales	160 units

You are required to show the cost of each sale and the value of the stock remaining at the end of the month under each of the following stock valuation methods:

a) FIFO
b) LIFO
c) AVCO

chapter 13:
FROM TRIAL BALANCE TO FINAL ACCOUNTS – SOLE TRADER

1   A sole trader had a capital balance of £32,569 on 1 May 2006. During the year ended 30 April 2007 the business made a net profit of £67,458 and the owner withdrew cash totalling £35,480 and goods with a cost of £1,680.

What is the capital balance at 30 April 2007?

2   A sole trader has just prepared his draft initial trial balance. The total of the debits was £526,504 and the total of the credits was £519,475. What is the balance on the suspense account and is it a debit or a credit balance?

3   A sole trader took goods from his business with a cost of £560 for his own personal use. What is the double entry for this event?

4   A sole trader has drafted his initial trial balance and found that the balance on the rent account is a debit of £3,600 and the balance on the insurance account is £4,250. Rent of £1,200 is due to be paid for the final quarter of the year and the insurance payments include £850 which relate to the following accounting period.

What are the profit and loss account charges for rent and insurance?

5   A sole trader has just prepared his initial draft trial balance for the year ended 30 June. This includes the following balances:

	£
Machinery at cost	140,000
Motor vehicles at cost	68,000
Fixtures and fittings at cost	23,000
Accumulated depreciation – machinery	64,500
Accumulated depreciation – motor vehicles	31,200
Accumulated depreciation – fixtures and fittings	13,400

The depreciation charges for the year to 30 June have not yet been accounted for and the sole trader's depreciation policies are:

Machinery	20% on cost
Motor vehicles	35% reducing balance
Fixtures and fittings	20% reducing balance

What is the total net book value of the fixed assets that will appear in the balance sheet at 30 June?

6 A sole trader has balanced off his ledger accounts as at 31 May 2007 and has now asked for your help in producing his final accounts. The ledger account balances at 31 May 2007 are as follows:

Bank

		£				£
			31 May	Balance b/d		1,650

Capital

		£				£
			31 May	Balance b/d		74,000

Creditors

		£				£
			31 May	Balance b/d		40,800

Debtors

		£				£
31 May	Balance b/d	61,500				

Discount allowed

		£				£
31 May	Balance b/d	2,100				

Discount received

		£				£
			31 May	Balance b/d		1,800

Drawings

		£				£
31 May	Balance b/d	30,000				

Fixtures and fittings at cost

		£				£
31 May	Balance b/d	24,500				

Electricity

		£				£
31 May	Balance b/d	2,300				

Insurance

		£				£
31 May	Balance b/d	3,000				

Miscellaneous expenses

		£			£
31 May	Balance b/d	1,200			

Motor expenses

		£			£
31 May	Balance b/d	3,400			

Motor vehicles at cost

		£			£
31 May	Balance b/d	48,000			

Purchases

		£			£
31 May	Balance b/d	245,000			

Provision for doubtful debts

		£			£
			31 May	Balance b/d	1,000

Provision for depreciation – fixtures and fittings

		£			£
			31 May	Balance b/d	6,100

Provision for depreciation – motor vehicles

		£			£
			31 May	Balance b/d	22,000

Rent

		£			£
31 May	Balance b/d	4,200			

Sales

		£			£
			31 May	Balance b/d	369,000

Stock

		£			£
31 May	Balance b/d	41,000			

Telephone

		£			£
31 May	Balance b/d	1,600			

VAT

		£			£
			31 May	Balance b/d	4,100

Wages

		£			£
31 May	Balance b/d	52,000			

a) You are required to draft the initial trial balance – check all of your additions carefully and if necessary enter a suspense account balance in order to make the trial balance equal.

b) A number of year end adjustments have yet to be made to the trial balance figures:

   i) Stock at 31 May 2007 has been valued at £43,500

   ii) The provisions for depreciation are as at 1 June 2006. Depreciation is to be provided at 30% on the reducing balance basis on motor vehicles and at 10% on cost of the fixtures and fittings.

   iii) It has been decided that a bad debt of £1,500 should be written off and that the provision for doubtful debts is to remain at 2% of remaining debtors.

   iv) There are accruals of £650 of electricity and £350 of telephone.

   v) Rent of £800 has already been paid for the quarter ended 31 August 2007 and insurance includes £1,200 for the year ended 31 December 2007.

   You are required to draft the journal entries required for these year end adjustments.

c) Since the drafting of the initial trial balance a number of errors have come to light:

   i) Motor expenses have been charged with £300 of miscellaneous expenses.

   ii) Discounts allowed of £425 and discounts received of £100 had been entered on the wrong side of the respective discounts accounts.

   You are required to draft the journal entries needed to correct these errors. (Once the errors have been corrected this should clear any suspense account balance in the trial balance.)

d) Amend each of the ledger accounts affected by any of the journal entries for year end adjustments or the correction of errors showing clearly the amended balance on the ledger account.

e) Redraft the trial balance after having put through the year end adjustments and the corrections of the errors.

f) Prepare the final accounts for the year ended 31 May 2007.

7   Given below is the initial trial balance of a sole trader for his year ended 30 June 2007.

	£
Administration expenses	7,250
Bank	3,280 (debit balance)
Capital	60,000
Carriage inwards	1,210
Carriage outwards	1,530
Creditors	20,200
Debtors	16,840
Discount allowed	2,510
Discount received	1,860
Drawings	14,600
Machinery at cost	58,400
Motor vehicles at cost	22,100
Purchases	121,200
Provision for doubtful debts	300
Provision for depreciation machinery	23,360
motor vehicles	9,680
Sales	167,400
Stock at 1 July 2006	15,400
Selling expenses	5,800
VAT	3,690 (credit balance)
Wages	16,700

Since drawing up the initial trial balance a number of errors have been discovered:

i)   Selling expenses of £340 paid by cheque have been omitted from the accounts completely.

ii)   Carriage inwards of £180 was entered on the wrong side of the account although the entry to the bank account was correctly made.

iii)   Discounts allowed of £690 were credited to debtors, and debited to both the discounts allowed account and the discounts received account.

There are also a number of year end adjustments which have yet to be accounted for:

i)   The closing stock at 30 June 2006 has been valued at £18,200.

ii)   A bad debt of £2,840 is to be written off and a provision of 2% is to be maintained of the remaining debtors.

iii)   Invoices for administration expenses for June 2007 totalling £680 were not received until after the trial balance had been drawn up.

iv)   Included in administration expenses are payments of £440 which relate to the period after 30 June 2007.

v)   Depreciation has not yet been charged for the year. The machinery is depreciated at 20% per annum on cost and the motor vehicles are depreciated on the reducing balance basis at a rate of 25%.

You are required to:

a) draft the initial trial balance and set up a suspense account if required.

b) draft journal entries to correct the errors found and put through the year end adjustments.

c) draft the ledger accounts that have been altered by the journal entries in part b) showing clearly the amended balances.

d) draft an amended trial balance after the journal entries have been put through.

e) prepare the final accounts of the sole trader for the year ended 30 June 2007.

8   You have been asked by Sandro Venus to assist in the preparation of the year end financial statements of his business. He is a sole trader who runs a trading business which specialises in ornaments decorated with sea shells. His trial balance as at 31 March 2007 is set out on the next page.

You are given the following further information:

i) A general provision for doubtful debts is to be set up at 5% of the year end debtors' balance.

ii) During the year Sandro Venus took goods which had cost £500 for his own personal use in decorating his flat.

iii) At the end of the year, one of the motor vehicles which had cost £5,500 and on which there was accumulated depreciation of £2,400 was sold for £3,500. Payment for the vehicle sold has not yet been received by Sandro Venus and no entry to reflect the sale has been made in the trial balance.

iv) At 31 March 2007 stock on hand was valued at £30,229.

SANDRO VENUS
Trial balance 31 March 2007

Description	Trial Balance	
	Debit £	Credit £
Wages and NIC	29,344	
Capital as at 1 April 2006		83,696
Postage and stationery	524	
Accumulated depreciation – motor vehicles		14,219
Accumulated depreciation – office equipment		2,750
Accumulated depreciation – fixtures and fittings		5,560
Purchases	103,742	
Trade creditors		17,725
Carriage inwards	923	
Motor vehicles (cost)	32,500	
Office equipment (cost)	13,745	
Fixtures and fittings (cost)	27,800	
Sales		187,325
Returns outwards		1,014
Trade debtors	18,740	
Drawings	14,400	
Depreciation – motor vehicles	6,094	
Depreciation – office equipment	1,375	
Depreciation – fixtures and fittings	2,780	
Prepayments	320	
Accruals		1,131
Stock as at 1 April 2006	27,931	
Returns inwards	1,437	
Cash at bank	9,473	
Cash in hand	166	
Bank deposit interest		972
Carriage outwards	657	
Rents, rates and insurance	7,721	
Bad debts	830	
Discounts allowed	373	
Bank charges	693	
Telephone	4,307	
Lighting and heating	3,755	
Motor expenses	4,762	
	314,392	314,392

You are required to:

a)   prepare Journal entries for any adjustments you feel necessary to the balances in the trial balance as a result of the matters set out in the further information above.

   Note. Narratives are not required.

b)   prepare a profit and loss account for the year ended 31 March 2007.

c)   prepare a balance sheet for the year ended 31 March 2007.

9   A sole trader has prepared his final accounts from his trial balance. Extracts from that trial balance are given below:

	£	£
Sales		184,321
Purchases	91,201	
General expenses	16,422	

You are required to prepare journal entries showing how these accounts would be closed off at the year end.

chapter 14:
THE EXTENDED TRIAL BALANCE

1   Given below is the list of balances for a business at its year end of 31 May 2007.

	£
Stock at 1 June 2006	1,600
Motor vehicles at cost	23,800
Computer at cost	2,400
Fixtures and fittings at cost	12,800
Provision for depreciation at 1 June 2006:	
Motor vehicles	12,140
Computer	600
Fixtures and fittings	2,560
Wages	16,400
Telephone	900
Electricity	1,200
Advertising	400
Stationery	600
Motor expenses	1,700
Miscellaneous expenses	300
Insurance	1,000
Sales	86,400
Purchases	38,200
Debtors	7,200
Provision for doubtful debts at 1 June 2006	200
Bank (debit balance)	1,300
Petty cash	100
Creditors	3,180
VAT (credit balance)	960
Capital	25,000
Drawings	21,140

You are also provided with the following information:

a) The depreciation charge for the year has not yet been accounted for:

- Motor vehicles are to be depreciated at 30% on the reducing balance basis
- The computer is being depreciated at 25% on the straight-line basis
- The fixtures and fittings are being depreciated at 20% on the straight-line basis

b) There is an accrual for electricity of £400

c) There is £300 of prepaid insurance

d) The provision for doubtful debts is to be 4% of the year end debtors

e) £100 of advertising costs have been included in the stationery account

f) The closing stock has been valued at £2,100.

You are required to:

a) enter the initial balances onto the extended trial balance given and check that the trial balance does balance

b) enter each of the adjustments into the adjustments columns on the extended trial balance and total the adjustments columns

c) extend the figures into the profit and loss account and balance sheet columns and total the columns including calculating the profit and entering it into the balance sheet columns

d) prepare the final accounts for the year ended 31 May 2007

Account name		Ledger balance		Adjustments		Profit and loss account		Balance sheet	
		DR £	CR £	DR £	CR £	DR £	CR £	DR £	CR £

Account name	Ledger balance		Adjustments		Profit and loss account		Balance sheet	
	DR £	CR £	DR £	CR £	DR £	CR £	DR £	CR £

2   Given below is the list of balances for a business at the end of June 2007.

	£
Capital	150,000
Creditors	40,400
Debtors	114,500
Sales	687,000
Stock at 1 July 2006	40,400
Plant at cost	68,000
Fixtures and fittings at cost	32,400
Wages	98,700
Sales returns	4,800
Telephone	4,100
Purchases	485,000
Heat and light	3,400
Advertising	8,200
Purchases returns	3,000
Selling costs	9,400
Discount received	4,700
Discount allowed	3,900
Administrative expenses	14,800
Miscellaneous expense	400
Provision for depreciation at 1 July 2006:	
Plant and machinery	34,680
Fixtures and fittings	6,480
Provision for doubtful debts at 1 July 2006	2,000
Drawings	36,860
Bank	6,400
VAT (credit balance)	1,800
HM Revenue and Customs	1,400
Suspense account (debit balance)	200

You are also given the following information:

a) The depreciation charges for the year are to be accounted for:

- Depreciation on plant and machinery is at the rate of 30% reducing balance
- Depreciation on fixtures and fittings is at the rate of 20% straight line

b) The suspense account balance has been investigated and the following errors have been discovered:

- Discounts received of £450 had been posted to the creditors account but not to the discount account

- Sales returns of £480 were correctly posted to the debtors account but were posted as £840 in the sales returns account

- A subtotal in the cash payments book of £1,010 for heat and light was not posted to the heat and light account

c) A bad debt of £1,500 is to be written off and a provision of 2% of debtors is required

d) There is an accrual for telephone expenses of £400 and the administrative expenses include prepaid amounts of £700

e) Closing stock has been valued at £42,800

You are required to:

a) enter the ledger balances (including the suspense account) onto the extended trial balance given and total the trial balance to ensure that it agrees

b) enter the adjustments in the adjustments columns and total them

c) extend the extended trial balance into the profit and loss account and balance sheet columns, total the columns to find the profit or loss and extend this into the balance sheet columns

d) prepare the final accounts for the year ended 30 June 2007

Account name	Ledger balance		Adjustments		Profit and loss account		Balance sheet	
	DR £	CR £	DR £	CR £	DR £	CR £	DR £	CR £

Account name	Ledger balance		Adjustments		Profit and loss account		Balance sheet	
	DR £	CR £	DR £	CR £	DR £	CR £	DR £	CR £

3 Below is an alphabetical list of balances taken from the ledger of Clegg and Co, a sole trader, as at 31 May 2007. Clegg & Co operates a computerised cash book but memorandum sales and purchase ledgers. You are also provided with some additional information.

	£
Administration costs	72,019.27
Bank overdraft	8,290.12
Capital	50,000.00
Loan	100,000.00
Depreciation charge	12,000.00
Drawings	36,000.00
Fixed assets: cost	120,287.00
Fixed assets: depreciation	36,209.28
Interest paid and payable	12,182.26
Interest received and receivable	21.00
Labour	167,302.39
Raw materials	104,293.38
Stock as at 1 June 2006	25,298.30
Purchase ledger control	42,190.85
Sales	481,182.20
Sales ledger control	156,293.00
VAT	4,938.20

a) Enter the balances in the format trial balance provided below. Set up a suspense account if necessary.

Account name		Trial balance		Adjustments		Profit and loss account		Balance sheet	
		DR £	CR £	DR £	CR £	DR £	CR £	DR £	CR £

b) With reference to the additional information below, clear the suspense account.

    i)   The debit side of the journal to record depreciation expense of £15,000.00 for the second six months of the period has been omitted.

    ii)   An examination of administration costs shows that there is a prepayment for insurance of £320.00 and an accrual for electricity of £480.00.

    iii)   One page of the sales returns day book was left out of the total posted to the sales ledger control account, although it was included in the other totals posted. The total value of credit notes on this page was £6,092.35.

    iv)   Invoices totalling £6,283.38 have not been recorded in the purchase ledger accounts.

    v)   The payment by BACS of wages in May of £14,248.40 has not been posted to the labour account, and nor has the purchase in May of a fixed asset for £4,000.00 been posted. This asset should be depreciated at a rate of 25% straight line, with a full year's depreciation being charged in the year of purchase.

    vi)   A cash receipt of £10,000.00 was recorded in the cash book but, as it was not identified, it has not yet been posted. It has now been clarified that this represents additional capital from the proprietor.

    vii)   Interest due of £650.00 on the loan needs to be accrued.

    viii)   At 31 May 2007 stock on hand was valued at £32,125.28.

c) With reference to the additional information above, make whatever other adjustments to the trial balance are necessary.

d)   i)   Extend the trial balance
    ii)   Total all columns of the extended trial balance.
    iii)   Make entries to record the net profit or loss for the year ended 31 May 2007.

e) Showing labour as an expense after gross profit, prepare a profit and loss account for the year ended 31 May 2007 and a balance sheet at that date.

chapter 15:
PARTNERSHIPS

1   Jim, Rob and Fiona are in partnership sharing profits in the ratio of 4 : 3 : 2. At 1 January 2007 the balances on their current accounts were:

Jim   £2,000
Rob   £1,000 (debit)
Fiona   £3,500

During the year to 31 December 2007 the partnership made a net profit of £135,000 and the partners' drawings during the year were:

Jim   £58,000
Rob   £40,000
Fiona   £32,000

Write up the partners' current accounts for the year ended 31 December 2007.

2   Josh and Ken are in partnership sharing profits in a ratio of 2 : 1. Ken is allowed a salary of £8,000 per annum and both partners receive interest on their capital balances at 3% per annum. An extract from their trial balance at 30 June 2007 is given below.

		£
Capital	Josh	40,000
	Ken	25,000
Drawings	Josh	21,000
	Ken	17,400
Current account	Josh	1,300
	Ken	800

The partnership made a net profit for the year ended 30 June 2007 of £39,950.

Write up the appropriation account and the partners' current accounts and show the balances that would appear in the balance sheet for the capital accounts and current accounts.

3   Given below is the trial balance of a partnership between Jo, Emily and Karen at 30 June 2007.

		£
Advertising		3,140
Bank		1,400 (debit)
Capital	Jo	25,000
	Emily	15,000
	Karen	10,000
Creditors		33,100
Current accounts	Jo	1,000 (credit)
	Emily	540 (credit)
	Karen	230 (credit)
Debtors		51,300
Drawings	Jo	12,000
	Emily	10,000
	Karen	10,000
Electricity		3,860
Fixtures and fittings at cost		12,500
Fixtures and fittings - accumulated depreciation		5,200
HM Revenue and Customs		680 (credit)
Insurance		2,500
Machinery at cost		38,000
Machinery - accumulated depreciation		15,700
Provision for doubtful debts		1,250
Purchases		199,000
Sales		306,000
Stock at 1 July 2006		23,400
Sundry expenses		2,480
Telephone		2,150
VAT		1,230 (credit)
Wages		43,200

You are also given the following information:

i)   Closing stock is valued at £24,100

ii)   Depreciation has yet to be charged for the year at the rate of 20% on cost for machinery and 25% reducing balance for fixtures and fittings

iii) A bad debt of £1,300 is to be written off and the provision for doubtful debts to be maintained at 3% of the remaining debtors

iv)   Electricity costs of £400 are to be accrued for and insurance includes a prepayment of £700

v)   Jo, Emily and Karen share profits in the equally. Emily has a salary of £4,000 per annum and each partner receives interest on their capital account balance at 5% per annum

You are required to:

a) draft the initial trial balance

b) draft journal entries to record the year end adjustments i) to iv)

c) write up the ledger accounts that are affected by the year end adjustments i) to iv) clearly showing the amended balance

d) draft a final trial balance after the year end adjustments have been put through (before any profit share to the partners)

e) prepare the profit and loss account for the year ended 30 June 2007

f) write up the partners' current accounts showing their share of profits and their drawings

g) prepare the balance sheet as at 30 June 2007

4   Bess, Charles and George are in partnership together. They operate a retail jewellery business. They are considering dissolving the partnership next year. They have asked you to assist in the preparation of the year end financial statements of their business. The trial balance as at 31 March 2007 is set out below.

BESS, CHARLES AND GEORGE
Trial balance as at 31 March 2007

	Debit £	Credit £
Motor expenses	3,769	
Drawings: Bess	46,000	
Charles	42,000	
George	38,000	
Capital account: Bess		60,000
Charles		40,000
George		20,000
Sales		568,092
Returns outwards		7,004
Carriage inwards	872	
Trade creditors		9,904
Returns inwards	8,271	
Purchases	302,117	
Carriage outwards	617	
Salespersons' commission	6,659	
Rent, rates and insurance	32,522	
Current account: Bess		4,670
Charles		5,600
George		3,750
Stock as at 1 April 2006	127,535	
Motor vehicles at cost	37,412	
Office equipment at cost	2,363	
Fixtures and fittings at cost	8,575	
Wages and NIC	48,317	
Lighting and heating	3,240	
Postage and stationery	705	
Accumulated depreciation: motor vehicles		18,651
office equipment		1,285
fixtures and fittings		3,754
Depreciation charge: motor vehicles	4,765	
office equipment	236	
fixtures and fittings	1,613	
Telephone	2,926	
Sundries	868	
Trade debtors	21,895	
Cash at bank	2,085	
Cash in hand	228	
Accruals		880
	743,590	743,590

You are also provided with the following information:

a)   The stock at the close of business on 31 March 2007 was valued at cost at £143,936.

b)   The partners are entitled to the following salaries per annum.

	£
Bess	30,000
Charles	25,000
George	17,000

c)   Interest on capital is to be paid to the partners at a rate of 5% on the balance at the end of the year on the capital accounts. No interest is to be paid on the current accounts.

d)   The profit sharing ratios in the partnership are:

Bess	5/12
Charles	4/12
George	3/12

You are required to:

1)   draft a profit and loss account for the year ended 31 March 2007

2)   prepare an appropriation account for the partnership for the year ended 31 March 2007

3)   prepare the balance sheet for the partnership, showing clearly the capital and current account balances

5   Given below is a list of the ledger account balances of a partnership at their year end of 30 April 2007. The two partners are Julian and Nigel Clark who share all profits equally. Julian also has a salary of £7,000 per annum.

	£
Sales	483,400
Stock at 1 May 2006	10,700
Purchases	279,600
Capital – Nigel Clark	60,000
Julian Clark	50,000
Current – Nigel Clark	2,000
Julian Clark	4,000
Drawings – Nigel Clark	30,000
Julian Clark	25,700
Building at cost	80,000
Motor vehicles at cost	28,600
Provision for depreciation:	
Buildings	9,600
Motor vehicles	14,500
Wages	63,800
Administration expenses	23,700
Selling costs	42,100
Debtors	60,400
Bank (debit balance)	2,200
Creditors	23,300

You are also given the following information:

i)   The closing stock at 30 April 2007 was valued at £11,200

ii)   Administration expenses of £1,200 are to be accrued and the selling costs include advertising fees paid in advance of £800

iii) The depreciation charge for the year needs to be accounted for – the building is being depreciated over 50 years straight line and the motor vehicles are depreciated at 30% reducing balance.

You are required to show the ledger account balances and adjustments on the extended trial balance given and to extend the figures into the profit and loss account and balance sheet columns showing the final share of the profit.

You are also required to prepare the final accounts for the partnership for the year ended 30 April 2007.

Account name		Ledger balance		Adjustments		Profit and loss account		Balance sheet	
		DR £	CR £	DR £	CR £	DR £	CR £	DR £	CR £

Account name		Ledger balance		Adjustments		Profit and loss account		Balance sheet	
		DR £	CR £	DR £	CR £	DR £	CR £	DR £	CR £

6 Ian and Max have been in partnership for a number of years sharing profits in the ratio of Ian two thirds and Max one third. The net assets of the partnership total £145,000 and it is believed that the partnership has goodwill of £18,000. Len is to be admitted to the partnership on 1 June 2007 and is to pay in £32,600 of capital. After Len has been admitted the profits will be shared as to two fifths to Ian and Max and one fifth to Len.

Write up the partners' capital accounts given below to reflect the goodwill adjustment and the admission of the new partner.

Capital accounts

	Ian	Max	Len		Ian	Max	Len
	£	£	£		£	£	£
				Bal b/d	85,000	60,000	

7 Theo, Deb and Fran have been in partnership for a number of years but on 31 December 2007 Deb is to retire. The balances on the partners' capital and current accounts at that date are:

		£
Capital	Theo	84,000
	Deb	62,000
	Fran	37,000
Current	Theo	4,500
	Deb	1,300
	Fran	6,200

Before the retirement of Deb the partners had shared profits in the ratio of 3 : 2 : 1. However after Deb's retirement the profit sharing ratio between Theo and Fran is to be 2 : 1. The goodwill of the partnership on 31 December 2007 is estimated to be £54,000. The agreement with Deb is that she will be paid £10,000 at the date of retirement and the remainder of the amount that is due to her will take the form of a loan to the partnership.

Write up the partners' capital and current accounts to reflect Deb's retirement.

8 During the year to 30 September 2007 the partnership of Will and Clare Evans made a net profit of £90,000. From 1 October 2006 until 30 June 2007 the partnership agreement was as follows:

		Per annum £
Salaries	Will	10,000
	Clare	15,000
Interest on capital 3% of the opening capital balance		
Profit share	Will	two thirds
	Clare	one third

However on 1 July 2007 the partnership agreement was changed as follows:

		£
Salaries	Will	12,000
	Clare	20,000
Interest on capital 3% of opening capital balance		
Profit share	Will	three quarters
	Clare	one quarter

The opening balances at 1 October 2006 on their capital and current accounts were as follows:

		£
Capital	Will	80,000
	Clare	50,000
Current	Will	2,000 (credit)
	Clare	3,000 (debit)

During the year ended 30 September 2007 Will made drawings of £44,000 and Clare made drawings of £37,000.

Prepare the partnership appropriation account in three column format and the partners' current accounts for the year ended 30 September 2007.

9 Mary Rose, Nelson Victory and Elizabeth Second are in partnership together hiring out river boats. Mary has decided to retire from the partnership at the end of the day on 31 March 2007. You have been asked to finalise the partnership accounts for the year ended 31 March 2007 and to make the entries necessary to account for the retirement of Mary from the partnership on that day.

You have been given the following information:

1) The profit for the year ended 31 March 2007 was £106,120.

2) The partners are entitled to the following salaries per annum.

	£
Mary	18,000
Nelson	16,000
Elizabeth	13,000

3) Interest on capital is to be paid at a rate of 12% on the balance at the beginning of the year on the capital accounts. No interest is paid on the current accounts.

4) Cash drawings in the year amounted to:

	£
Mary	38,000
Nelson	30,000
Elizabeth	29,000

5) The balances on the current and capital accounts at 1 April 2006 were as follows.

Capital accounts		Current accounts	
	£		£
Mary	28,000 (credit)	Mary	£2,500 (credit)
Nelson	26,000 (credit)	Nelson	£2,160 (credit)
Elizabeth	22,000 (credit)	Elizabeth	£1,870 (credit)

6) The profit-sharing ratios in the partnership are currently:

Mary	4/10
Nelson	3/10
Elizabeth	3/10

On the retirement of Mary, Nelson will put a further £40,000 of capital into the business. The new profit-sharing ratios will be:

Nelson	6/10
Elizabeth	4/10

7) The goodwill in the partnership is to be valued at £90,000 on 31 March 2007. No separate account for goodwill is to be maintained in the books of the partnership. Any adjusting entries in respect of goodwill are to be made in the capital accounts of the partners.

8) Any amounts to the credit of Mary on the date of her retirement should be transferred to a loan account.

You are required to:

a) prepare the partners' capital accounts as at 31 March 2007 showing the adjustments that need to be made on the retirement of Mary from the partnership

b) prepare an appropriation account for the partnership for the year ended 31 March 2007

c) prepare the partners' current accounts for the year ended 31 March 2007

d) show the balance on Mary's loan account as at 31 March 2007

chapter 16:
INCOMPLETE RECORDS

1 The net assets of a business totalled £14,689 at 1 January 2007 and £19,509 at 31 December 2007. The owner did not pay any additional capital into the business but did withdraw £9,670 in drawings.

What was the profit of the business for the year?

2 A business has net assets of £31,240 on 31 May 2007. On 1 June 2006 the net assets of the business were £26,450. The owner knows that he took £12,300 of drawings out of the business during the year in cash and £560 of goods for his own use.

What was the profit of the business for the year?

3 A business had net assets at the start of the year of £23,695 and at the end of the year of £28,575. The business made a profit of £17,370 for the year.

What were the owner's drawings for the year?

4 The owner of a small retail business provides you with the following information about the transactions for the month of May 2007:

	£
Till rolls showing amounts paid into till	5,430
Paying in slip showing amount paid into bank from till	4,820
Cheques to creditors totalling	3,980

The till always has a £100 cash float and the balance on the bank account at 1 May was £368 and at 30 May was £414. The owner has taken cash drawings out of the till and out of the bank account directly.

What is the total of the owner's drawings for the month?

Cash account	
£	£

Bank account	
£	£

5 A small retail business keeps a cash float of £250 in the till. The bank statement for the month of March 2007 shows that the amount of cash paid into the bank for the month was £7,236. The owner keeps a record of the amounts of cash paid directly out of the till and knows that these consisted of wages of £320, cleaning costs of £50 and drawings of £1,050.

What were the sales for the month?

Cash account	
£	£

6   A business has a balance on its debtors account of £1,589 at the start of October 2007 and this has risen to £2,021 by the end of October. The paying in slips for the month show that £5,056 was received from debtors during the month and discounts of £127 were allowed.

What are the sales of the business for the month?

Debtors account

£	£

7   The balance on a business's creditors account at 1 March 2007 was £4,266 and by 31 March was £5,111. During the month cheques paid to creditors totalled £24,589 and discounts received were £491.

What were the credit purchases for the month?

Creditors account

£	£

8   A retail business operates with a mark up on cost of 20%. The purchases for the month of May totalled £3,600 and the stock at the start of May was £640 and at the end of May was £570.

What were the sales for the month?

9   A retail business operates with a mark up on cost of 30%. The sales for the period were £5,200 and the stock at the start and end of the period were £300 and £500.

What were the purchases for the period?

10 A retail business operates on the basis of a gross profit margin of 20%. The purchases for the month of April totalled £5,010 and the stock at the start and the end of the month was £670 and £980 respectively.

What are the sales for the period?

11 Kuldipa Potiwal runs a small computer games retail and mail order business, but she does not keep proper accounting records. She has provided you with the following bank account summary for the year ended 31 October 2007.

Bank account summary

	£
Balance at bank (1 November 2006)	
Bank overdraft	3,250
Receipts	
Cash paid in	56,000
Cheques from debtors	46,000
Investment income	1,500
Rent received	2,500
Payments	
Payments to trade creditors	78,000
Rent and rates	6,400
Postage and packing costs	2,200
Motor expenses	5,050
Administration expenses	4,600

Additional information is provided as follows:

i) Kuldipa sells all her computer games at cost plus 50%.

ii) Before paying cash receipts into the bank, Kuldipa used some of the cash received to make a number of payments:

Wages of shop assistant and driver	£350 per week
Drawings	£220 per week
Administration expenses	£750 per annum

All cash is paid into the bank daily.

iii) The investment income was interest on her private investment account.

iv) Other balances were as follows.

	31 October 2006	31 October 2007
	£	£
Delivery van (valuation)	17,500	12,500
Stock of games	12,200	13,750
Trade creditors	9,000	13,400
Trade debtors	6,000	7,200
Rates paid in advance	500	200
Rent receivable	-	250
Administration expenses owing	175	215

v) During the year a vanload of games being delivered to credit customers was stolen. The van was recovered, undamaged, but the games have not been recovered. The insurance company has agreed to pay for 50% of the cost of the stolen games, but payment has not yet been received.

Kuldipa Potiwal calculated from the copy delivery notes that the selling price value of the games stolen was £6,000.

vi) At Christmas 2006 Kuldipa Potiwal gave games as presents to her young relatives. The selling price of these games was £480.00.

You are required to:

a) prepare a detailed calculation of the net profit of the business for the year ended 31 October 2007

Note. You should prepare a two column cash/bank account to help you in this calculation.

b) calculate the balance of Kuldipa's capital account at 31 October 2007.

12 Sheena Gordon has been trading for just over twelve months as a dressmaker. She has kept no accounting records at all, and she is worried that she may need professional help to sort out her financial position, and she has approached you.

You meet with Sheena Gordon and discuss the information that you require her to give you. Sometime later, you receive a letter from Sheena Gordon providing you with the information that you requested, as follows:

i) She started her business on 1 October 2006. She opened a business bank account and paid in £5,000 of her savings.

ii) During October she bought the equipment and the stock of materials that she needed. The equipment cost £4,000 and the stock of materials cost £1,800. All of this was paid for out of the business bank account.

iii) A summary of the business bank account for the twelve months ended 30 September 2007 showed the following.

	£		£
Capital	5,000	Equipment	4,000
Cash banked	27,000	Opening stock of materials	1,800
		Purchases of materials	18,450
		General expenses	870
		Drawings	6,200
		Balance c/d	680
	32,000		32,000

iv) All of the sales are on a cash basis. Some of the cash is paid into the bank account while the rest is used for cash expenses. She has no idea what the total value of her sales is for the year, but she knows that she has spent £3,800 on materials and £490 on general expenses. She took the rest of the cash not banked for her private drawings. She also keeps a cash float of £100.

v) The gross profit margin on all sales is 50%.

vi) She estimates that all the equipment should last for five years. You therefore agree to depreciate it using the straight line method.

vii) On 30 September 2007, the creditors for materials amounted to £1,400.

viii) She estimates that the cost of stock of materials that she had left at the end of the year was £2,200.

You are required to:

a) calculate the total purchases for the year ended 30 September 2007.
b) calculate the total cost of sales for the year ended 30 September 2007.
c) calculate the sales for the year ended 30 September 2007.
d) show the entries that would appear in Sheena Gordon's cash account.
e) calculate the total drawings made by Sheena Gordon throughout the year.
f) calculate the figure for net profit for the year ended 30 September 2007.

13 Given below is a summary of the bank statement for a business for the year ended 30 June 2007.

	£
Receipts	
Bankings	62,800
Payments	
Creditors	48,600
Electricity	1,400
Insurance	800
Telephone	1,300
Drawings	10,700
Computer	2,000

All money from cash sales and from debtors is paid into the till and then paid into the bank. Before paying the money into the bank the owner has informed you that cash wages of £1,600 were paid out of the till and that she took cash drawings from the till of £2,400.

The business operates at a gross profit margin of 30%.

The assets and liabilities of the business at the start and end of the year are given below although, due to the stock records being mislaid, the owner does not know the value of the closing stock.

	1 July 2006	30 June 2007
	£	£
Motor vehicle at cost	12,000	12,000
Computer at cost	–	2,000
Stock	3,400	not known
Debtors	4,100	6,300
Bank	6,700	4,700
Till float	200	200
Creditors	2,100	1,600
Accruals – electricity	120	150
Prepayments – insurance	180	200

The motor vehicle was purchased on 1 March 2006 and is being depreciated at 25% per annum on the straight-line basis. The computer purchased during the year was purchased on 1 January 2007 and is being depreciated at 20% per annum on the straight-line basis.

You are required to prepare the profit and loss account for the year ended 30 June 2007 and the balance sheet at that date.

PRACTICE SIMULATION 1

CANDLE CONTRACTS

Diploma Pathway students

Please note that if you are studying for the AAT qualification via the Diploma Pathway route, you will not be required to take a simulation for Unit 5, just the exam.

However, it would be good practice for you to try this simulation as it provides a good test of your understanding of the content and techniques required in the exam itself.

SIMULATION

COVERAGE OF PERFORMANCE CRITERIA

The following performance criteria are covered in this Simulation.

Element   **PC Coverage**

5.2 A   Correctly prepare reconciliations of final accounts.

5.2 B   Identify any discrepancies in the reconciliation process and either take steps to rectify them or refer them to the appropriate person.

5.2 C   Accurately prepare a trial balance and open a suspense account to record any imbalance.

5.2 D   Establish the reasons for any imbalance and clear the suspense account by correcting the errors, or reduce them and resolve outstanding items to the appropriate person.

5.2 F   Correctly identify, calculate and record appropriate adjustments.

5.3 B   Prepare final accounts of partnerships in proper form and in compliance with partnership agreement, from the trial balance.

INTRODUCTION

This Simulation is designed to test your ability to maintain financial records and prepare accounts.

The situation is provided below.

The tasks you are to perform are set out on Pages 133 and 134.

You are provided with data which you must use to complete the tasks.

Your answers should be set out in the Answer Booklet on Pages 138 to 153.

You are allowed four hours to complete your work.

A high level of accuracy is required. Check your work carefully.

THE SITUATION

Your name is Darcy Graham and you are an accounts assistant working for Candle Contracts, a small business owned by two partners, Keith Buxted and Fred Simons, which specialises in supplying stores and shops with candles and related products which are purchased from a number of manufacturers. You report to the accountant Meg Halliwell.

Both sales and purchases are made exclusively on credit with settlement discounts being offered to some credit customers and Candle Contracts being offered settlement discounts from some of its suppliers. All sales are standard rated for VAT purposes.

Books and records

The accounting system for Candle Contracts is entirely manual and a full set of ledger accounts is kept in the main ledger. The exception to this is the cash book which is kept physically separate as a primary record but is also part of the main ledger.

Subsidiary ledgers are kept for debtors, the sales ledger, and for creditors, the purchases ledger. These include a memorandum ledger account for each debtor and creditor.

Accounting policies and procedures

The balances on the sales ledger and purchases ledger control accounts are reconciled to the total of the individual balances in the subsidiary ledgers at the end of each month.

Candle Contracts has three categories of fixed assets. The motor vehicles used for delivery of products are depreciated at a rate of 30% on the reducing balance. The fixtures and fittings are depreciated at 20% straight line. The office equipment is depreciated at a rate of 25% on the reducing balance. A full year's depreciation is charged in the year of acquisition and none is charged in the year of disposal. There have been no additions or disposals of fixed assets during the year.

The simulation

In this simulation you will be required to perform a number of tasks leading up to the preparation of an extended trial balance for the year ended 30 June 2007.

TASKS TO BE COMPLETED

In the Answer Booklet on Pages 138 to 153 complete the tasks outlined below. Data for this assessment is provided on Pages 135 to 136.

1   Refer to the cash books given on Page 138 of the Answer Booklet. Post the entries for June to the main ledger accounts on Pages 139 to 143. Balance the cash book to find the balance that will appear in the extended trial balance. The balance on the cash book at 1 June 2007 was an overdraft balance of £3,206.16.

2   The depreciation charges for the year have not yet been calculated. Calculate the depreciation charge for the year for each class of fixed asset on Page 144 of the Answer Booklet and post the amounts to the main ledger accounts on Pages 139 to 143.

3   Refer to the list of debtor account balances from the subsidiary sales ledger given on Page 135 and compare this total to the balance on the sales ledger control account in the main ledger, which you must calculate. Refer also to the memo from Meg Halliwell given on Page 135. Prepare a reconciliation of the balance on the sales ledger control account to the total of the list of balances from the subsidiary sales ledger by redrafting the sales ledger control account on Page 145 of the Answer Booklet. Do not adjust the sales ledger control account in the main ledger at this stage.

4   Prepare the journal entries for the adjustments required from the sales ledger control account reconciliation in the journal given on Page 146 of the Answer Booklet with full narratives. Post the journal entries to the main ledger accounts including the sales ledger control account.

5   As at 30 June 2007 the totals from the purchases day book and purchases returns day book for the last week of June had not been posted to the main ledger accounts although the individual entries had been posted to the subsidiary purchases ledger accounts. Refer to the day book totals on Page 135 and post these totals to the main ledger accounts.

6   Refer to the list of creditor account balances from the subsidiary purchases ledger on Page 136. Balance the purchases ledger control account in the main ledger and check that the balance on the purchases ledger control account does agree to the total of the list of creditor account balances on Page 147 of the Answer Booklet (the totals should agree).

7   Balance all of the remaining ledger accounts in the main ledger and enter these balances in the first two columns of the Extended Trial Balance given on Pages 148 and 149 of the Answer Booklet. Do not forget the cash book balance. Total the first two columns of the extended trial balance to ensure that they are equal.

8   The suspense account must now be cleared. The suspense account balance is made up of two credit entries.

One credit entry for £366.75 was an amount received from a former customer for a debt that was written off in the year ended 30 June 2006. When the cheque was received you entered it into the cash receipts book but did not know what to do with the credit entry and therefore used the suspense account.

The other credit entry for £128.30 was for the cost of goods that Keith Buxted, one of the partners, informed you that he had taken out of the business for his own use. Your accounting treatment was to debit the owner's drawings account and to credit the suspense account.

Meg Halliwell has since offered advice to you as to the accounting treatment of these two items and you should now draft journal entries on Page 150 of the Answer Booklet to clear the suspense account – full narratives are required.

9   On the extended trial balance make adjustments in the adjustments columns for the following matters:

   ■   the journal entries prepared in Task 8
   ■   the closing stock valued at £7,188.15
   ■   the accruals and prepayments identified – see Page 136

Check that the totals of the adjustments columns agree.

10 Extend the trial balance. This includes totalling all columns of the trial balance and making entries to record the net profit or loss for the year ended 30 June 2007.

11 Having calculated the net profit for the year prepare the appropriation account for the year on Page 151. Fred has a salary of £12,500 per annum and the remaining profits are split between the partners with Keith receiving two thirds and Fred one third. Write up the partners' current accounts transferring balances from their drawings account.

12 Using the extended trial balance prepare a profit and loss account for the year ended 30 June 2007 and a balance sheet at that date, on Pages 152 and 153 of the Answer Booklet.

DATA

Debtor balances at 30 June 2007

	£
Jones Stores	4,628.49
Wax Wonders	7,321.18
Fantasy Isle Store	3,006.11
Treasures Untold	960.32
Candlistic Ltd	2,896.80
Fairtown Department Store	7,486.92
XTC Trading	3,212.27

MEMO

To: Darcy Graham
From: Meg Halliwell
Date: 7 July 2007
Subject: Debtors balances

When you prepare the reconciliation of debtors balances from the subsidiary ledger with the control account you should be aware of the following:

- a debt from Fantasy Isle Store has been written off as bad due to a disagreement totalling £102.50 – this has been entered into the subsidiary ledger account but not the main ledger account

- discounts allowed to customers in March were posted to the individual accounts in the subsidiary ledger but not to the main ledger – the total of the discounts was £186.79.

Purchases day book and purchases returns day book totals

Purchases day book

	Total £	VAT £	Net £
30 June	10,721.64	1,596.84	9,124.80

Purchases returns day book

	Total £	VAT £	Net £
30 June	824.38	122.78	701.60

Creditor balances at 30 June 2007

	£
Wax Suppliers	1,024.83
Endeavour Partners	201.60
Simply Six Ltd	521.86
Candlemania	406.21
J T Roberts	786.20
Jonathan Brown	331.30
F L Furle	100.00
Wax Wizards	261.96

Accruals and prepayments

Included in administration overheads there is an insurance prepayment of £543.33.

There is an accrual for rent of £2,050.00.

PRACTICE SIMULATION 1

CANDLE CONTRACTS

Task 1

Cash receipts book

Date	Details	Total £	VAT £	Sales ledger £	Other £	Discounts allowed £
7 June	Paying in slip 114	6,478.90		6,478.90		66.11
9 June	Paying in slip 115	2,570.36		2,570.36		26.22
13 June	Paying in slip 116	3,105.68		3,105.68		31.69
16 June	Paying in slip 117	1,055.79		1,055.79		10.77
20 June	Paying in slip 118	5,790.45		5,790.45		59.08
23 June	Paying in slip 119	3,612.56		3,612.56		36.86
28 June	Paying in slip 120	1,581.39		1,581.39		16.13
30 June	Paying in slip 121	2,046.57		2,046.57		20.88
		26,241.70		26,241.70		267.74

Cash payments book

Date	Details	Cheque no	Total £	VAT £	Purchases ledger £	Other £	Discounts received £
2 June	JT Roberts	01546	2,510.47		2,510.47		51.23
5 June	Wax Suppliers	01547	1,946.58		1,946.58		
9 June	BR Telephone	01548	681.50	101.50		580.00	
12 June	Candlemania	01549	3,015.37		3,015.37		61.53
15 June	Simply Six Ltd	01550	1,723.44		1,723.44		
19 June	Advertising	01551	940.00	140.00		800.00	
23 June	Wax Wizards	01552	2,061.57		2,061.57		
26 June	FL Furle	01553	3,000.00		3,000.00		
28 June	Endeavour Ptnrs	01554	995.47		995.47		
30 June	Council rates	SO	560.00			560.00	
30 June	Bank interest		53.18			53.18	
			17,487.58	241.50	15,252.90	1,993.18	112.76

Tasks 1, 2, 4, 5, and 11

Main ledger accounts

Administration overheads

	£		£
31 May Balance b/d	14,589.34		

Bad debts expense

	£		£
30 June Balance b/d	748.20		

Bank interest payable

	£		£
31 May Balance b/d	495.68		

Capital account – Keith Buxted

	£		£
		1 July Balance b/d	38,500.00

Capital account – Fred Simons

	£		£
		1 July Balance b/d	21,500.00

Current account – Keith Buxted

	£		£
		1 July Balance b/d	3,821.35

Current account – Fred Simons

	£		£
		1 July Balance b/d	1,959.00

Purchases ledger control

	£		£
		31 May Balance b/d	9,102.36

Sales ledger control

	£		£
30 June Balance b/d	56,310.82		

Discount allowed

	£		£
31 May Balance b/d	2,310.58		

Discount received

	£		£
		31 May Balance b/d	931.44

Drawings account – Keith Buxted

	£		£
30 June Balance b/d	20,357.50		

Drawings account – Fred Simons

	£		£
30 June Balance b/d	19,703.00		

Fixtures and fittings – at cost

	£		£
30 June Balance b/d	14,760.00		

Fixtures and fittings – depreciation expense

	£		£

Fixtures and fittings – accumulated depreciation

	£		£
		1 July Balance b/d	5,680.50

Motor vehicles at cost

	£		£
30 June Balance b/d	76,200.00		

Motor vehicles – depreciation expense

	£		£

Motor vehicles – accumulated depreciation

	£		£
		1 July Balance b/d	38,400.00

Office equipment – at cost

	£		£
30 June Balance b/d	10,845.50		

Office equipment – depreciation expense

	£		£

Office equipment – accumulated depreciation

	£		£
		1 July Balance b/d	3,750.32

Purchases

	£		£
31 May Balance b/d	101,383.33		

Purchases returns

	£		£
		31 May Balance b/d	6,523.45

Sales

	£		£
		30 June Balance b/d	290,446.12

Sales returns

	£		£
30 June Balance b/d	15,365.66		

Selling overhead

	£		£
31 May Balance b/d	9,254.67		

Stock

	£		£
30 June Balance b/d	10,256.38		

Suspense

	£		£
		30 June Balance b/d	495.05

VAT

	£		£
		30 June Balance b/d	2,105.47

Wages

	£		£
30 June Balance b/d	73,840.56		

Task 2

Depreciation calculations

Task 3

Sales ledger control account reconciliation

Task 4

Journal entries

	DR £	CR £

Task 6

Purchases ledger control account reconciliation

Tasks 7, 9 and 10

Account name		Ledger balance DR £	Ledger balance CR £	Adjustments DR £	Adjustments CR £	Profit and loss account DR £	Profit and loss account CR £	Balance sheet DR £	Balance sheet CR £

Account name		Ledger balance		Adjustments		Profit and loss account		Balance sheet	
		DR £	CR £	DR £	CR £	DR £	CR £	DR £	CR £

Task 8

Journal entries

	DR £	CR £

Task 11

Appropriation account for the year ended 30 June 2007

Task 12

Profit and loss account for the year ended 30 June 2007

Balance sheet as at 30 June 2007

PRACTICE SIMULATION 2

BRINTON LONGHAUL SERVICES

Diploma Pathway students

Please note that if you are studying for the AAT qualification via the Diploma Pathway route, you will not be required to take a simulation for Unit 5, just the exam.

However, it would be good practice for you to try this simulation as it provides a good test of your understanding of the content and techniques required in the exam itself.

SIMULATION

COVERAGE OF PERFORMANCE CRITERIA

The following performance criteria are covered in this Simulation.

Element	PC Coverage
5.2 A	Correctly prepare reconciliations of final accounts.
5.2 B	Identify any discrepancies in the reconciliation process and either take steps to rectify them or refer them to the appropriate person.
5.2 C	Accurately prepare a trial balance and open a suspense account to record any imbalance.
5.2 D	Establish the reasons for any imbalance and clear the suspense account by correcting the errors, or reduce them and resolve outstanding items to the appropriate person.
5.2 F	Correctly identify, calculate and record appropriate adjustments.
5.3 B	Prepare final accounts of partnerships in proper form and in compliance with partnership agreement, from the trial balance.

INTRODUCTION

This Simulation is designed to test your ability to maintain financial records and prepare accounts.

The Simulation is divided into five parts and 15 tasks. You are advised to look through the whole simulation first to gain a general appreciation of your tasks.

Your answers should be set out in the Answer Booklet on Pages 176 to 204.

You are allowed four hours to complete your work.

A high level of accuracy is required. Check your work carefully.

THE SITUATION

Brinton Longhaul Services is a business that transports goods by truck for customers within Europe. It also provides breakdown and repair services to trucks from its specialist workshop. All its customers are based in the UK.

- The business was set up as a sole tradership by Matthew Brinton in 2002.

- The business operates from a depot and offices rented on a short lease. It employs ten members of staff, mostly drivers and mechanics.

Your name is Karim Persaud. You are an Accounting Technician and you have recently been recruited to provide maternity cover to Avril Baker, the person who normally keeps the accounting records. You report directly to Matthew Brinton.

Today's date is 27 January 2007, and you have been asked to prepare draft accounts for Brinton Longhaul Services for the year ended 31 December 2006.

You have also been asked to contribute your expertise to two other businesses with which Matthew and his family are involved, Brinton Taxis and Cassandra's Cosmetics.

Accounting records

Brinton Longhaul Services maintains a manual system of accounts. The plant register, purchase ledger, sales ledger, cash book and petty cash book are not part of the main ledger.

The business is registered for VAT and all sales are standard rated at 17.5%.

TASKS TO BE COMPLETED

PART 1 ACCOUNTING FOR FIXED ASSETS

Background information

Brinton Longhaul Services owns the following fixed assets:

- trucks and cars
- office equipment
- workshop equipment

The main ledger includes accounts for cost and accumulated depreciation (ie the balance sheet provision) for each category of fixed asset. The depreciation charge (ie the expense recorded in the profit and loss account) is recorded in a single main ledger depreciation expense account.

Depreciation rates and methods are as follows:

Trucks and cars	25% pa on net book value (reducing balance basis)
Office equipment	25% pa on cost (straight line basis)
Workshop equipment	20% pa on net book value (reducing balance basis)

- A full year's depreciation is charged in the year of an asset's acquisition, regardless of the exact date of acquisition.

- No depreciation is charged in the year of an asset's disposal.

- Residual value is assumed to be nil in all cases.

Details of purchases and disposals of individual fixed assets are recorded in the plant register. The plant register also includes details of depreciation calculations.

Individual items costing less than £100 are not capitalised, but are treated as revenue expenses.

All purchase invoices (including fixed asset purchases) must be approved for payment by Matthew Brinton, who is the only signatory on the bank account. Fixed asset disposals are authorised by a memo from Matthew.

Purchases of fixed assets are recorded via the journal, not the purchases day book.

Task 1

Refer to the supplier's invoice, which has not yet been paid, and the memo on Pages 164 and 165 of this booklet. These relate to one purchase and one disposal of cars, plus a disposal of workshop equipment. Note that VAT on cars cannot be recorded as input tax, and that delivery charges are treated as transport supplies.

- Record the acquisition and the disposals in the plant register on Pages 176 to 177 of the Answer Booklet.

- Prepare journals to record the acquisition and both disposals in the main ledger. Use Page 178 of the Answer Booklet.

Task 2

With reference to the main ledger accounts on Pages 181 to 189 of the Answer Booklet, calculate the depreciation charge for the year to 31 December 2006 on the office equipment. Note that £10,000 of office equipment has already been fully depreciated. Use Page 179 of the Answer Booklet.

Calculate the depreciation for the year on the trucks and cars, and workshop equipment, and record the relevant amounts in the plant register on Pages 176 to 177 of the Answer Booklet.

Prepare journals on Page 178 of the Answer Booklet to record all depreciation in the main ledger.

Task 3

Refer to the memo from Matthew Brinton on Page 166 of this booklet.

- Write a reply to this memo, giving the advice that he has requested. Use the memo form on Page180 of your Answer Booklet.

- Prepare a journal on Page 178 of the Answer Booklet if required.

PART 2 LEDGER ACCOUNTING AND THE TRIAL BALANCE

Background information

All sales and purchases are on credit.

Sales and sales credits are recorded in the sales day book, which is posted to the sales ledger control account, the VAT control account and the transport sales and workshop sales accounts in the main ledger.

Purchases and purchases returns are recorded in the purchases day book, which is posted to the purchases ledger control account, the VAT control account, and the transport supplies, workshop purchases and administration costs accounts in the main ledger.

The sales ledger and the purchases ledger contain details of transactions with individual customers and suppliers. They are not part of the double entry system.

Receipts and payments into and from the bank account are recorded in a manual cash book. This is posted to the main ledger at the end of each month. Matthew's drawings are posted to the drawings account.

Receipts and payments into and from the petty cash box are recorded in a manual petty cash book. This is posted to the main ledger at the end of each month.

The sales and purchases day books have been written up and posted to the main ledger for the eleven months to 30 November 2006. The cash book and petty cash book have been written up and posted for the full year.

Task 4

Refer to the sales day book and the purchases day book on Page 167 of this book.

Write up the ledger accounts on Pages 181 to 189 of the Answer Booklet as follows for December 2006:

- post the journals that you have prepared in Tasks 1 to 3 to the main ledger
- post from the sales day book to the main ledger
- post from the purchases day book to the main ledger

Task 5

Refer to the sales ledger accounts on Pages 169 to 170 of this book and the sales ledger control account on Page 185 of the Answer Booklet.

- List and total the balances on the sales ledger accounts at 31 December 2006. Use Page 189 of the Answer Booklet.

- Compare this total with the balance on the sales ledger control account at 31 December 2006. Note the reason for the difference between the two on Page 189 of the Answer Booklet.

Task 6

Refer to the list of purchases ledger balances on Page 190 of the Answer Booklet and the purchases ledger control account on Page 184 of the Answer Booklet.

- Total the list of balances on the purchases ledger accounts at 31 December 2006.

- Compare this total with the balance on the purchases ledger control account at 31 December 2006. With reference to the purchases day book and cash book on Pages 167 and 168 of this book, establish the reason for the difference between the two.

- Prepare a journal on Page 191 of the Answer Booklet to correct any errors.

- Post this journal entry to the main ledger.

Task 7

Refer to the stock valuation schedule on Page 192 of the Answer Booklet for the parts that are held in the workshop on 31 December 2006. Refer also to the stock control account on Page 186 of the Answer Booklet, and the memo from Matthew on Page 171 of this book.

- On Page 192 of the Answer Booklet, total the stock valuation schedule and compare it with the balance on the stock control account at 31 December 2006.

- In the space provided, note the reason for the difference between the two.

- Prepare a journal on Page 193 of the Answer Book to correct any errors.

- Post this journal entry to the main ledger.

Task 8

Bring down a balance as at 31 December 2006 on each account in the main ledger.

Enter the balances in the trial balance columns of the schedule on Page 194 of the Answer Booklet. The totals of the two columns will not be equal. Enter any difference in a suspense account on the face of the trial balance.

PART 3 ADJUSTING AND EXTENDING THE TRIAL BALANCE

Task 9

On 31 December 2006 an amount of £10,000 was withdrawn from the business bank account via the local branch. The payment has been entered in the cash book, but the narrative column is blank. This amount forms part of the balance on the suspense account (only one side of the double entry – credit bank – was recorded).

- Describe how you would attempt to discover what this payment represents. Set out your answer on Page 195 of the Answer Booklet.

   The other item in the suspense account is the result of errors in the recording of bad debt expenses. Refer to Matthew's memo on Page 172 of this book.

- Draft journal entries, dated 31 December 2006, to correct these errors. Use Page 196 of the Answer Booklet. You should provide full narratives.

Task 10

Enter adjustments in the second two columns of the extended trial balance on Page 194 of the Answer Booklet:

- for the journal entries you prepared in Task 9
- for the accruals and prepayments listed on Page 173 of this booklet

There will still be a balance on the suspense account.

Task 11

- Extend the trial balance, putting the suspense account balance under current assets in the balance sheet.

- Total all columns of the extended trial balance.

- Make entries on the extended trial balance to record the net profit or loss for the year ended 31 December 2006.

- Transfer all relevant ledger account balances to the profit and loss ledger account on Page 197 of the Answer Booklet.

- Calculate the balance on the profit and loss ledger account and ensure it agrees with the amount calculated on the extended trial balance.

PART 4 PREPARING DRAFT ACCOUNTS

Task 12

- Prepare the profit and loss account of Brinton Longhaul Services for the year ended 31 December 2006 on Page 198 of the Answer Booklet.

- Prepare the balance sheet of Brinton Longhaul Services at 31 December 2006 on Page 198 of the Answer Booklet.

You should work to the nearest £.

Background information

As a totally separate enterprise, Matthew operates a taxi firm in partnership with his sister Cassandra, called Brinton Taxis. Their partnership agreement states that:

- Interest on capital is to be paid at 5% on the fixed balance on the capital accounts. No interest is paid on the current accounts.

- The partners are entitled to the following salaries for the year ended 31 December 2006:

	£
Matthew Brinton	10,000
Cassandra Brinton	25,000

- Profits and losses, after deducting interest on capital and salaries, are shared between the partners in the following ratio:

	%
Matthew Brinton	30
Cassandra Brinton	70

Matthew has presented you with a trial balance for Brinton Taxis (see Page 173 of this booklet), and asked you to produce final accounts.

Task 13

- Prepare the profit and loss account of Brinton Taxis for the year ended 31 December 2006 on Page 199 of the Answer Booklet.

- Prepare an appropriation account for the partnership for the year ended 31 December 2006.

- Prepare the partners' current accounts for the year ended 31 December 2006.

- Prepare the balance sheet of Brinton Taxis at 31 December 2006.

You should work to the nearest penny.

PART 5 RESTRUCTURING ACCOUNTS FROM INCOMPLETE EVIDENCE

As well as being in partnership with her brother, Cassandra Brinton also runs a small business selling cosmetics to people who attend parties at her home. She has been doing this for two years, but while things went well to begin with, her second year of trading (to 31 December 2006) has been difficult, mainly because her car was broken into on the last day of the year. A lot of stock, and most of her records, were stolen.

Cassandra provides you with some information, including:

- a list of assets and liabilities at 1 January 2006

- a list of customers who still owe her money at 31 December 2006, and a list of suppliers to whom she owes money

- a summary of her bank statements for 2006 (she has confirmed that all receipts relate to money from customers)

- confirmation that petty cash brought forward, plus cash withdrawals during the year, were used partly for her drawings of £200 per month and partly for cash expenses of the business.

Task 14

With reference to the information from Cassandra on Page 174 of this book:

On page 201 of the answer booklet, prepare a profit and loss account and a balance sheet for Cassandra's Cosmetics for the year ended 31 December 2006. Show all your workings on Page 202 of the Answer Booklet.

Task 15

Both Matthew and Cassandra feel that they have a lot to learn about the financial side of their businesses. They asked Avril Baker to put together a list of responses to some of their specific queries. Some of these responses are still incomplete.

Complete the responses as indicated on Pages 203 to 204 of the Answer Booklet.

DATA

CarsRUs Ltd

67-72 Main Street, Southmoor, Windale GH6 9MA

INVOICE
Invoice No 4534354
VAT registration 368813836
Date/Tax point: 30 December 2006

M Brinton
Brinton Longhaul Services,
Unit 15 Fernham Trading Estate
Windale GH7 8FG

	£	£
Trima RGS 2000 diesel registration MB56 FER		18,500.00
VAT @ 17.5%		3,237.50
Road fund licence (no VAT)		160.00
20 litres diesel	16.00	
Delivery charge	200.00	
VAT on diesel and delivery	37.80	
		253.80
Total due		22,151.30
Part exchange value of FE02 GHJ		(5,000.00)
Balance to pay		17,151.30

Terms: net, 30 days

Approved for payment 3 January 2007   *Matthew Brinton*

MEMORANDUM

To: Avril Baker
From: Matthew Brinton
Subject: Disposal of workshop equipment   **Date:** 5 December 2006

I have managed to sell some workshop equipment to my friend Lucas for £2,000. He will pay us at the end of January. It is the sundry equipment bought on 14 April 2002.

I am also trading in my old car for a new one at the end of the month. We will not have to pay the balance on the new car until the end of January 2007.

Matthew

MEMORANDUM

To: Karim Persaud
From: Matthew Brinton
Subject: Various fixed asset matters   Date: 25 January 2007

I have been meaning to mention that in August 2006 I scrapped a printer that we bought in January 2002 for £500. I'm not sure if this affects the 2006 accounts at all – please advise.

Another thing I'm not sure about – yesterday I acquired a new printer for the office for £99.99. Can we include this in fixed assets?

Finally, I want to acquire a new truck to fulfil a new long-term contract as soon as possible. It will cost £60,000, but I'm reluctant to pay more than £20,000 in cash right now. I estimate the truck will be used in the business for at least seven years. What alternatives are there, and what will be their effect on our assets and liabilities? Please set out the accounting entries with some figures as examples.

Matthew

Purchases day book for December 2006 (summary)

	£
Administration costs	1,170.50
Transport supplies	3,193.80
Workshop purchases	2,380.90
VAT	1,180.40
Total	7,952.60

Sales day book for December 2006

Date	Customer	Sales: transport £	Sales: workshop £	VAT £	Total £
1 December	RetailHeaven plc	6,781.00		1,186.67	7,967.67
5 December	ARC Ltd		150.00	26.25	176.25
8 December	Wemble & Co	1,896.35		331.86	2,228.21
10 December	TRILOGISTIX		1,520.00	266.00	1,786.00
15 December	TRILOGISTIX		3,741.65	654.78	4,396.43
17 December	RetailHeaven plc	4,637.50		811.56	5,449.06
21 December	Wemble & Co	7,512.50		1,314.68	8,827.18
28 December	ARC Ltd		2,133.65	373.38	2,507.03
		20,827.35	7,545.30	4,965.18	33,337.83

Cash receipts book

Date	Details	Total	Sales ledger control
		£	£
2006			
1 Dec	TRILOGISTIX	5,687.35	5,687.35
3 Dec	Wemble & Co	189.00	189.00
8 Dec	ARC Ltd	2,422.65	2,422.65
11 Dec	RetailHeaven plc	4,161.85	4,161.85
15 Dec	TRILOGISTIX	6,845.65	6,845.65
18 Dec	RetailHeaven plc	3,121.75	3,121.75
21 Dec	ARC Ltd	2,887.05	2,887.05
24 Dec	Wemble & Co	1,754.00	1,754.00
		27,069.30	27,069.30

Cash payments book (extract)

Details	
	£
Administration costs	117.50
Drawings	2,455.00
Purchases ledger control	6,985.00
Transport supplies	308.85
VAT	2,957.80
Wages and salaries	9,140.45
	10,000.00
Workshop purchases	241.20
TOTALS FOR DECEMBER	32,205.80

Sales ledger

ARC Ltd

Date	Details	Amount £	Date	Details	Amount £
2006			2006		
1 Dec	Balance b/d	3,333.40	8 Dec	Bank	2,422.65
5 Dec	Sales day book	176.25	15 Dec	Bank	2,887.05
15 Dec	Sales day book	2,507.03	31 Dec	Balance c/d	706.98
		6,016.68			6,016.68
2007					
1 Jan	Balance b/d	706.98			

Lewin Haulage

Date	Details	Amount £	Date	Details	Amount £
2006			2006		
1 Dec	Balance b/d	419.50	31 Dec	Balance c/d	419.50
		419.50			419.50
2007					
1 Jan	Balance b/d	419.50			

RetailHeaven plc

Date	Details	Amount £	Date	Details	Amount £
2006			2006		
1 Dec	Balance b/d	7,283.60	11 Dec	Bank	4,161.85
1 Dec	Sales day book	7,967.67	18 Dec	Bank	3,121.75
17 Dec	Sales day book	5,449.06	31 Dec	Balance c/d	13,416.73
		20,700.33			20,700.33
2007					
1 Jan	Balance b/d	13,416.73			

TRILOGISTIX

Date	Details	Amount £	Date	Details	Amount £
2006			*2006*		
1 Dec	Balance b/d	12,533.00	1 Dec	Bank	5,687.35
10 Dec	Sales day book	1,786.00	15 Dec	Bank	6,845.65
15 Dec	Sales day book	4,396.43	31 Dec	Balance c/d	6,182.43
		18,715.43			18,715.43
2007					
1 Jan	Balance b/d	6,182.43			

Wemble & Co

Date	Details	Amount £	Date	Details	Amount £
2006			*2006*		
1 Dec	Balance b/d	1,943.00	3 Dec	Bank	189.00
8 Dec	Sales day book	2,228.21	24 Dec	Bank	1,754.00
21 Dec	Sales day book	8,827.18	31 Dec	Balance c/d	11,055.39
		12,998.39			12,998.39
2007					
1 Jan	Balance b/d	11,055.39			

MEMORANDUM

To: Karim Persaud
From: Matthew Brinton
Subject: Stock valuation   Date: 25 January 2007

We do a physical count of stock on 30 December and value the cost on a FIFO basis, using the lower of cost and net realisable value. We then adjust the balance on the stock account and the workshop purchases account by a journal.

Avril prepared an initial stock valuation at 30 December and put through the journal as usual. However, on 31 December I took some parts from the workshop for my own use. The cost of these parts on a FIFO basis was £125.00. I updated the stock valuation schedule to reflect this, but Avril did not have the chance to make any book entries.

Matthew

MEMORANDUM

To: Karim Persaud
From: Matthew Brinton
Subject: Bad debts
                                                    Date: 25 January 2007

I am a little concerned that we have made a bit of a mess of our accounting for the bad debts provision, which we created in August this year. The amount of the general provision is £2,000, but we were unsure how to account for this beyond crediting the provision account.

In December, after legal advice we recognised a bad debt from Lewin Haulage of £419.50. Again we were unsure how to account for this beyond crediting the sales ledger control account.

Matthew

Accruals and prepayments at 31 December 2006

All calculations are made to the nearest month.

Only two items are expected to give rise to accruals or prepayments:

Business rates

On I November 2006 the business paid six months rates in advance of £6,900 (included in administration costs).

Legal fees

Following the dispute with Lewin Haulage a legal bill of £500 is expected, though it has not yet been received (to be included in administration costs).

BRINTON TAXIS

Trial balance for year ended 31 December 2006

	£	£
Accruals		32
Bank loan		50,000
Capital at 31 December 2006: Cassandra		7,500
Capital at 31 December 2006: Matthew		7,500
Cash at bank	6,823	
Cash in hand	98	
Current account at 1 January 2006: Cassandra	800	
Current account at 1 January 2006: Matthew		1,500
Depreciation expense	4,875	
Drawings: Cassandra	23,450	
Drawings: Matthew	12,645	
Fixed assets: accumulated depreciation		11,375
Fixed assets: cost	70,000	
Loan interest	3,000	
Other expenses	1,865	
Prepayments	200	
Profit on disposal of taxis		1,995
Purchases	21,645	
Sales		85,852
Sundry creditors		300
Sundry debtors	1,000	
Trade creditors		1,960
Trade debtors	8,246	
VAT		2,375
Wages	15,742	
	170,389	170,389

CASSANDRA'S COSMETICS

List of assets and liabilities at 1 January 2006

	£
Fixed assets (car) at cost	10,000
Stock	2,875
Debtors	1,975
Cash at bank	2,430
Petty cash	55
Creditors	935
Bank loan	4,500

Trading policy

All sales are on a 50% margin

Accounting policies

Depreciation – 25% straight line, residual value at end of four years: 10% of cost

Summary of bank statements for 2006

	£
Opening balance	2,430
Cheque payments to suppliers	7,535
Receipts from customers	12,645
Cash withdrawals	5,340
Loan interest	270
Closing balance	1,930

Customers who owe money as at 31 December 2006:	£3,820
Suppliers who are owed money at 31 December 2006:	£860
Fixed amount owed by insurance company re stolen stock:	£2,000
Cost of stock not stolen:	£500

PRACTICE SIMULATION 2

BRINTON LONGHAUL SERVICES

ANSWER BOOKLET

Task 1

PLANT REGISTER			25% pa NBV					
TRUCKS AND CARS								
	Acquisition date	Cost	Dep'n	NBV	Funding method	Disposal proceeds	Disposal date	
		£	£	£		£		
FE01 KJH	1 January 2002	50,000.00						
Truck								
31/12/02			12,500.00	37,500.00	Cash			
31/12/03			9,375.00	28,125.00				
31/12/04			7,031.25	21,093.75				
31/12/05			5,273.44	15,820.31				
P983 GHA	1 January 2003	28,000.00			Cash			
Truck								
31/12/02			7,000.00	21,000.00				
31/12/03			5,250.00	15,750.00				
31/12/04			3,937.50	11,812.50				
31/12/05			2,953.13	8,859.37				
FE02 GHJ	1 January 2002	20,000.00			Cash			
Car								
31/12/02			5,000.00	15,000.00				
31/12/03			3,750.00	11,250.00				
31/12/04			2,812.50	8,437.50				
31/12/05			2,109.38	6,328.12				

WORKSHOP EQUIPMENT			20% pa NBV				
	Acquisition date	Cost	Dep'n	NBV	Funding method	Disposal proceeds	Disposal date
		£	£	£			
Service equipment	1 April 2002	40,000.00			Cash		
31/12/02			8,000.00	32,000.00			
31/12/03			6,400.00	25,600.00			
31/12/04			5,120.00	20,480.00			
31/12/05			4,096.00	16,384.00			
Sundry equipment	14 April 2002	6,345.00			Cash		
31/12/02			1,269.00	5,076.00			
31/12/03			1,015.20	4,060.80			
31/12/04			812.16	3,248.64			
31/12/05			649.74	2,598.90			

Tasks 1 to 3

Journal

Date 2006	Account names and narrative	Debit £	Credit £
	Journal 1		
	Journal 2		
	Journal 3		
	Journal 4		
	Journal 5		

Task 2

Calculation of depreciation charge on office equipment

£

Task 3

MEMORANDUM

To: Matthew Brinton
From: Karim Persaud
Subject: Re: Various fixed asset matters   **Date:** 27 January 2007

Task 8 and 11

MAIN LEDGER

Administration costs

Date 2006	Details	Amount £	Date 2006	Details	Amount £
1 Dec	Balance b/d	12,875.65			
31 Dec	Petty cash book	56.40			
31 Dec	Bank	117.50			

Bad debt expense

Date 2006	Details	Amount £	Date 2006	Details	Amount £
1 Dec	Balance b/d	248.90			

Bank control

Date 2006	Details	Amount £	Date 2006	Details	Amount £
1 Dec	Balance b/d	37,764.55	31 Dec	Payments	32,205.80
31 Dec	Receipts	27,069.30			

Capital

Date 2006	Details	Amount £	Date 2006	Details	Amount £
			1 Dec	Balance b/d	110,000.00

Depreciation expense

Date 2006	Details	Amount £	Date 2006	Details	Amount £

Drawings

Date 2006	Details	Amount £	Date 2006	Details	Amount £
1 Dec	Balance b/d	27,000.00			
31 Dec	Bank	2,455.00			

Disposals

Date 2006	Details	Amount £	Date 2006	Details	Amount £

Office equipment: Cost

Date 2006	Details	Amount £	Date 2006	Details	Amount £
1 Dec	Balance b/d	22,000.00			

Office equipment: Accumulated depreciation

Date 2006	Details	Amount £	Date 2006	Details	Amount £
			1 Dec	Balance b/d	19,000.00

Petty cash control

Date	Details	Amount	Date	Details	Amount
2006		£	2006		£
1 Dec	Balance b/d	100.00	31 Dec	Payments	56.40

Provision for doubtful debts

Date	Details	Amount	Date	Details	Amount
2006		£	2006		£
			1 Dec	Balance b/d	2,000.00

Purchases ledger control account

Date	Details	Amount	Date	Details	Amount
2006		£	2006		£
31 Dec	Bank	6,985.00	1 Dec	Balance b/d	8,860.00

Sales ledger control account

Date	Details	Amount	Date	Details	Amount
2006		£	2006		£
1 Dec	Balance b/d	25,512.50	31 Dec	Bank	27,069.30
			31 Dec	Journal – Lewin	
				bad debt	419.50

Sales: Transport

Date	Details	Amount	Date	Details	Amount
2006		£	2006		£
			1 Dec	Balance b/d	105,395.55

Sales: Workshop

Date	Details	Amount	Date	Details	Amount
2006		£	2006		£
			1 Dec	Balance b/d	104,758.60

Stock

Date 2006	Details	Amount £	Date 2006	Details	Amount £
1 Dec	Balance b/d	4,356.05	31 Dec	Journal	352.46

Sundry creditors

Date 2006	Details	Amount £	Date 2006	Details	Amount £

Sundry debtors

Date 2006	Details	Amount £	Date 2006	Details	Amount £

Transport supplies

Date	Details	Amount	Date	Details	Amount
2006		£	2006		£
1 Dec	Balance b/d	35,131.85			
31 Dec	Bank	308.85			

Trucks and cars: Cost

Date	Details	Amount	Date	Details	Amount
2006		£	2006		£
1 Dec	Balance b/d	98,000.00			

Trucks and cars: Accumulated depreciation

Date	Details	Amount	Date	Details	Amount
2006		£	2006		£
			1 Dec	Balance b/d	66,992.20

VAT control

Date	Details	Amount	Date	Details	Amount
2006		£	2006		£
31 Dec	Bank	2,957.80	1 Dec	Balance b/d	2,841.00

Wages and salaries

Date	Details	Amount	Date	Details	Amount
2006		£	2006		£
1 Dec	Bal b/d	109,685.30			
31 Dec	Bank	9,140.45			

Workshop equipment: Cost

Date	Details	Amount	Date	Details	Amount
2006		£	2006		£
1 Dec	Bal b/d	46,345.00			

Workshop equipment: Accumulated depreciation

Date 2006	Details	Amount £	Date 2006	Details	Amount £
			1 Dec	Balance b/d	27,362.10

Workshop purchases

Date 2006	Details	Amount £	Date 2006	Details	Amount £
1 Dec	Balance b/d	26,189.65			
31 Dec	Journal	352.46			
31 Dec	Bank	241.20			

Task 5

Sales ledger account balances at 31 December 2006

£

ARC Ltd
Lewin Haulage
RetailHeaven plc
TRILOGISTIX
Wemble & Co

Sales ledger control account:
Balance at 31 December 2006

Difference   £

Task 6

Purchases ledger account balances at 31 December 2006

	£
Bronwen & Co	1,546.32
Eddlestone Ltd	2,576.38
HighDry plc	1,963.72
Ormskirk Parts Ltd	975.29
Runcorn plc	1,552.06
Viscount Ltd	1,186.83

Purchases ledger control account:
Balance at 31 December 2006

Difference   £

Journal

Date 2006	Account names and narrative	Debit £	Credit £
	Journal 6		

Task 7

Workshop stock valuation schedule at 31 December 2006

Part number	FIFO cost £	NRV £	Valuation £
15674	21.23	58.00	
43430	465.65	525.00	
45446	801.28	789.65	
46876	549.00	678.65	
55564	1,158.45	1,500.00	
68368	640.02	756.05	
97531	254.59	482.70	
Total			

Stock ledger control account balance at 31 December 2006

Difference   £_____

Journal

Date 2006	Account names and narrative	Debit £	Credit £
	Journal 7		

Task 8, 10 and 11

Brinton Longhaul Services year ended 31 December 2006

Account name	Trial balance DR £	Trial balance CR £	Adjustments DR £	Adjustments CR £	Profit and loss account DR £	Profit and loss account CR £	Balance sheet DR £	Balance sheet CR £
Administration costs								
Bad debt expense								
Bank control								
Capital								
Depreciation expense								
Disposals								
Drawings								
Office equipment: acc dep'n								
Office equipment: cost								
Petty cash control								
Provision for doubtful debts								
Purchases ledger control								
Sales ledger control								
Sales: transport								
Sales: workshop								
Stock								
Sundry creditors								
Sundry debtors								
Transport supplies								
Trucks and cars: acc dep'n								
Trucks and cars: cost								
VAT control								
Wages and salaries								
Workshop equipment: acc dep'n								
Workshop equipment: cost								
Workshop purchases								
Suspense								
Accruals								
Prepayments								
Profit for the year								

Task 9

Withdrawal of £10,000

Journal

Date 2006	Account names and narrative	Debit £	Credit £

Task 11

Profit and loss account

Date	Details	Amount £	Date	Details	Amount £
2006			2006		

Task 12

BRINTON LONGHAUL SERVICES

Profit and loss account for the year ended 31 December 2006

	£	£
Sales		
Less: Cost of sales		
Transport supplies		
Workshop purchases	————	
		————
Gross profit		
Expenses		
Wages and salaries		
Bad debts		
Admin costs		
Depreciation		
Loss on disposals	————	
		————
Net profit		════

Balance sheet at 31 December 2006

	£	£	£
Fixed assets			
Office equipment			
Trucks and cars			
Workshop equipment	————	————	————
	————	————	
Current assets			
Stock			
Trade debtors			
Provision			
Sundry debtors			
Prepayments			
Suspense			
Cash at bank			
Cash in hand		————	
		————	
Current liabilities			
Trade creditors			
Sundry creditors			
VAT			
Accruals		————	
		————	
Net current assets			————
Net assets			
			————
Capital b/f			
Net profit for the year			
Drawings			————
			════

Task 13

BRINTON TAXIS

Profit and loss account for the year ended 31 December 2006

	£	£
Sales		
Purchases		
Gross profit		
Profit on disposal		
Expenses		
Wages		
Depreciation		
Other expenses		
Loan interest		
Net profit		

Balance sheet at 31 December 2006

	£	£	£
Fixed assets			
Current assets			
Stock			
Trade debtors			
Sundry debtors			
Prepayments			
Cash at bank			
Cash in hand			
Current liabilities			
Trade creditors			
Sundry creditors			
VAT			
Accruals			
Net current assets			
Bank Loan			
Net assets			
Capital: Matthew			
Capital: Cassandra			
Current account: Matthew			
Current account: Cassandra			

199

Appropriation account for year ended 31 December 2006

		£	£
Net profit			
Salary			
Matthew			
Cassandra			
Interest on capital			
Matthew			
Cassandra			
Balance of net profit			
Share of profit			
Matthew			
Cassandra			

Current accounts

Date	Details	Matthew £	Cassandra £	Date	Details	Matthew £	Cassandra £
2006				2006			

Task 14

CASSANDRA'S COSMETICS

Profit and loss account for the year ended 31 December 2006

	£	£
Sales		
Cost of sales		
Opening stock		
Purchases		
Closing stock	_____	
		_____
Gross profit		
Expenses		
Depreciation		
Net cost of stolen stock		
Loan interest	_____	
		_____
Net profit		_____

Balance sheet at 31 December 2006

	£	£	£
Fixed assets			
Current assets			
Stock			
Trade debtors			
Sundry debtors – insurance			
Cash at bank			
Cash in hand		_____	
		_____	
Trade creditors			
Net current assets			_____
Bank loan			_____
Net assets			_____
Opening capital			
Profit for the year			
Drawings			_____
			_____

Workings

£   £

Task 15

MEMO

To: Matthew and Cassandra Brinton
From: Avril Baker
Date: 27 January 2007

RESPONSES TO YOUR FINANCIAL QUERIES

1   Sole traders and partnerships in the UK *are/are not bound by the Companies Act 1985. (*Delete as applicable.)

2   The legislation by which partnerships are affected on points where they do not have a partnership agreement is _____.

3   If partners do not have a formal agreement as to how much salary they should receive and how profits should be split, the legislation states that:

_____.

_____.

4   Accounting regulations which have a strong influence on the accounts of sole traders and partnerships are: _____ and _____.

5   The selection of accounting policies is governed by: _____.

6   The basic accounting concepts that underlie the selection of accounting policies are

_____ and _____.

7   Definition of the accruals concept: _____

_____.

8   Definition of the going concern concept: _____

_____.

9   When selecting accounting policies, according to the Statement of Principles the objective is to have information that is: _____, _____, _____ and _____.

10 An item is material in the context of a set of accounts when its omission or misstatement would

_____.

11 The accounting regulation which states that depreciation should be charged on fixed assets is

_____.

12 If a fixed asset is most likely to wear out at an even rate, the most suitable depreciation method would be *straight line/reducing balance. (*Delete as applicable.)

13 While the Companies Act allows the valuation of stock on the LIFO basis, this is prevented by

_____.

14   Stocks should be valued at the lower of _____ and _____.

15   Under the FIFO basis, stock is deemed to comprise items bought *most recently/longest ago. (*Delete as applicable.)

16   Assets acquired under leasing or hire purchase arrangements are governed by _____.

17   Value added tax should be *included/excluded from the sales figure in the profit and loss account. VAT owed to HM Revenue & Customs should be shown under _____ in the balance sheet, This is covered by _____.

AAT

PRACTICE EXAM 1

AMMAR

These tasks were set by the AAT in December 2007.

Time allowed: 3 hours plus 15 minutes' reading time.

This exam paper is in TWO sections.

You have to show competence in BOTH sections. So, try to complete EVERY task in BOTH sections.

Section 1 contains 10 tasks and Section 2 contains 7 tasks.

You should spend about 90 minutes on Section 1, and 90 minutes on Section 2.

You should show your workings in the spaces provided.

SECTION 1 (Suggested time allowance: 90 minutes)

DATA

Ammar is the proprietor of a business which repairs and maintains buildings.

He keeps a sales day-book and a purchases day-book but he does not keep a double entry bookkeeping system. All payments and receipts pass through the business bank account. The business is registered for VAT.

You are an accounting technician at Harper and Co., the accounting firm that prepares the final accounts for Ammar. The financial year end is 31 October.

You have the following information:

Balances as at:	31 October 2006	31 October 2007
	£	£
Vehicle at cost	18,000	18,000
Vehicle accumulated depreciation	4,500	To be calculated
Stock at cost	6,400	7,200
Trade debtors	10,500	12,900
Prepayment	750	To be calculated
Accrual	200	To be calculated
Trade creditors	5,800	6,300
VAT payable	2,200	To be calculated
Capital	26,650	26,650

Bank summary for the year ended 31 October 2007

	£		£
Balance b/f	3,700	Rent	6,250
Receipts from trade debtors	142,800	Payroll expenses	22,000
		Payments to trade creditors	70,000
		General expenses – including VAT	4,700
		VAT – paid to HMRC	11,025
		Drawings	30,000
		Balance c/f	2,525
	146,500		146,500

Day book summaries for the year ended 31 October 2007

	Net £	VAT £	Total £
Sales	125,000	21,875	146,875
Purchases	60,000	10,500	70,500

Task 1.1

You need to find the figure for discounts allowed.

Prepare the sales ledger control account for the year ended 31 October 2007, showing clearly the figure for discounts allowed. There are no other missing figures.

Sales ledger control account

	£		£

Task 1.2

The prepayment in the list of balances is for rent. The bank summary includes £1,500 for rent, for the quarter ending 31 December 2007. Ammar is not charged VAT on rent.

Prepare the rent account, showing clearly the rent for the year ended 31 October 2007.

Rent		
	£	£

Workings

Task 1.3

The bank summary shows general expenses of £4,700 which includes VAT at 17.5%.

Note. General expenses are not included in the purchases day book.

a)   Calculate the general expenses net of VAT.

_____

_____

_____

_____

b)   Calculate the VAT on general expenses that you must include in the VAT account.

_____

_____

_____

_____

Task 1.4

You need to find the closing balance figure for VAT.

Using the information you have been given already and your answer to Task 1.3b), complete the VAT account.

VAT

	£		£
		Balance b/f	2,200

Task 1.5

The accrual of £200 in the list of balances is for payroll expenses. In November 2007, £320 was paid for payroll expenses incurred in October 2007.

Prepare the payroll expenses account, showing clearly the payroll expenses for the year ended 31 October 2007. You will need to refer to the data earlier in the question.

Payroll expenses

£	£

Task 1.6

Depreciation is provided at 25% on a reducing balance basis.

a)   Calculate the depreciation charge for the year ended 31 October 2007.

_____

_____

_____

_____

b)   Calculate the updated accumulated depreciation.

_____

_____

_____

_____

Task 1.7

Your supervisor has suggested to Ammar that he makes a provision for doubtful debts of 5% of his outstanding trade debtors.

a)   Calculate the provision for doubtful debts that you must include in the trial balance.

_____

_____

_____

_____

b)   Explain briefly to Ammar why he might need a provision for doubtful debts in his accounts.

_____

_____

_____

_____

Task 1.8

Complete the trial balance below as at 31 October 2007. Take into account your answers to the above tasks, and all the other information you have been given.

Ammar		
Trial balance as at 31 October 2007		
	DR £	CR £
Total		

Task 1.9

One of the functions of a trial balance is to help in the detection of errors. However, not all errors are detected by the trial balance.

Using the table below, indicate whether the trial balance would detect each of the errors.

Note. You do not need to make any adjustments.

Would the errors below be detected by the trial balance?	Yes	No
a) A bank payment has been entered into the bank account but no other entries have been made.		
b) A sales invoice for £420 + VAT has been entered as follows: DR Sales £420 CR Sales ledger control account £420		
c) Discounts received of £101 have been credited to discounts received as £110 and debited to the purchases ledger control account as £101.		
d) Payroll expenses of £890 have been debited to payroll expenses and credited to the bank account. The correct amount should have been £980.		

Task 1.10

Ammar needs to buy a replacement van for his business. He asks how he could fund this.

Name TWO different methods of funding which Ammar could consider.

_____

_____

_____

SECTION 2 (Suggested time allowance: 90 minutes)

DATA

Asma, Ben and Chris are the owners of Great Gifts, a partnership business that sells gifts to the public from a retail store.

You are an accounting technician at Harper and Co., the accounting firm that prepares the final accounts for Great Gifts.

The financial year end is 30 September.

- The partners maintain a double entry accounting system consisting of a main ledger and a purchases ledger. They also keep computerised stock records.

- There are no credit sales.

- Great Gifts is registered for VAT.

- The trial balance as at 30 September 2007 is shown on the next page.

Great Gifts – Trial balance as at 31 September 2007

	Ledger balances	
	DR £	CR £
Administration expenses	24,530	
Advertising expenses	11,250	
Bank	10,125	
Capital account – Asma		30,000
Capital account – Ben		30,000
Capital account – Chris		30,000
Cash	2,200	
Current account – Asma	6,000	
Current account – Ben	23,000	
Current account – Chris	23,000	
Depreciation expense	20,650	
Equipment at cost	25,000	
Equipment accumulated depreciation		9,000
Fixtures and fittings at cost	131,500	
Fixtures and fittings accumulated depreciation		13,150
Opening stock	36,000	
Payroll expenses	52,000	
Purchases	290,820	
Purchases ledger control account		38,250
Rent	56,500	
Sales		550,000
Suspense		500
VAT		11,675
TOTAL	**712,575**	**712,575**

DATA

You have investigated the balance on the suspense account and discovered some errors that need to be corrected. There are also some year end adjustments to be made. You do not need to adjust for VAT.

a) Administration expenses of £820 were debited to the purchases account. The credit entry was correct.

b) i) Equipment costing £2,500 was purchased for cash during the year. The correct entry was made to the bank, but no other entries were made.

   ii) Depreciation needs to be provided on this new equipment for the year ended 30 September 2007 at 30% using the straight line method. A full year's depreciation is charged in the year of purchase.

c) Accrued advertising expenses of £1,500 were debited to the advertising expenses account twice. No other entries were made.

d) The figure for closing stock needs to be calculated. You have the following information:

   i)   Closing stock at cost from the computerised stock system £43,500
   ii) Obsolete items included in this figure cost £4,200 but were later sold for £1,700.

Task 2.1

Prepare journal entries to account for the information given above. Use the blank journal below. You do not need to give dates and narratives.

Note. There is space for your workings on the next page.

Journal		
	DR £	CR £
a)		
b) i)		
ii)		
c)		
d)		

Workings

Task 2.2

Prepare a profit and loss account for the partnership for the year ended 30 September 2007, showing clearly the gross profit and the net profit. Use the trial balance above and your journal adjustments from above.

Workings	Great Gifts Profit and loss account for the year ended 30 September 2007		
		£	£

ADDITIONAL DATA

Asma retired from the partnership on 31 March 2007. You have the following information about the partnership agreement.

- Partners' annual salaries

  Asma £20,500 (£10,250 for 1 October 2006 to 31 March 2007)
  Ben £25,000
  Chris nil

- Interest on capital accounts

  5% per annum on the balance at the beginning of the year.

- Profit share, effective until 31 March 2007

  Asma 50%
  Ben 25%
  Chris 25%

- Profit share, effective from 1 April 2007

  Ben 60%
  Chris 40%

You can assume that profits accrued evenly during the year.

Task 2.3

Complete the following table to show the interest on capital for each of the partners. Show your workings below.

Interest on capital	1 October 2006 to 31 March 2007	1 April 2007 to 30 September 2007	Total
	£	£	£
Asma			
Ben			
Chris			

Workings

Task 2.4

Prepare the appropriation account for the partnership for the year ended 30 September 2007. There is extra space for your workings below if you need it.

GREAT GIFTS

Appropriation account for the year ended 30 September 2007

	1 October 2006 to 31 March 2007	1 April 2007 to 30 September 2007	Total
	£	£	£
Net profit			
Salaries			
Asma			
Ben			
Interest on capital			
Asma			
Ben			
Chris			
Profit available for distribution			
Profit share			
Asma			
Ben			
Chris			
Balance			

Workings

Task 2.5

- Goodwill was valued at £50,000 on 31 March 2007.
- Goodwill is to be eliminated from the accounts.

Prepare the goodwill account for the partnership for the year ended 30 September 2007. Show clearly the individual transfers to and from each partner's capital account. Show your workings below.

Goodwill account

	£		£

Workings

Task 2.6

There is not enough cash available to repay Asma's capital account. Asma agrees to leave the balance due to her as a loan to the new partnership.

a) Which one of the following would be the correct journal entry to clear Asma's capital account to a loan account? Tick ONE correct box.

☐	Dr Capital – Asma	Cr Trade creditors
☐	Dr Loan – Asma	Cr Capital – Asma
☐	Dr Capital – Asma	Cr Loan – Asma
☐	Dr Bank	Cr Capital – Asma

b)   Some businesses retain goodwill in their accounts. In which category of asset should goodwill be included? Tick ONE correct box.

☐   Tangible fixed assets

☐   Intangible fixed assets

☐   Current assets

Task 2.7

The closing stock valuation figure was taken from the computerised records. These are updated in the stock room when stock is received, and automatically updated at the point of sale when stock is sold. The partners of Great Gifts inform you that there are sometimes differences between the quantity showing on the computer and the physical stock actually on the shelves.

Draft a note to the partners of Great Gifts. In your note:

■   List THREE reasons why the computer records and the physical stock might not agree.
■   Explain briefly how the profit is affected if these stock records are incorrect.

_____

_____

_____

_____

_____

_____

_____

_____

_____

_____

_____

_____

_____

_____

_____

_____

_____

_____

AAT

PRACTICE EXAM 2

MARK GOSS

These tasks were set by the AAT in June 2007.

Time allowed: 3 hours plus 15 minutes' reading time.

This exam paper is in TWO sections.

You must show competence in BOTH sections. So, try to complete EVERY task in BOTH sections.

Section 1 contains 10 tasks and Section 2 contains 7 tasks.

You should spend about 80 minutes on Section 1 and 100 minutes on Section 2.

There is blank space for your workings in the spaces provided.

SECTION 1 (Suggested time allowance: 80 minutes)

DATA

Mark Goss started trading on 1 April 2006. He is a computer technician working for small businesses. He does not keep a double entry bookkeeping system. The business is not registered for VAT.

You are an accounting technician at Harper and Co., the accounting firm that Mark has asked to prepare his first set of accounts for the year ended 31 March 2007. Mark has already summarised the bank account, which is shown below.

Mark Goss – Bank summary for the year ended 31 March 2007

	£		£
Capital introduced 1 April 2006	5,000	Rent of premises	4,500
Receipts from trade debtors	25,800	Creditors for supplies	8,840
		Travel expenses	2,100
		General expenses	1,750
		Equipment rental payments	1,000
		Drawings	12,000
		Closing balance	610
	30,800		30,800

ADDITIONAL DATA

- Mark Goss transferred his own vehicle to the business on 1 April 2006. It was valued at £6,000.

- The vehicle is to be depreciated at 25% on a reducing balance basis.

- On 31 March 2007, trade debtors owed £3,400.

- On 31 March 2007, £1,195 was owed to creditors for supplies. During the year the total supplies were £11,200.

- The bank summary includes a payment of £900 for rent of premises for the period 1 April 2007 to 30 June 2007.

- During May 2007, a payment of £135 was made for electricity used during the period 1 February 2007 to 30 April 2007. Electricity is charged to general expenses.

Task 1.1

Prepare the capital account as at 1 April 2006, showing clearly all the capital introduced.

Capital account

	£		£

Task 1.2

Prepare the sales ledger control account for the year ended 31 March 2007, showing clearly the credit sales as the balancing figure.

Sales ledger control account

	£		£

Task 1.3

Prepare the purchases ledger control account for the year ended 31 March 2007, showing the difference as discounts received.

Purchases ledger control account

	£		£

Task 1.4

Calculate the depreciation charge for the year ended 31 March 2007.

Task 1.5

Prepare the rent account, showing clearly the rent for the year ended 31 March 2007.

Rent

	£		£

Task 1.6

Calculate the adjusted general expenses for the year ended 31 March 2007.

_____

_____

_____

_____

_____

_____

_____

_____

Task 1.7

Mark Goss has just discovered that one of his customers, Unready Limited, has gone out of business. The company owes him £290, which is included in the closing trade debtors figure. Mark knows he will not be able to recover any of the debt.

Draft the journal entry required to account for this. Include a narrative.

Journal		
	DR £	CR £
Narrative		

Task 1.8

Complete the trial balance as at 31 March 2007, taking into account your answers to the above tasks, and all the other information you have been given.

Mark Goss Trial balance as at 31 March 2007		
	DR £	CR £
Total		

Task 1.9

In Task 1.4 you calculated depreciation using the reducing balance method.

a) Explain briefly the purpose of depreciation.

_____

_____

_____

_____

_____

_____

Mark Goss is going to buy some office furniture. He expects it to be of equal use to the business for each of the next five years.

b) Tick the box which shows the method of depreciation you should recommend him to use.

☐ 25% straight line method

☐ 25% reducing balance method

☐ 20% straight line method

☐ 20% reducing balance method

Task 1.10

As Mark Goss's business grows, he will have to make decisions about accounting policies. FRS 18 names four objectives which should be considered when selecting accounting policies.

Name TWO of the objectives listed in FRS 18 which should be considered when selecting accounting policies.

1) _____

_____

_____

2) _____

_____

_____

SECTION 2 (Suggested time allowance: 100 minutes)

DATA

Neru and Rob are the owners of NR Copiers, a partnership business that sells photocopiers.

You are an accounting technician at Harper and Co., the accounting firm that prepares the final accounts for NR Copiers.

- The financial year end is 31 March.

- The partners maintain an integrated accounting system consisting of a main ledger, a purchases ledger, a sales ledger and a stock ledger.

- Stock records are maintained at cost in the stock ledger which is updated every time a sale or stock purchase is made.

- NR Copiers is registered for VAT.

- The proforma extended trial balance for the year ended 31 March 2007 is shown on the next two pages.

Most of the year-end adjustments have been made in the accounts, but there are some further adjustments you now need to make:

a) Administration expenses of £1,500 need to be accrued. Ignore VAT.

b) A cheque for £50 paid from the bank for cash has been debited to selling expenses. This needs to be corrected. The credit entry is correct.

c) The provision for doubtful debts needs to be changed to £800.

d) A vehicle has been disposed of during the year.

    i) The original cost of the vehicle was £12,000.

    ii) The accumulated depreciation on the vehicle was £5,250.

    iii) Thee vehicle was sold for £5,000. This amount was credited to sales and debited to the bank account.

You need to make all the adjustments required to deal with this disposal. You do not need to adjust the depreciation charge for the year. You do not need to make any adjustments for VAT.

Task 2.1

Make entries in the adjustments columns of the extended trial balance on the next two pages to account for the above.

Task 2.2

Extend the profit and loss and balance sheet columns of the extended trial balance. Make entries to record the net profit or loss for the year ended 31 March 2007.

NR Copiers – Extended trial balance		
	Ledger balances	
	DR £	CR £
Administration expenses	70,400	
Bank	34,505	
Capital account – Neru		40,000
Capital account – Rob		40,000
Cash	120	
Closing stock	24,000	24,000
Current account – Neru	30,100	
Current account – Rob	20,700	
Depreciation charge for the year	10,500	
Opening stock	19,000	
Provision for doubtful debts		500
Purchases	158,500	
Purchases ledger control account		25,000
Rent	11,000	
Sales		359,000
Sales ledger control account	30,700	
Selling expenses	55,650	
VAT		8,175
Vehicles at cost	56,000	
Vehicles accumulated depreciation		24,500
TOTAL	**521,175**	**521,175**

As at 31 March 2007

Adjustments		Profit and loss account		Balance sheet	
DR £	CR £	DR £	CR £	DR £	CR £

ADDITIONAL DATA

Neru and Rob share the profits of the partnership equally.

Task 2.3

Update the partners' current accounts to account for the profit or loss for the year ended 31 March 2007. Balance off the accounts, showing the balances carried down.

Capital accounts

	Neru £	Rob £		Neru £	Rob £
31 March 2007					
Balance b/f	30,100	20,700			

Workings

Task 2.4

Prepare a balance sheet for NR Copiers as at 31 March 2007.

Use this column for any workings	NR Copiers Balance sheet as at 31 March 2007	Cost	Depreciation	Net book value
		£	£	£

ADDITIONAL DATA

On 1 April 2007 Kim was admitted to the partnership.

■ She introduced £80,000 to the bank account.

■ Goodwill was valued at £150,000 on 1 April 2007.

■ Goodwill is to be eliminated from the accounts.

■ The new profit sharing percentages are:

	%
Neru	45
Rob	35
Kim	20

Task 2.5

Update the capital accounts for the partners. Show clearly:

■ the introduction of cash by Kim
■ the introduction of goodwill
■ the elimination of goodwill
■ the balances carried down

Capital accounts

	Neru £	Rob £	Kim £		Neru £	Rob £	Kim £
				Balance b/f	40,000	40,000	

Task 2.6

Your friend knows Kim, the new partner at NR Copiers. He knows you are involved in preparing the accounts for the partnership. He asks you how much money Kim has invested in NR Copiers.

Outline how you should respond to your friend's question.

_____

_____

_____

_____

_____

Task 2.7

One model of photocopier the partnership sells is the ZX70. The partnership buys it for £900 excluding VAT.

a)   What would the selling price be, excluding VAT, if a 40% mark-up was applied?

_____

_____

_____

_____

_____

b)   What would the selling price be, excluding VAT, if the sales margin was 40%?

_____

_____

_____

_____

_____

_____

AAT

PRACTICE EXAM 3

ACE CARS

These tasks were set by the AAT in December 2006.

Time allowed: 3 hours plus 15 minutes' reading time.

This exam is in TWO sections.

You must show competence in BOTH sections.

You should therefore attempt and aim to complete EVERY task in EACH section.

You should spend about 80 minutes on Section 1, and about 100 minutes on Section 2.

All essential calculations should be included within your answer.

SECTION 1 (Suggested time allowance: 80 minutes)

DATA

Alex and Charlie Ellis are the owners of Ace Cars, a partnership business that operates a small fleet of taxis used by businesses and the public. They do not keep a double entry bookkeeping system. The business is registered for VAT.

You are an accounting technician at Harper and Co., the accounting firm that prepares the final accounts for Ace Cars. You are working on the accounts for Ace Cars for the year ended 30 September 2006.

Sales for the year ended 30 September 2006:

- Credit sales amounted to £46,000 net of VAT
- Cash sales amounted to £212,000 net of VAT
- All sales are standard-rated for VAT at 17.5%

Payments from the bank account for the year ended 30 September 2006:

■	Payroll expenses	£48,000
■	Administration expenses	£6,400 Ignore VAT
■	Vehicle running expenses	£184,475 *including* VAT at 17.5%
■	Drawings Alex	£19,800
■	Drawings Charlie	£22,000
■	VAT	£17,300

Summary of balances available:

Balances as at	30 September 2005 £	30 September 2006 £
Accrued payroll expenses	Nil	950
Bank account	5,630	9,215
Capital account Alex	20,000	20,000
Capital account Charlie	20,000	20,000
Current account Alex (credit balance)	5,590	To be calculated
Current account Charlie (credit balance)	3,190	To be calculated
Trade debtors	4,120	5,710
VAT (credit balances)	4,200	4,575
Vehicles – cost	60,000	60,000
Vehicles – accumulated depreciation	16,770	To be calculated

Task 1.1

Calculate the total sales figure for inclusion in the trial balance.

_____

_____

_____

_____

Task 1.2

a) Calculate the figure for credit sales inclusive of VAT for entry into the sales ledger control account.

_____

_____

_____

b) Using your answer to a) and the data on the previous page, prepare the sales ledger control account for the year ended 30 September 2006, showing clearly the receipts paid into the bank as the balancing figure.

Sales ledger control account

	£		£

Task 1.3

a) Calculate the cash sales inclusive of VAT which have been paid into the bank account. All cash sales are banked.

_____

_____

_____

_____

b) Show a summarised bank account for the year ended 30 September 2006.

Bank account

	Dr £		Cr £
Opening balance	5,630		
	_____	Closing balance	9,215

Task 1.4

Calculate the figure for vehicle running expenses, net of VAT, for inclusion in the trial balance.

_____

_____

_____

_____

ADDITIONAL DATA

The following adjustments need to be made before preparing the trial balance.

- Depreciation needs to be provided on the vehicles at 30% using the reducing balance method. There were no acquisitions or disposals of vehicles during the year.

- Administration expenses need to include an accrual for accountancy fees of £675. Ignore VAT.

- Drawings of £2,200 by Alex have been debited to payroll expenses in error.

Task 1.5

a) Calculate the depreciation charge for the year ended 30 September 2006.

_____

_____

_____

_____

b) Calculate the accumulated depreciation as at 30 September 2006.

_____

_____

_____

_____

Task 1.6

Calculate the adjusted administration expenses.

_____

_____

_____

_____

Task 1.7

Calculate the adjusted payroll expenses, using the Data on Page 240 and the Additional Data on Page 243.

_____

_____

_____

_____

Task 1.8

Update the partners' current accounts, showing clearly the balances carried forward.

Use the Data on Page 240 and the Additional Data on Page 243.

Note. Do not make any appropriation account adjustments.

Current accounts

	Alex	Charlie		Alex	Charlie
	£	£		£	£
			Balance b/f	5,590	3,190

Task 1.9

Complete the proforma trial balance as at 30 September 2006, taking into account your answers to the above tasks, and all the other data you have been given.

Ace Cars Trial balance as at 30 September 2006		
	DR £	CR £
Accrual for administration expenses (accountancy fee)		
Accrual for payroll expenses		
Administration expenses		
Bank		
Capital account – Alex		
Capital account – Charlie		
Current account – Alex		
Current account – Charlie		
Depreciation expense		
Payroll expenses		
Sales		
Sales ledger control account		
VAT		
Vehicles – cost		
Vehicles – accumulated depreciation		
Vehicle running expenses		
Total		

Task 1.10

The partners are asking for advice on improving their accounting system. You have been asked to consider the records they keep for fixed assets. The partners give you this information that they have about the vehicles:

Registration Number	Cost £
PR04KTR	17,000
KV05WBY	14,500
MR05GTR	12,500
HY06PON	16,000

a) Name the accounting record that you would suggest the partners use to keep the details of their vehicles.

_____

_____

_____

_____

b) Name FOUR additional items of information (other than registration number and cost) about each of the vehicles that you would suggest the partners keep in the accounting record you named in a).

_____

_____

_____

_____

c) List TWO advantages of keeping the additional items of information you named in b).

_____

_____

_____

_____

Task 1.11

a) One of the drivers, who is an employee of Ace Cars, would like a new vehicle for business use. Who should authorise the purchase of a new vehicle for the business? Tick the correct box.

☐ The driver

☐ One of the partners of Ace Cars

☐ One of the partners of Harper and Co.

☐ The receptionist of Ace Cars

b) The partners of Ace Cars ask you at what level of expenditure items should be capitalised. What would be most appropriate for their business? Tick the correct box.

☐ Over £5

☐ Over £500

☐ Over £50,000

SECTION 2 (Suggested time allowance: 100 minutes)

DATA

Mohammed Gaafar is the owner of Impact, a business that makes and sells signs for homes and businesses.

You are an accounting technician at Harper and Co., the accounting firm that prepares the final accounts for Impact.

- The financial year end is 30 September 2006.

- Mohammed keeps a manual bookkeeping system consisting of a main ledger and a subsidiary sales ledger.

- Double entry takes place in the main ledger. Individual accounts of debtors are kept in memorandum accounts in the sales ledger.

- A sales day book is used. Totals from the day-book are transferred into the main ledger.

- The business is not registered for VAT.

The trial balance available to you is shown below.

IMPACT
Trial balance as at 30 September 2006

	DR £	CR £
Bank		1,100
Capital		7,500
Cash	150	
Depreciation expense	900	
Drawings	15,000	
Equipment at cost	5,000	
Equipment accumulated depreciation		1,900
General expenses	3,700	
Loan		2,500
Loan interest	165	
Opening stock	3,320	
Provision for doubtful debts		150
Purchases	24,700	
Rent	4,500	
Sales		47,260
Sales ledger control account	2,975	
Total	60,410	60,410

The individual balances of the accounts in the sales ledger were listed, totalled and compared with the £2,975 balance on the sales ledger control account. The total came to £2,990 and after investigation the following errors were found:

a)   A customer account with a debit balance of £83 was omitted from the list.
b)   A customer account with a debit balance of £157 was listed as £175.
c)   A credit note for £25 had been entered in a customer account as an invoice.
d)   Discount of £30 had been taken but not entered into the customer account.

Task 2.1

Make appropriate adjustments to the total of the list using the table below. For each adjustment show clearly the amount involved and whether the amount is to be added or subtracted.

	£
Total from listing of balances	2,990
Adjustment for a) – add/subtract	
Adjustment for b) – add/subtract	
Adjustment for c) – add/subtract	
Adjustment for d) – add/subtract	
	———
Revised total to agree with sales ledger control account	≡≡≡

Task 2.2

Rita Bunn, a junior colleague at your firm, is interested in the reconciliation you did between the sales ledger and the sales ledger control account in Task 2.1. She does not understand why it was necessary.

Using the headed paper below, write a memo to Rita Bunn. Your memo should explain:

- the purpose of the sales ledger
- whether the sales ledger is part of the double entry accounting system
- the purpose of the sales ledger control account
- whether the sales ledger control account is part of the double entry accounting system
- the reason for doing the reconciliation

MEMO

To: **Rita Bunn**   **Subject:** **Reconciliation**
From: **Accounting Technician**   **Date:**   **6 December 2006**

This page is for the continuation of your memo. You may not need all of it.

MEMO CONT'D

ADDITIONAL DATA

You need to make the following year-end adjustments.

a)   Included in the figure for rent is an amount of £900 for the quarter ending 31 December 2006.

b)   The provision for doubtful debts needs to be adjusted to 4% of the balance on the sales ledger control account.

c)   An accrual needs to be made for loan interest. The charge to the profit and loss account should be 7.2% of the balance on the loan account.

d)   Mohammed has given you a figure for closing stock at cost of £4,238. This includes some material which he will have to scrap which cost £138.

e)   Mohammed sold an item of equipment during the year.

   i)   He sold it for £275, which was debited to the bank account and credited to the sales account.

   ii)   The original cost of the equipment was £500.

   iii) It was purchased during the year ended 30 September 2003.

   iv)   Depreciation is provided at 20% on a straight line basis. A full year's depreciation is made in the year of acquisition and none in the year of disposal.

You need to make all the adjustments required to deal with this disposal. You do not need to adjust the depreciation charge for the year.

Task 2.3

Prepare journal entries to account for the above. Use the blank journal on the next page.

Note. You do not need to give dates and narratives.

Workings

JOURNAL

	DR £	CR £
a)		
b)		
c)		
d)		
e)		

Task 2.4

Enter your journal entries into the adjustment columns of the extended trial balance on Page 255.

Task 2.5

Complete the profit and loss and balance sheet columns of the extended trial balance on Page 255. Make entries to record the net profit or loss for the year ended 30 September 2006.

Impact – Extended trial balance as at 30 September 2006

	Ledger balances		Adjustments		Profit and loss account		Balance sheet	
	DR £	CR £	DR £	CR £	DR £	CR £	DR £	CR £
Bank		1,100						
Capital		7,500						
Cash	150							
Depreciation expense	900							
Drawings	15,000							
Equipment at cost	5,000							
Equipment accumulated depreciation		1,900						
General expenses	3,700							
Loan		2,500						
Loan interest	165							
Opening stock	3,320							
Provision for doubtful debts		150						
Purchases	24,700							
Rent	4,500							
Sales		47,260						
Sales ledger control account	2,975							
Accruals								
Prepayments								
Closing stock – balance sheet								
Closing stock – profit and loss account								
Adjustment to provision for doubtful debts								
Disposal of fixed assets								
Net profit/loss for the year								
Total	60,410	60,410						

Task 2.6

Prepare a profit and loss account for Impact for the year ended 30 September 2006, showing clearly the gross profit and the net profit.

You may use this column for workings if you need to.	**Impact** **Profit and loss account for the year ended 30 September 2006**		
		£	£

Task 2.7

a) Name TWO accounts listed in the extended trial balance that would appear in the current assets section of Impact's balance sheet.

_____

_____

_____

_____

b) In which section of the balance sheet will drawings be included?

Tick the correct box.

☐ Fixed Assets

☐ Current Assets

☐ Liabilities

☐ Capital

AAT

PRACTICE EXAM 4

EBONY GEE

These tasks were set by the AAT in June 2006.

Time allowed: 3 hours plus 15 minutes' reading time.

This exam paper is in TWO sections.

You have to show competence in BOTH sections.

You should therefore attempt and aim to complete EVERY task in EACH section.

You should spend about 80 minutes on Section 1, and about 100 minutes on Section 2.

Please show your workings in the spaces provided.

SECTION 1 (Suggested time allowance: 80 minutes)

DATA

Ebony Gee owns an Internet trading business, buying and selling clothes. The business is not registered for VAT.

She keeps a bank account, but she does not keep a double entry bookkeeping system. All transactions pass through the business bank account.

You are an accounting technician at Harper and Co., the accounting firm that prepares the final accounts for Ebony Gee. The financial year end is 31 March.

You have the following information.

Balance as at 31 March 2006

	£
Equipment at cost	3,100
Equipment accumulated depreciation	1,593
Stock at cost	1,750
Prepayment	1,100
Accrual	205
Capital	5,157

Bank summary for the year ended 31 March 2007

	£		£
Balance brought down	1,005	Rent	4,900
Sales	55,000	Purchases	26,300
Capital introduced	10,000	Postage and packing expenses	4,200
Balance carried down	1,090	Payroll expenses	18,000
		Selling expenses	2,395
		Office expenses	3,600
		Purchase of new equipment	1,700
		Drawings	6,000
	67,095		67,095

Task 1.1

The prepayment in the list of balances is for rent. The figure for rent in the bank summary on the previous page includes £1,200 for the quarter ended 30 June 2007.

Prepare the rent account, showing clearly the rent for the year ended 31 March 2007.

Rent			
	£		£

Task 1.2

The accrual in the list of balances is for selling expenses. During May 2007 Ebony paid £390 for selling expenses relating to the quarter ended 30 April 2007. You can assume that selling expenses accrued evenly over that quarter.

Prepare the selling expenses account, showing clearly the selling expenses for the year ended 31 March 2007.

Selling expenses			
	£		£

Task 1.3

Update the capital account to show the capital introduced during the year, and balance the account.

Capital			
	£		£
		Balance brought down	5,157

Task 1.4

During the year some equipment was part-exchanged.

- It was bought in September 2004 for £1,200.
- A part-exchange allowance of £300 was given.
- Depreciation is provided at 35% on a reducing balance basis.
- A full year's depreciation is charged in the year of acquisition and none in the year of disposal.

a) Calculate the net book value of the equipment that was part-exchanged during the year.

_____

_____

_____

_____

_____

_____

_____

_____

_____

_____

_____

b) Prepare the disposals account for the year ended 31 March 2007.

<table>
<tr><th colspan="2" align="center">Disposals</th></tr>
<tr><td align="center">£</td><td align="center">£</td></tr>
<tr><td></td><td></td></tr>
</table>

Task 1.5

a)   Calculate the cost of the equipment purchased during the year ended 31 March 2007.

_____

_____

_____

_____

b)   Calculate the revised total equipment cost as at 31 March 2007.

_____

_____

_____

_____

_____

c)   Calculate the depreciation charge for the year ended 31 March 2007.

_____

_____

_____

_____

_____

d)   Calculate the updated accumulated depreciation as at 31 March 2007.

_____

_____

_____

_____

_____

Task 1.6

On 31 March 2007, stock was checked and the following list produced.

	Cost £	Selling price £	Net realisable value £
Stock for sale	1,980	4,000	3,800
Stock included in sales but not yet dispatched to customers	90	150	150
Stock paid for but not yet received (in transit)	120	230	230

Calculate the closing stock figure for inclusion in the trial balance.

_____

_____

_____

_____

Task 1.7

Prepare the trial balance as at 31 March 2007, taking into account your answers to the above tasks, and all the other information you have been given.

	DR £	CR £
Ebony Gee **Trial balance as at 31 March 2007**		
Total		

Task 1.8

Your junior colleague, Paul Chin, is looking at the work you have done. He does not understand why you have calculated depreciation. He asks whether the cost of the new equipment could all be charged to the profit and loss account this year because it has been paid for out of the bank account.

Explain to Paul Chin why depreciation cannot be dealt with in the way he suggests.

Your e-mail should briefly explain:

- the purpose of depreciation
- the accruals concept
- how depreciation is an application of the accruals concept.

From:	accounting.technician@harper.co.uk
To:	paul.chin@harper.co.uk
Date:	14 June 2006
Subject:	Depreciation

Task 1.9

Your supervisor tells you that Ebony's last accounts showed a loss, and she is expecting to show a loss again this year.

Which ONE of the following accounting terms would you particularly need to consider if Ebony continues to make a loss?

Tick the correct box.

☐ Relevance

☐ Accruals

☐ Comparability

☐ Materiality

☐ Going concern

☐ Reliability

SECTION 2 (Suggested time allowance: 100 minutes)

DATA

Ade, Jon and Pat are the partners of a restaurant trading as Jadon. Pat joined the partnership on 1 February 2007. There is more information about this later.

You are an accounting technician at Harper and Co., the accounting firm that prepares the final accounts for Jadon.

- The financial year end is 30 April.

- The partners maintain a double entry accounting system consisting of a main ledger and a purchases ledger.

- The business is registered for VAT.

- The trial balance as at 30 April 2007 is shown on the next page.

JADON
Trial balance as at 30 April 2007

	Ledger balances	
	DR £	CR £
Accruals		4,900
Bank	41,000	
Capital account as at 1 May 2006 – Ade		30,000
Capital account as at 1 May 2006 – Jon		35,000
Cash	150	
Closing stock – balance sheet	2,200	
Closing stock – profit and loss account		2,200
Current account as at 1 May 2006 – Ade		6,800
Current account as at 1 May 2006 – Jon		3,100
Depreciation expense	14,062	
Drawings – Ade	60,000	
Drawings – Jon	60,000	
Drawings – Pat	7,500	
Equipment at cost	90,000	
Equipment accumulated depreciation as at 1 May 2006		9,000
General expenses	19,500	
Opening stock	1,900	
Prepayments	5,700	
Purchases	124,920	
Purchases ledger control account		14,080
Rent	22,500	
Sales		365,000
Suspense account		78,120
VAT		8,720
Vehicles at cost	75,000	
Vehicles accumulated depreciation		18,750
Wages	51,238	
TOTAL	575,670	575,670

DATA

You have investigated the balance on the suspense account. You have discovered some errors that need to be corrected.

a) Rent of £7,500 has been debited to the general expenses account. You do not need to adjust for VAT.

b) Pat introduced capital of £80,000 during the year. This was debited to the bank account but no other entries were made.

c) Accrued wages of £1,150 have been credited to both the accruals account and the wages account. No other entries have been made.

d) No entries have been made for the depreciation charge of £9,000 for equipment for the year.

e) The figures from the columns of the purchases day book for 14 April 2007 have been totalled correctly as follows:

Purchases column	£2,400
VAT column	£420
Total column	£2,820

The amounts have been posted as follows:

Dr	Purchases	£2,820
Cr	Purchases ledger control account	£2,400

Task 2.1

Prepare journal entries to account for items a) to e) above. Use the blank journal on the next page. You do not need to give dates and narratives.

Workings

JOURNAL

	DR £	CR £

Task 2.2

Prepare a profit and loss account for Jadon for the year ended 30 April 2007, showing clearly the gross profit and the net profit.

Workings	Jadon Profit and loss account for the year ended 30 April 2007		
		£	£
	Sales		
	Opening stock		
	Purchases		
	Closing stock		
	Cost of goods sold		
	Gross profit		
	Wages		
	Rent		
	General expenses		
	Depreciation (vehicles and equipment)		
	Net profit		

ADDITIONAL DATA

Pat joined the partnership on 1 February 2007. You have the following information about the partnership agreement:

- Goodwill was valued at £150,000 on 31 January 2007. Goodwill is to be eliminated from the accounts.

- Profit share, effective until 31 January 2007

Ade	50%
Jon	50%

  Profit share, effective from 1 February 2007

Ade	40%
Jon	40%
Pat	20%

- You can assume that profits accrued evenly during the year.

- Interest on capital accounts

  6% per annum on the balance, calculated on a monthly basis.

- Partners' annual salaries

Ade	£10,900 per year
Jon	£15,000 per year
Pat	£6,600 for the period from 1 February 2006 to 30 April 2007.

Task 2.3

Update the capital accounts for the partners for the year ended 30 April 2007. Show clearly:

- the introduction of goodwill
- the introduction of cash by Pat
- the elimination of goodwill
- the balances carried down.

You will need to refer to the Data on Page 269 and the Additional Data above.

Capital accounts

	Ade £	Jon £	Pat £		Ade £	Jon £	Pat £
Goodwill eliminated				Balance b/d as at 1 May 06	30,000	35,000	
				Goodwill introduced			
				Bank			
Balance c/d							

Workings

Task 2.4

Complete the following table to show the interest on capital for each of the partners.

Show your workings.

Interest on capital	1 May 06 – 31 Jan 07	1 Feb 07 – 30 April 07	Total
Ade			
Jon			
Pat			

Workings

Task 2.5

Prepare the appropriation account for the partnership for the year ended 30 April 2007.

Show your workings.

Jadon
Appropriation account for the year ended 30 April 2007

Interest on capital	1 May 06 – 31 Jan 07	1 Feb 07 – 30 April 07	Total
Net profit			
Salaries:			
Ade			
Jon			
Pat			
Interest on capital:			
Ade			
Jon			
Pat			
Profit available for distribution			
Profit share:			
Ade			
Jon			
Pat			

Workings

Task 2.6

Prepare the current accounts for the partners for the year ended 30 April 2007. Show clearly the balances carried down. You will need to refer to the trial balance on Page 269 and your answer to Task 2.5.

Capital accounts

	Ade £	Jon £	Pat £		Ade £	Jon £	Pat £
				Balance b/d as at 1 May 06	6,800	3,100	

Task 2.7

When the balance sheet of Jadon is drawn up, in which section will:

a)   the partners' current accounts be included? Tick the correct box.

☐   Assets

☐   Liabilities

☐   Capital

b)   equipment accumulated depreciation be included? Tick the correct box.

☐   Assets

☐   Liabilities

☐   Capital

Task 2.8

In Task 2.1 you prepared journals to correct errors. If you were in the workplace, you would then post the journals. Which account balance would you check next, before preparing the final accounts?

AAT

PRACTICE EXAM 5

PL TRADING

These tasks were set by the AAT in December 2005.

Time allowed: 3 hours plus 15 minutes' reading time.

This examination paper is in TWO sections.

You must show competence in BOTH sections.

You should therefore attempt and aim to complete EVERY task in EACH section.

You should spend about 90 minutes on Section 1, and 90 minutes on Section 2.

All essential calculations should be included within your answer.

SECTION 1 (Suggested time allowance: 90 minutes)

DATA

Pat and Lee are the owners of PL Trading, a partnership that sells office equipment to businesses.

They keep a sales day book and a purchases day book but they do not keep a double entry bookkeeping system. All transactions pass through the business bank account. The business is registered for VAT.

You are an accounting technician at Harper and Co., the accounting firm that prepares the final accounts for PL Trading. The financial year end is 31 October.

You have the following information available to you.

Balances as at	31 October 2006 £	31 October 2007 £
Vehicles at cost	40,000	40,000
Vehicles accumulated depreciation	15,000	To be calculated
Stock at cost	17,700	To be calculated
Trade debtors	63,200	68,400
Prepayment	NIL	To be calculated
Accrual	1,000	To be calculated
Trade creditors	36,800	41,300
VAT	5,300	To be calculated
Capital – Pat	40,000	40,000
Capital – Lee	32,000	32,000
Current – Pat	750	To be calculated
Current – Lee	1,050	To be calculated

Bank summary for the year ended 31 October 2007

	£		£
Balance brought forward	11,000	Rent	15,000
Receipts from trade debtors	418,975	Payroll expenses	38,500
		Payments to trade creditors	251,870
		General expenses	27,824
		VAT	20,575
		Drawings – Pat	30,000
		Drawings – Lee	24,000
		Balance carried forward	22,206
	429,975		429,975

Day book summaries for the year ended 31 October 2007

	Net £	VAT £	Total £
Sales	361,000	63,175	424,175
Purchases	220,000	38,500	258,500

Task 1.1

You need to find the figure for discounts received.

Prepare the purchases ledger control account for the year ended 31 October 2007, showing clearly the figure for discounts received.

Note. There are no other missing figures.

Purchases ledger control account

£		£

Task 1.2

The accrual in the list of balances is for rent. The figure for rent in the bank summary on the previous page includes £3,000 for the quarter starting 1 October 2007.

a)   Prepare the rent account, showing clearly the rent for the year ended 31 October 2007.

Rent

£		£

b)   Name the main accounting concept that you have applied.

Task 1.3

The bank summary shows general expenses of £27,824 which includes VAT at 17.5%.

Note. General expenses are not included in the purchases day book.

a)   Calculate the general expenses figure for inclusion in the trial balance.

_____

_____

_____

_____

b)   Calculate the VAT figure on general expenses for inclusion in the VAT account.

_____

_____

_____

_____

Task 1.4

You need to find the closing balance figure for VAT.

Using the information you have been given on Page 279, and your answer to Task 1.3 b), complete the VAT account.

VAT

	£		£
		Opening balance	5,300

Task 1.5

Depreciation is provided at 25% on a straight line basis.

a)   Calculate the depreciation charge for the year ended 31 October 2007.

_____

_____

_____

_____

b)   Calculate the updated accumulated depreciation.

_____

_____

_____

_____

Task 1.6

On 31 October 2007, closing stock was valued at selling price at £22,750 excluding VAT. The mark-up on these goods is 40%.

Calculate the closing stock figure for inclusion in the trial balance.

_____

_____

_____

_____

ADDITIONAL DATA

- During the year, Pat took furniture which cost £1,200 from the business for private use at home. No entries have been made to account for this. Ignore VAT.

- The partnership agreement provides for interest on capital to be charged at 5% per annum. There is no provision for interest on drawings.

Task 1.7

Calculate the adjusted purchases figure for inclusion in the trial balance.

Note. You will also need to refer to the information on Page 279.

Task 1.8

a) Update the partners' current accounts for drawings and interest on capital, and balance them off.

Note. You do not need to make any entries for profit or loss for the year.

Current accounts

	Pat £	Lee £			Pat £	Lee £
			2006			
			31 Oct	Balance b/d	750	1,050

b) Calculate the TOTAL figure for interest on capital, for inclusion in the trial balance.

_____

_____

_____

_____

Task 1.9

Complete the trial balance below as at 31 October 2007, taking into account your answers to the above tasks, and all the other information you have been given.

PL Trading Trial Balance as at 31 October 2007		
	DR £	CR £
Trade debtors		
Trade creditors (purchases ledger control account)		
Capital – Pat		
Capital – Lee		
Bank		
Discounts received		
Payroll expenses		
Rent		
General expenses		
VAT		
Depreciation charge		
Vehicles at cost		
Vehicles accumulated depreciation		
Opening stock		
Closing stock – balance sheet		
Closing stock – profit and loss account		
Purchases		
Sales		
Current account – Pat		
Current account – Lee		
Interest on capital		
Prepayment		
Total		

Task 1.10

In Task 1.6 you calculated the closing stock figure.

a) Explain why you had to do this, making appropriate reference to SSAP 9 *Stocks and long-term contracts*.

_____

_____

_____

_____

_____

_____

_____

b) Indicate what the effect on the profit would be if the closing stock were included in the final accounts at selling price. Tick the correct answer.

☐ Profit would be overstated

☐ Profit would be understated

☐ There would be no effect on the profit

SECTION 2 (Suggested time allowance: 90 minutes)

DATA

Sam James is the owner of a business that sells books and newspapers to the general public and local businesses.

You are an accounting technician at Harper and Co., the accounting firm that prepares the final accounts for Sam James.

- The financial year end is 30 September.

- Sam James maintains a double entry accounting system consisting of a main ledger, a purchases ledger, and a sales ledger.

- Sam James is not registered for VAT.

- The trial balance as at 30 September 2007 is shown on the next page.

Sam James –Trial Balance as at 30 September 2007		
	Ledger balances	
	DR £	CR £
Administration expenses	8,700	
Bank	3,532	
Capital account		20,000
Cash	250	
Closing stock – balance sheet	4,890	
Closing stock – profit and loss account		4,890
Drawings	24,000	
Equipment at cost	15,800	
Equipment accumulated depreciation		12,496
Opening stock	4,250	
Purchases	89,440	
Purchases ledger control account		8,700
Rent	8,000	
Sales		146,520
Sales ledger control account	5,600	
Vehicles at cost	22,000	
Vehicles accumulated depreciation		5,856
Wages	12,000	
TOTAL	**198,462**	**198,462**

DATA

Most of the year-end adjustments have been entered, but there are some adjustments you now need to make.

a)   Sales of £790 have been credited to the purchases account.

b)   Depreciation on equipment needs to be provided at 25% reducing balance.

c)   Sam James part-exchanged his business vehicle during the year.

    i)   The original cost of the vehicle which was part-exchanged was £12,000.

    ii)   The net book value of the vehicle which was part-exchanged was £6,144.

    iii)   £10,000 was paid from the bank account. The amount was credited to the bank account and debited to the vehicles at cost account.

    iv)   A part-exchange allowance of £3,500 was given.

d)   A full year's depreciation needs to be provided on the new vehicle at 25% reducing balance.

e)   One of Sam James' debtors has gone bankrupt. The amount owing was £400. This needs to be written off.

f)   Sam James has agreed to introduce a provision for doubtful debts of 2% of the remaining debtors.

Task 2.1

Make entries in the adjustments columns of the extended trial balance below to account for the above.

Sam James –Trial Balance as at 30 September 2007				
	Ledger balances		Adjustments	
	DR £	CR £	DR £	CR £
Administration expenses	8,700			
Bank	3,532			
Capital account		20,000		
Cash	250			
Closing stock – balance sheet	4,890			
Closing stock – profit and loss account		4,890		
Drawings	24,000			
Equipment at cost	15,800			
Equipment accumulated depreciation		12,496		
Opening stock	4,250			
Purchases	89,440			
Purchases ledger control account		8,700		
Rent	8,000			
Sales		146,520		
Sales ledger control account	5,600			
Vehicles at cost	22,000			
Vehicles accumulated depreciation		5,856		
Wages	12,000			
TOTAL	**198,462**	**198,462**		

Task 2.2

Prepare a profit and loss account for Sam James for the year ended 30 September 2007, showing clearly the gross profit and the net profit.

Workings	Sam James Profit and loss account for the year ended 30 September 2006		
		DR £	CR £

Task 2.3

Prepare a balance sheet for Sam James as at 30 September 2007.

Workings	Sam James Balance sheet as at 30 September 2007	DR £	CR £

Task 2.4

After discussion with Sam James, you think that some items of equipment are included in administration expenses but should be recorded as equipment.

a)   What is the main difference in the accounting treatment between administration expenses and equipment?

_____

_____

_____

_____

_____

b)   What information would you need to decide into which account the items belong?

_____

_____

_____

_____

c)   How would you obtain this information?

_____

_____

_____

_____

d)   List the accounts which would be affected if you found you needed to make an adjustment. You do not need to show any figures.

_____

_____

_____

_____

_____

ANSWERS

answers to chapter 1:
REVISION OF HOW ACCOUNTING SYSTEMS WORK

1 a) When a sale is made today but payment is not to be made for two weeks this is a **credit** sale.

  b) When goods are purchased on credit the business will owe money to a **creditor**.

  c) When a customer returns goods that have been purchased these are known as **sales returns**.

  d) When a business purchases an item for long term use it is known as **capital** expenditure.

  e) If goods are returned to a supplier we would expect to receive a **credit note** from the supplier.

  f) When cheques are received from customers through the post they are initially recorded on a **remittance list**.

2

	Transaction	Primary record
a)	Credit note received from a supplier	Purchases returns day book
b)	Invoice sent out to a customer	Sales day book
c)	Payment by cheque to a supplier	Cash payments book
d)	Payment by cheque for goods	Cash payments book
e)	Credit note sent out to a customer	Sales returns day book
f)	Cheque received from a customer	Cash receipts book
g)	Payment of the telephone bill	Cash payments book
h)	Reimbursement in cash for a business expense paid by an employee	Petty cash book
i)	Invoice received from a supplier	Purchases day book

3   a), b) and d)

CASH BOOK: RECEIPTS

Date	Details	Cash	Discount allowed	Sales Ledger Control	Cash sales	VAT	Capital	Interest
		£	£	£	£	£	£	£
2007								
5 October	Cash/cheques	7,309.83	245.02	6,959.41	298.23	52.19		
9 October	BACS receipt	1,293.94		1,293.94				
12 October	Cash/cheques	2,738.64	67.00	1,212.86	1,298.54	227.24		
17 October	Cash/cheques	800.00			800.00			
24 October	Cash/cheques	5,309.30	278.27	3,663.72	1,400.50	245.08		
31 October	Cheques paid in	6,293.66		6,088.66	174.47	30.53		
27 October	BACS receipt	5,000.00					5,000.00	
27 October	Interest	459.35						459.35
		29,204.72	590.29	20,018.59	3,171.74	555.04	5,000.00	459.35

CASH BOOK: PAYMENTS

Date	Details	Cheque no	Cash	Discount received	Purchase Ledger Control	Other
2007						
1 October	Jedburgh County Council	DD	1,092.87			1,092.87
1 October	Society of Picture Framers	DD	250.00			250.00
2 October	Timbmet Wood Ltd	1397	3,298.93	45.00	3,298.93	
3 October	Glass Products Ltd	1398	5,209.36		5,209.36	
7 October	Lamination Ltd	1399	1,376.84	24.50	1,376.84	
10 October	The Contract Cleaning Co	1400	563.37		563.37	
11 October	Just A Minute Courier Co	1401	357.00		357.00	
12 October	Lynn's Caterers	1402	175.00		175.00	
15 October	Thor Stationery	1403	736.83	13.00	736.83	
16 October	Kinetic Electricity Ltd	DD	200.00			200.00
20 October	High Stick Adhesives	1404	245.09		245.09	
21 October	Big Gas Co Ltd	BACS	150.00			150.00
22 October	Quality Paper Co	1405	1,983.09		1,983.09	
24 October	Glass Ceramics Ltd	1406	3,736.94	51.00	3,736.94	
27 October	Chrome Sheeting Ltd	1407	398.65		398.65	
28 October	Salaries	BACS	3,378.24			3,378.24
25 October	ATM withdrawal	Debit card	100.00			100.00
25 October	Debit card payment	Debit card	248.97			248.97
			23,501.18	133.50	18,081.10	5,420.08
	Analysis:					
	Direct labour					3,378.24
	Administration					1,692.87
	Drawings					348.97
						5,420.08

	£
Cash book balance at 1 October 2007	(2,190.87)
Receipts in October	29,204.72
Payments in October	(23,501.18)
Balance on the cash book at 30 October 2007	3,512.67

c)

MEMO

To: Harry Gold
From: A Student
Date: 1 November 2007
Re: Items appearing on the bank statement at 31 October 2007

There are three items appearing on the bank statement that have no supporting documentation, so I hoped you may be able to shed some light on them.

First, there is a BACS receipt on 27 October for £5,000.00 which is stated to be from 'Harry Gold Personal Account'. Please could you confirm the exact nature of this receipt?

Second, there is an ATM withdrawal of £100.00 on 25 October, and finally a debit card payment to Siren.com on the same date. Again, could you please confirm the exact nature of these payments?

Thank you.

answers to chapter 2:
REVISION OF DOUBLE ENTRY BOOKKEEPING

1 **Transaction** **Two effects**

a) Payment of £15,000 into a business bank account by an individual in order to start up a business

Increase in bank account
Increase in capital

b) Payment by cheque of £2,000 for rent of a business property

Decrease in bank account
Increase in rent expense

c) Payment by cheque of £6,200 for purchase of a delivery van

Decrease in bank account
Increase in fixed asset

d) Payment by cheque of £150 for vehicle licence for the van

Decrease in bank account
Increase in van expenses

e) Payment by cheque of £2,100 for goods for resale

Decrease in bank account
Increase in purchases

f) Sale of goods for cash and cheques of £870

Increase in bank account
Increase in sales

g) Purchase of goods for resale on credit for £2,800

Increase in purchases
Increase in creditors

h) Payment by cheque for petrol of £80

Decrease in bank account
Increase in van expenses

i) Sale of goods on credit for £3,400

Increase in sales
Increase in debtors

j) Payment by cheque of £1,500 to creditors

Decrease in bank account
Decrease in creditors

k) Payment by cheque of electricity bill of £140

Decrease in bank account
Increase in electricity expense

l) Receipt of cheque from debtor of £1,600

Increase in bank account
Decrease in debtors

m) Withdrawal of £500 of cash for the owner's personal living costs

Decrease in bank account
Increase in drawings

n) Payment by cheque for petrol of £70

Decrease in bank account
Increase in van expenses

2

Capital account

	£		£
		Bank	15,000

Bank account

	£		£
Capital	15,000	Rent	2,000
Sales	870	Van	6,200
Debtors	1,600	Van expenses	150
		Purchases	2,100
		Van expenses	80
		Creditors	1,500
		Electricity	140
		Drawings	500
		Van expenses	70

Rent account

Bank	2,000		£

Van account

	£		£
Bank	6,200		

Van expenses account

	£		£
Bank	150		
Bank	80		
Bank	70		

Purchases account

	£		£
Bank	2,100		
Creditors	2,800		

Sales account

	£		£
		Bank	870
		Debtors	3,400

Creditors account

	£		£
Bank	1,500	Purchases	2,800

Debtors account

	£		£
Sales	3,400	Bank	1,600

Electricity account

	£		£
Bank	140		

Drawings account

	£		£
Bank	500		

3

Capital account

	£		£
		Bank	15,000

Bank account

	£		£
Capital	15,000	Rent	2,000
Sales	870	Van	6,200
Debtors	1,600	Van expenses	150
		Purchases	2,100
		Van expenses	80
		Creditors	1,500
		Electricity	140
		Drawings	500
		Van expenses	70
		Balance c/d	4,730
	17,470		17,470
Balance b/d	4,730		

Rent account

	£		£
Bank	2,000		

Van account

	£		£
Bank	6,200		

Van expenses account

	£		£
Bank	150		
Bank	80		
Bank	70	Balance c/d	300
	300		300
Balance b/d	300		

Purchases account

	£		£
Bank	2,100		
Creditors	2,800	Balance c/d	4,900
	4,900		4,900
Balance b/d	4,900		

Sales account

	£		£
		Bank	870
Balance c/d	4,270	Debtors	3,400
	4,270		4,270
		Balance b/d	4,270

Creditors account

	£		£
Bank	1,500	Purchases	2,800
Balance c/d	1,300		
	2,800		2,800
		Balance b/d	1,300

Debtors account

	£		£
Sales	3,400	Bank	1,600
		Balance c/d	1,800
	3,400		3,400
Balance b/d	1,800		

Electricity account

	£		£
Bank	140		

Drawings account

	£		£
Bank	500		

Trial balance

	£	£
Capital		15,000
Bank	4,730	
Rent	2,000	
Van	6,200	
Van expenses	300	
Purchases	4,900	
Sales		4,270
Creditors		1,300
Debtors	1,800	
Electricity	140	
Drawings	500	
	20,570	20,570

4

Main ledger

Sales account

	£		£
		21 May Balance b/d	12,370
		28 May SDB	700
28 May Balance c/d	13,280	28 May CRB	210
	13,280		13,280
		Balance b/d	13,280

Sales returns account

	£		£
21 May Balance b/d	1,050		
28 May SRDB	50	28 May Balance c/d	1,100
	1,100		1,100
Balance b/d	1,100		

Sales ledger control account

	£		£
21 May Balance b/d	990	28 May SRDB	50
28 May SDB	700	28 May CRB	480
		28 May CRB – discount	16
		28 May Balance c/d	1,144
	1,690		1,690
Balance b/d	1,144		

Discounts allowed account

	£		£
21 May Balance b/d	124		
28 May CRB	16	28 May Balance c/d	140
	140		140
Balance b/d	140		

Subsidiary ledger

K Finch

	£		£
21 May Balance b/d	290	28 May CRB	280
28 May SDB	300	28 May CRB – discount	10
		28 May Balance c/d	300
	590		590
Balance b/d	300		

T Weller

	£		£
21 May Balance b/d	220	28 May SRDB	20
28 May SDB	160	28 May CRB	80
		28 May CRB – discount	2
		28 May Balance c/d	278
	380		380
Balance b/d	278		

F Simpson

	£		£
21 May Balance b/d	480	28 May SRDB	30
28 May SDB	240	28 May CRB	120
		28 May CRB – discount	4
		28 May Balance c/d	566
	720		720
Balance b/d	566		

5   a), b) and c)

CASH BOOK: RECEIPTS

Date	Details	Bank	Discount allowed	Sales Ledger Control	Cash Sales	VAT	Other
2007		£	£	£	£	£	£
2 Feb	Cheques etc paid in	2,244.27	25.00	1,928.20	269.00	47.07	
6 Feb	Interest paid	54.00					54.00
7 Feb	Cheques etc paid in	3,160.47	19.00	2,298.02	734.00	128.45	
10 Feb	BACS – StraightCall Insurance	200.00					200.00
12 Feb	Cheques etc paid in	1,584.02	14.50	1,290.27	250.00	43.75	
14 Feb	Cheques etc paid in	896.28		896.28			
17 Feb	Cheques etc paid in	3,746.95	65.00	3,291.29	387.80	67.86	
21 Feb	Cheques etc paid in	4,887.27	32.00	4,182.27	600.00	105.00	
23 Feb	Cheques etc paid in	582.33		582.33			
26 Feb	Cheques etc paid in	8,539.54	15.00	8,209.54	280.86	49.14	
		25,895.13	170.50	22,678.20	2,521.66	441.27	254.00
25 Feb	BACS receipt – Assignia plc	6,283.02		6,283.02			
		32,178.15	170.50	28,961.22	2,521.66	441.27	254.00
Analysis	Disposals						200.00
	Interest						54.00
							254.00

CASH BOOK: PAYMENTS

Date	Details	Cheque No	Bank £	Discount received £	Purchase ledger control £	Other £
1 Feb	South Oxon Council (rates)	DD	231.50			231.50
1 Feb	Thanet Pension Fund (rent)	DD	500.00			500.00
2 Feb	Drake Bicycles	6295	2,638.39	20.00	2,638.39	
3 Feb	David Lett Shopfitting	6296	4,029.38	55.00	4,029.38	
7 Feb	Sama Newsagents	6297	176.93		176.93	
10 Feb	Mike Cuthbertson – drawings	S/O	3,000.00			3,000.00
11 Feb	Essex Cycles	6298	2,378.49	35.00	2,378.49	
12 Feb	Firebrand Tyres	6299	1,287.35	10.00	1,287.35	
15 Feb	Patrick's Pumps	6300	1,243.66		1,243.66	
16 Feb	South Oxon Council (waste collection)	DD	35.00			35.00
20 Feb	Crutchleys Accountants (fees)	6301	235.00		235.00	
21 Feb	Lurrells & Co (fees)	6302	293.75		293.75	
22 Feb	Heartlands Electric	DD	150.00			150.00
24 Feb	Midland Gas	DD	90.00			90.00
27 Feb	Salaries	BACS	4,622.12			4,622.12
			20,911.57	120.00	12,282.95	8,628.62
25 Feb	Handley & Co (cheque returned unpaid)		352.50			352.50
25 Feb	ATM withdrawal		200.00			200.00
			21,464.07	120.00	12,282.95	9,181.12
	Analysis:					
	Sales ledger control					352.50
	Staff costs					4,622.12
	Administration/overheads					1,006.50
	Drawings					3,200.00
						9,181.12

c)

Administration/overheads

Date	Details	Amount £	Date	Details	Amount £
28/2	Cash book	1,006.50			

Bank

Date	Details	Amount £	Date	Details	Amount £
1/2	Balance b/d	5,920.39	28/2	February payments	21,464.07
28/2	February receipts	32,178.15	28/2	Balance c/d	16,634.47
		38,098.54			38,098.54

Discount allowed and received

Date	Details	Amount £	Date	Details	Amount £
28/2	Cash book	170.50	28/2	Cash book	120.00

Disposals

Date	Details	Amount £	Date	Details	Amount £
			28/2	Insurance receipt	200.00

Drawings

Date	Details	Amount £	Date	Details	Amount £
28/2	Cash book	3,200.00			

Interest received

Date	Details	Amount £	Date	Details	Amount £
			28/2	Cash book	54.00

Purchase ledger control

Date	Details	Amount £	Date	Details	Amount £
28/2	Cash paid	12,282.95			
28/2	Discount received	120.00			

Sales

Date	Details	Amount £	Date	Details	Amount £
			28/2	Cash sales	2,521.66

Sales ledger control

Date	Details	Amount £	Date	Details	Amount £
28/2	Cheque returned unpaid	352.50	28/2	Cash received	28,961.22
			28/2	Discount allowed	170.50

Staff costs

Date	Details	Amount £	Date	Details	Amount £
28/2	Cash book	4,622.12			

VAT

Date	Details	Amount £	Date	Details	Amount £
			28/2	Cash sales	441.27

6   The trial balance of Pooley will appear as follows at 31 December 2007.

	Debit £	Credit £
Stock as at 1 January 2007	22,000	
Purchases	223,000	
Sales		340,700
Discounts allowed	4,600	
Discounts received		5,500
Returns in	6,700	
Returns out		5,600
Wages and salaries	34,500	
Bad debts	3,100	
Carriage in	1,400	
Carriage out	2,200	
Other operating expenses	24,500	
Trade debtors	34,000	
Trade creditors		21,600
Provision for bad debts		450
Cash on hand	800	
Bank overdraft		23,400
Capital		38,550
Property	50,000	
Equipment	64,000	
Provisions for depreciation at 1 January 2007		
Property		10,000
Equipment		25,000
	470,800	470,800

7   Rather than write out the ledger accounts all over again, the question may be answered as follows.

a)   The postings necessary for each transaction are:

		£	£
Debit	Purchases	2,000	
Credit	Cash		1,000
	Purchase ledger control		1,000
Debit	Interest	20	
Credit	Cash		20
Debit	Electricity	25	
Credit	Cash		25
Debit	Telephone	12	
Credit	Cash		12
Debit	Cash	500	
	Sales ledger control	3,000	
Credit	Sales		3,500
Debit	Cash	220	
Credit	Sales ledger control		220

b) Once these have been posted and the accounts balanced off, the trial balance is:

Account	Debit	Credit £
Cash	18,083	
Capital		9,500
Bank loan		3,000
Sales		19,300
Debtors (sales ledger control)	6,980	
Rent	2,750	
Purchases	4,100	
Creditors (purchase ledger control)		2,400
Interest	370	
Electricity	425	
Telephone	192	
Drawings	1,300	
	34,200	34,200

Tutorial note. If you are not confident of your arithmetic, you may find it safer to write out and balance off all the ledger accounts individually.

answers to chapter 3:
INTRODUCTION TO FINANCIAL STATEMENTS

1

	Balance	**Category**
a)	Salaries	Expense
b)	Bank overdraft	Liability
c)	Carriage inwards	Expense
d)	Bank loan	Liability
e)	Capital	Liability
f)	Debtors	Asset
g)	Purchases	Expense

2 Trial balance

	£	£	**Category**
Rent	11,400		Expense
Sales		143,000	Income
Stock	2,400		Expense
Creditors		6,000	Liability
Purchases	86,200		Expense
Drawings	17,910		Reduction of liability
Telephone	1,250		Expense
Discount received		80	Income
Carriage outwards	400		Expense
Motor vehicles	32,600		Asset
Debtors	11,900		Asset
Discount allowed	120		Expense
Capital		40,000	Liability
Wages	20,600		Expense
Heat and light	1,600		Expense
Computer	2,400		Asset
Bank	300		Asset
	189,080	189,080	

3

	£	£
Sales		867,450
Cost of sales:		
Opening stock	24,578	
Purchases	426,489	
	451,067	
Less: closing stock	(30,574)	
		(420,493)
Gross profit		446,957
Selling and distribution costs		(104,366)
Administration costs		(87,689)
Net profit		254,902

4   The main categories that appear on a balance sheet are:

■   fixed assets
■   current assets – stocks, debtors, bank and cash
■   current liabilities – creditors
■   long term liabilities – loans
■   capital
■   net profit
■   drawings

5   a)   Asset
b)   Expense
c)   Neither – it is a (long-term) liability
d)   Asset
e)   Asset – it relates to a future period and so is a 'prepayment'
f)   Asset
g)   Expense
h)   Expense
i)   Asset
j)   Expense
k)   Asset

6   a)   These are some of the main reasons for preparing accounts.

   i)   Most businesses are continuous, but periodic reports are needed to assess whether their trading activities are successful or not.

   ii)   Many businesses are managed by people other than their owners. The owners will wish to see how well their managers are performing.

   iii)   Accounting profit is used as the basis for the calculation of tax due and also to calculate other important numbers such as the profit due to individual partners in a partnership or the bonus due to managers.

   b)   A balance sheet is a list of the assets, liabilities and capital of a business at a given moment. Assets are divided into fixed assets and current assets. Liabilities may be current or long term.

   A profit and loss account matches the revenue earned in a period with the costs incurred in earning it. It is usual to distinguish between a gross profit (sales revenue less the cost of goods sold) and a net profit (being the gross profit less the expenses of selling, distribution, administration and so on).

7

	£
Assets 1 January 2007	10,000
Liabilities 1 January 2007	7,000
Owner's investment at 1 December 2007	3,000

	£
Assets 31 December 2007	15,000
Liabilities 31 December 2007	10,000
Owner's investment at 31 December 2007	5,000

Increase in net assets = £2,000

Profit = Increase in net assets + drawings – new capital introduced
      = 2,000 + 0 – 4,000
      = (2,000)

Therefore the business made a **loss** of £2,000.

8   a)   Materiality
   b)   Going concern
   c)   Accruals or matching

9 a) FRS 18, Accounting policies, identifies two accounting concepts which play a pervasive role in the preparation of final accounts and selection of accounting policies. These are the going concern concept and the accruals concept.

Final accounts should be prepared on the going concern basis unless the directors believe that the organisation is not a going concern. The going concern basis says that the final accounts are prepared with the underlying assumption that the business will continue for the foreseeable future. This concept or basis affects the values of assets shown in the balance sheet in particular. If the business is a going concern then assets will continue to be shown in the balance sheet at an amount based on the amount that they cost. However if the business were not a going concern and was due to close down in the near future then assets such as specialised premises or machinery may have a very low value as they would not easily be sold when the business closed.

Final accounts should also be prepared on the accruals basis of accounting. The accruals basis of accounting requires that the effects of transactions are reflected in the final accounts for the period in which they occur and not in the period in which any cash involved is received or paid.

This means that the amount of any income or expense that appears in the final accounts should be the amount that was earned or incurred during the accounting period rather than the amount of cash that was received or paid.

b) FRS 18 sets out four objectives against which an organisation should judge the appropriateness of accounting policies to its own particular circumstances. These objectives are relevance, reliability, comparability and understandability.

Relevance

Financial information is said to be relevant if it has the ability to influence the economic decisions of the users of that information and is provided in time to influence those decisions. Where an organisation faces a choice of accounting policies they should choose the one that is more relevant in the context of the final accounts as a whole.

Reliability

There are a number of aspects to providing reliable information in the final accounts:

- the figures should represent the substance of the transactions or events

- the figures should be free from bias or neutral

- the figures should be free of material errors

- a degree of caution has been applied in making judgements where there is uncertainty

Comparability

Information in final accounts is used by many different people and organisations from the employees and investors in the organisation to its creditors and bank. The information provided in the final accounts is much more useful to these users if it is comparable over time and also with similar information about other organisations. The selection of appropriate accounting policies and their consistent use should provide such comparability.

Understandability

Accounting policies should be chosen to ensure ease of understanding for users of final accounts. For this purpose users are assumed to have a reasonable knowledge of business and economic activities and accounting and a willingness to study the information diligently.

10   SSAPs and FRSs deal with the following matters.

a)   Requiring the description of the way in which a set of accounts has been prepared.
b)   Laying down rules for the presentation of certain types of information.
c)   Requiring the disclosure of information.
d)   Prescribing rules for asset valuation and profit measurement.

answers to chapter 4:
VALUE ADDED TAX

1 a) VAT on purchases is known as **input** tax.

b) VAT on sales is known as **output** tax.

c) VAT is paid by a VAT registered business to **HM Revenue & Customs**.

d) Postal costs are an example of a supply which is **exempt** from VAT.

e) If a car is purchased for use within a business the VAT is **irrecoverable**.

2

Sales account

	£		£
30 June Balance c/d	15,545.55	23 June Balance b/d	14,375.55
		30 June SDB	830.00
		30 June CRB	340.00
	15,545.55		15,545.55
		Balance b/d	15,545.55

Sales returns account

	£		£
23 June Balance b/d	1,552.68	30 June Balance c/d	1,576.68
30 June SRDB	24.00		
	1,576.68	Balance b/d	1,576.68
Balance b/d	1,576.68		

Sales ledger control account

	£		£
23 June Balance b/d	3,226.50	30 June SRDB	28.20
30 June SDB	975.25	30 June CRB	629.17
		30 June CRB – discount	5.75
		30 June Balance c/d	3,538.63
	4,201.75		4,201.75
Balance b/d	3,538.63		

VAT account

	£		£
30 June SRDB	4.20	23 June Balance b/d	1,263.50
30 June Balance c/d	1,464.05	30 June SDB	145.25
		30 June CRB	59.50
	1,468.25		1,468.25
		Balance b/d	1,464.05

Discounts allowed account

	£		£
23 June Balance b/d	235.47	30 June Balance c/d	241.22
30 June CRB	5.75		
	241.22		241.22
Balance b/d	241.22		

Subsidiary ledger – sales ledger

S David

	£		£
23 June Balance b/d	662.50	30 June CRB	135.12
30 June SDB	176.25	30 June CRB – discount	5.75
		30 June Balance c/d	697.88
	838.75		697.88
Balance b/d	697.88		

L Hibbard

	£		£
23 June Balance b/d	307.25	30 June CRB	336.25
30 June SDB	493.50	30 June Balance c/d	464.50
	800.75		800.75
Balance b/d	464.50		

P Timms

	£		£
23 June Balance b/d	612.80	30 June SRDB	28.20
30 June SDB	305.50	30 June CRB	157.80
		30 June Balance c/d	732.30
	918.30		918.30
Balance b/d	732.30		

3   a)   DR   Purchases   £1,200.00

           DR   VAT   £210.00

           CR   Bank   £1,410.00

     b)   DR   Purchases   £1,410.00

           CR   Bank   £1,410.00

4

VAT control account

	£		£
Purchases (£4,500 × 17.5%)	787.50	Balance b/d	2,165.00
Van (£10,460 × 17.5%)	1,830.50	Sales (£(6,000 − 300) × 17.5%)	997.50
Balance c/d	544.50		
	3,162.50		3,162.50

No VAT can be claimed on input tax on cars or on entertaining.

answers to chapter 5:
CAPITAL EXPENDITURE

1 a) Capital £12,000 + £400 + £250 = £12,650

       Revenue £100

  b) Capital £120,000 + £400 + £1,200 = £121,600

       Revenue £13,000

  c) Capital £10,600 – £1,100 + £2,450 = £11,950

       Revenue £1,100

  d) Capital £14,000 + £2,450 (VAT) + £50 = £16,500

       Revenue £150

2 SPK100 Revenue expenditure

   FL11 Capital expenditure

3 a) DR Motor vehicles account (12,000 x 1.175) £ 14,100.00

     DR Motor expenses account £ 150.00

     CR Bank account £ 14,250.00

  b) DR Machinery account (15,400 + 1,400) £ 16,800.00

     DR VAT account £ 2,695.00

     CR Creditors account (15,400 + 2,695) £ 18,095.00

     CR Wages account £ 1,400.00

c) DR   Computer account (3,800 – 150)   £ 3,650.00

    DR   Computer expenses account   £ 150.00

    DR   VAT account   £ 665.00

    CR   Bank account (3,800 + 665)   £ 4,465.00

d) DR   Building maintenance account   £   800.00

    CR   Bank account   £   800.00

e) DR   Computer expenses account   £   200.00

    CR   Bank account   £   200.00

4

Machinery account

	£		£
Balance b/d	103,400.00		
Bank	13,500.00		
Wages	400.00		
Purchases	850.00		

Buildings account

	£		£
Balance b/d	200,000.00		
Bank (150,000 + 20,000)	170,000.00		

VAT account

	£		£
Machinery (13,500 × 17.5%)	2,362.50	Balance b/d	13,289.60

Purchases account

	£		£
Balance b/d	56,789.50	Machinery	850.00

Wages account

	£		£
Balance b/d	113,265.88	Machinery	400.00

Buildings maintenance account

	£		£
Balance b/d	10,357.00		
Bank	4,000.00		

Bank account

	£		£
Balance b/d	214,193.60	Machinery	
		(13,500 + 2,362.50)	15,862.50
		Buildings	170,000.00
		Buildings maintenance	4,000.00

5   Borrowing

In order to finance the purchase of fixed assets by borrowing a loan must be taken out with a bank or finance company. The loan will normally have a fixed rate of interest which will have to be paid monthly or quarterly. The terms of the loan will also determine how it must be repaid. In some cases the entire amount of the loan will be repaid at the end of the loan period. However in many cases the loan will be repaid in instalments together with the interest on a monthly or quarterly basis. Once the loan money has been received then the business can purchase the fixed asset.

Hire purchase

Under a hire purchase agreement a deposit will normally be initially paid to the hire purchase company after which the business will have the right to use the fixed asset. Thereafter instalments will be paid on a monthly or quarterly basis to the hire purchase company which will include interest as well as payments of the cost of the asset. At the end of the hire purchase term on payment of the final instalment the fixed asset will become the legal property of the business.

Leasing

A leasing agreement is similar to a hire purchase agreement but with the major difference that under a leasing agreement the business never becomes the legal owner of the fixed asset. There are two types of leasing agreement – a finance lease and an operating lease.

Under a finance lease the business will make regular payments to the leasing company which cover the cost of the asset and the lease interest. The business never actually owns the asset but has the right to use it for normally its entire useful life. An operating lease is a shorter term lease where a fixed asset is hired for a period that is shorter than the asset's total life. The rental payments that are made will cover the finance costs of the leasing company.

6   Under SSAP 21 *Accounting for leases and hire purchase contracts*, the accounting treatment of finance leases is fundamentally different from the accounting treatment of operating leases.

A finance lease asset is treated as though it was an owned asset of the business. It is included in fixed assets in the balance sheet and is depreciated over its useful economic life. There is also a creditor in the balance sheet for the capital cost of the finance lease. Each period, the finance charge that is paid as part of the lease is charged to the profit and loss account and the creditor for the capital cost of the finance lease is reduced.

However, an asset leased under an operating lease does not appear on the balance sheet and the lease payments are simply charged to the profit and loss account each period.

answers to chapter 6:
DEPRECIATION OF FIXED ASSETS

1   Fixed assets are used within a business in order to generate the profits that the business makes. The nature of fixed assets is that they are purchased with the intention of using them for a number of years within the business. For this reason the cost of these assets is capitalised and included on the balance sheet rather than including the cost as an expense of the period in which they were purchased.

However, the nature of the fixed assets is that they will contribute to providing revenues of the business each year. Therefore in accordance with the fundamental accounting concept of accruals or matching a portion of the cost of the fixed asset should be charged as an expense for the period.

This is the basis for the annual depreciation charge for fixed assets. As they earn revenues for the business then a proportion of their cost must be charged to the business each year in order to match with those revenues.

2   a)   Annual charge   £17,400/5 years   =   £3,480

    Net book value   £17,400 – (3 x 3,480)   =   £6,960

    b)   Annual charge $\dfrac{12,800 - 2,000}{4 \text{ years}}$ =   £2,700

    Net book value   £12,800 – (2 x 2,700)   =   £7,400

    c)   Annual charge $\dfrac{4,600 - 700}{3 \text{ years}}$ =   £1,300

    Net book value   £4,600 – 1,300   =   £3,300

3 a)

		£
1 April 2006	Cost	24,600
31 March 2007	Depreciation	4,920
NBV		19,680

b)

		£
1 April 2004	Cost	18,700.00
31 March 2005	Depreciation	4,675.00
NBV		14,025.00
31 March 2006	Depreciation	3,506.25
NBV		10,518.75
31 March 2007	Depreciation	2,629.69
NBV		7,889.06

c)

1 April 2005	Cost	3,800.00
31 March 2006	Depreciation	1,140.00
NBV		2,660.00
31 March 2007	Depreciation	798.00
NBV		1,862.00

4 a) Depreciation charge £14,000 x 20% x 8/12 = £1,866.67

b) Depreciation charge £3,200 x 25% = £800.00

c) Depreciation charge £4,400 x 40% x 2/12 = £293.33

5

	Straight line 25% £	Reducing balance 55% £
Year 1	700	1,540
Year 2	700	693
Year 3	700	312
Year 4	700	255
	2,800	2,800

Workings

1) Straight line method

$$\text{Depreciation} = \frac{2,800 - 0}{4} = £700 \text{ pa or } 25\%$$

2) Reducing balance method

Year 1: £2,800 × 55% = £1,540

Year 2: (£2,800 − £1,540) × 55% = £1,260 × 55%
           = £693

Year 3: (£1,260 − £693) × 55% = £567 × 55%
           = £312

Year 4: £567 − £312 = £255

answers to chapter 7:
DISPOSAL OF FIXED ASSETS

1

	£
1 Apr 2005 Cost	12,500
31 Mar 2006 Depreciation	(3,750)
NBV	8,750
31 Mar 2007 Depreciation	(2,625)
NBV	6,125
Proceeds	(6,000)
Loss on disposal	125

2 Annual depreciation charge $= \dfrac{£25,000 - 3,000}{5}$

$= £4,400$

Fixed asset at cost account

	£		£
1 Jan 2005 Bank	25,000	31 Dec 2007 Disposal	25,000

Depreciation account

	£		£
31 Dec 2005 Provision	4,400	31 Dec 2005 P&L	4,400
31 Dec 2006 Provision	4,400	31 Dec 2006 P&L	4,400
31 Dec 2007 Provision	4,400	31 Dec 2007 P&L	4,400

Provision for depreciation account

	£		£
31 Dec 2006 Balance c/d	8,800	31 Dec 2005 Expense	4,400
		31 Dec 2006 Expense	4,400
	8,800		8,800
31 Dec 2007 Disposal	13,200	1 Jan 2007 Balance b/d	8,800
		31 Dec 2007 Expense	4,400
	13,200		13,200

Disposal account

	£		£
31 Dec 2007 Cost	25,000	31 Dec 2007 Provision	13,200
		31 Dec 2007 Bank	11,000
		31 Dec 2007 Loss on disposal	800
	25,000		25,000

3 Depreciation calculation:

		£
1 Apr 2005	Cost	13,800
31 Mar 2006	Depreciation	(4,140)
NBV		9,660
31 Mar 2007	Depreciation	(2,898)
NBV		6,762

Depreciation expense account

	£		£
31 Mar 2007 Provision	2,898		

Provision for depreciation account

	£		£
31 Mar 2007 Disposal	7,038	1 Apr 2006 Balance b/d	4,140
		31 Mar 2007 Expense	2,898
	7,038		7,038

Motor vehicle at cost account

	£		£
1 Apr 2005 Bank	13,800	31 Mar 2007 Disposal	13,800

Disposal account

	£		£
31 Mar 2007 Cost	13,800	31 Mar 2007 Provision	7,038
31 Mar 2007 Profit	238	31 Mar 2007 Bank	7,000
	14,038		14,038

4 a) A profit on disposal is sometimes described as **over** depreciation.

b) A loss on disposal is sometimes described as **under** depreciation.

5 Depreciation at the date of disposal:

		£
31 December 2005	15,600 x 25% x 6/12	1,950
31 December 2006	15,600 x 25%	3,900
31 December 2007	15,600 x 25% x 11/12	3,575
		9,425

Disposal account

	£		£
30 Nov 2007 Cost	15,600	30 Nov 2007 Provision	9,425
		30 Nov 2007 Bank	6,000
		30 Nov 2007 Loss on disposal	17
	15,600		15,600

6 Depreciation at date of disposal:

		£
31 July 2005	12,800 x 25%	3,200
31 July 2006	12,800 x 75% x 25%	2,400
31 July 2007	12,800 x 75% x 75% x 25%	1,800
		7,400

Disposal account

	£		£
30 Sept 2007 Cost	12,800	30 Sept 2007 Provision	7,400
		30 Sept 2007 Bank	4,000
		30 Sept 2007 Loss on disposal	1,400
	12,800		12,800

7

Cars at cost account

		£		£
1 Jan 2005	Bank	20,000	31 Dec 2007 Disposal	20,000
31 Dec 2007	Bank	18,000	31 Dec 2007 Bal c/d	24,000
	Disposal	6,000		
		44,000		44,000
1 Jan 2008	Bal b/d	24,000		

Disposal account

	£		£
30 Dec 2007 Cars at cost	20,000	31 Dec 2007 Provision for depreciation	15,000
31 Dec 2007 Profit on disposal	1,000	31 Dec 2007 Cars at cost	6,000
	21,000		21,000

8   a)

Motor vehicles: Cost

		£				£
2007			*2007*			
30 June	Balance b/f	63,500	30 June	Disposals (a)		1,000
	Disposals (trade in			Disposals (b)		2,500
	allowance (b))*	750		Disposals (c)		2,000
	Disposals (d)	1,250		Disposals (d)		5,000
				Balance c/d		55,000
		65,500				65,500

* Balance of cost of £3,250 already entered in accounts.

Motor vehicles: Accumulated depreciation

		£				£
2007			*2007*			
30 June	Van scrapped (a)	1,000	30 June	Balance b/f		38,000
	Disposals (b)	1,500		Profit and loss		
	Disposals (c)(W1)	1,375		account (charge		
	Disposals (d)(W2)	3,375		for year)		12,500
	Balance c/d	43,250				
		50,500				50,500

Motor vehicles: Disposals

		£			£
2007			*2007*		
30 June	Motor vehicles: cost (a)	1,000	30 June	Balance b/f	800
	Motor vehicles: cost (b)	2,500		Motor vehicles: cost	
	Motor vehicles: cost (c)	2,000		(trade in allowance (b))	750
	Motor vehicles: cost (d)	5,000		Accumulated	
				depreciation (a)	1,000
				Accumulated	
				depreciation (b)	1,500
				Accumulated	
				depreciation (c)(W1)	1,375
				Motor vehicles: cast	
				(sale proceeds (d))	1,250
				Accumulated	
				depreciation (d) (W2)	3,375
				Profit and loss account:	
				loss on disposals	450
		10,500			10,500

Workings

1) Accumulated depreciation on car 3)

	£
Cost	2,000
Accumulated depreciation (balancing figure)	1,375
Written down value	625

2) Accumulated depreciation on van 4)

	£
Cost	5,000
Accumulated depreciation (balancing figure)	3,375
Net book value	1,625
Sale proceeds	1,250
Loss on disposal	375

b) **EMMA & CO**
Balance sheet extract as at 30 June 2007

	£
Motor vehicles: cost	55,000
accumulated depreciation	43,250
	11,750

FIXED ASSET REGISTER

Description/serial no	Date acquired	Original cost £	Depreciation £	NBV £	Funding method	Disposal proceeds £	Disposal date
Office and shop equipment							
Depreciation: 25% p.a. on cost (straight line basis)							
Computer	1/9/04	3,000.00			Cash		
Year ended 31/8/05			600.00	2,400.00			
Year ended 31/8/06			600.00	1,800.00			
Year ended 31/8/07			600.00	1,200.00			
Printer and photocopier	1/9/04	2,000.00			Cash		
Year ended 31/8/05			400.00	1,600.00			
Year ended 31/8/06			400.00	1,200.00			
Year ended 31/8/07			400.00	800.00			
Fax machine	30/9/04	800.00			Cash		
Year ended 31/8/05			160.00	640.00			
Year ended 31/8/06			160.00	480.00			
Year ended 31/8/07			160.00	320.00			
Chiller cabinets	1/4/04	7,000.00			Cash		
Year ended 31/8/05			1,400.00	5,600.00			
Year ended 31/8/06			1,400.00	4,200.00			
Year ended 31/8/07			1,400.00	2,800.00			
Till	1/9/05	5,000.00					
Year ended 31/8/06			1,000.000	4,000.00	Cash	200.00	31/8/07
NBV at 31/8/07 c/f				**5,120.00**			

FIXED ASSET REGISTER

Description/serial no	Date acquired	Original cost £	Depreciation £	NBV £	Funding method	Disposal proceeds £	Disposal date
Office and shop equipment							
Depreciation: 20% p.a. on cost (straight line basis)							
Security shutters	30/9/04	6,000.00			Cash		
Year ended 31/8/05			1,200.00	4,800.00			
Year ended 31/8/06			1,200.00	3,600.00			
Year ended 31/8/07			1,200.00	2,400.00			
Desk	31/8/07	800.00			Cash		
Year ended 31/8/07			160.00	640.00			
Computerised till	31/8/07	3,500.00			Cash		
Year ended 31/8/07			700.00	2,800.00			
NBV at 31/8/07				**5,840.00**			
NBV at 31/8/07 b/f				**5,120.00**			
NBV at 31/8/07				**10,960.00**			

FIXED ASSET REGISTER

Description/serial no	Date acquired	Original cost £	Depreciation £	NBV £	Funding method	Disposal proceeds £	Disposal date
Butchery equipment							
20% p.a. on net book value (reducing balance basis)							
Workbenches (6)	1/9/04	6,000.00			Cash		
Year ended 31/8/05			1,200.00	4,800.00			
Year ended 31/8/06			960.00	3,840.00			
Year ended 31/8/07			768.00	3,072.00			
Grinding machine	1/9/04	3,600.00			Cash		
Year ended 31/8/05			720.00	2,880.00			
Year ended 31/8/06			576.00	2,304.00			
Year ended 31/8/07			460.80	1,843.20			
Slicer	1/9/04	2,350.00			Cash		
Year ended 31/8/05			470.00	1,880.00			
Year ended 31/8/06			376.00	1,504.00			
Year ended 31/8/07			300.80	1,203.20			
Freezer (600 cu ft)	1/9/05	9,000.00			Cash		
Year ended 31/8/06			1,800.00	7,200.00			
Year ended 31/8/07			1,440.00	5,760.00			
Freezer (1,200 cu ft)	31/8/07	15,500.00			Cash		
Year ended 31/8/07			3,100.00	12,400.00			
NBV at 31/8/07				**24,278.40**			

FIXED ASSET REGISTER

Description/serial no	Date acquired	Original cost £	Depreciation £	NBV £	Funding method	Disposal proceeds £	Disposal date
Delivery vehicles							
25% p.a. on cost (reducing balance basis)							
Van TY61 CVB	1/4/04	15,000.00			Cash		
Year ended 31/8/05			3,750.00	11,250.00			
Year ended 31/8/06			3,750.00	7,500.00			
Year ended 31/8/07			3,750.00	3,750.00			
Van GH62 UYT	1/4/05	12,000.00			Cash		
Year ended 31/8/06			3,000.00	9,000.00			
Year ended 31/8/07			3,000.00	6,000.00			
Van TY72 BNM	1/1/07	11,500.00			Cash		
Year ended 31/8/07			2,875.00	8,625.00			
NBV at 31/8/07				**18,375.00**			

a) Journal 1

Date 2007	Account names and narrative	Debit £	Credit £
31/8	Butchery equipment (cost)	15,500.00	
	Office and shop equipment (cost)	4,300.00	
	VAT	3,410.75	
	Sundry creditors		23,210.75
	Being new fixed assets acquired at 31 August		

b) Journal 2

Date 2007	Account names and narrative	Debit £	Credit £
31/8	Suspense	200.00	
	Disposals		200.00
	Office and shop equipment (accumulated depreciation)	1,000.00	
			1,000.00
	Disposals	5,000.00	
	Disposals		5,000.00
	Office and shop equipment (cost)		
	Being disposal of the old till		

c) Journal 3

Date 2007	Account names and narrative	Debit £	Credit £
31/8	Depreciation charge	20,314.60	
	Office and shop equipment: Accumulated depreciation (600.00 + 400.00 + 160.00 + 1,400.00 + 1,200.00 + 160.00 + 700.00))		4,620.00
	Butchery equipment: Accumulated depreciation (768.00 + 460.80 + 300.80 + 1,440.00 + 3,100.00)		6,069.60
	Delivery vehicles: Accumulated depreciation (3,750.00 + 3,000.00 + 2,875.00)		9,625.00
	Being depreciation for the year		

d)

Butchery equipment (accumulated depreciation)

Date	Details	Amount £	Date	Details	Amount £
2007			2007		
31/8	Balance c/d	12,171.60	31/8	Balance b/d	6,102.00
				Journal 3	6,069.60
		12,171.60			12,171.00

Butchery equipment (cost)

Date	Details	Amount £	Date	Details	Amount £
2007			2007		
31/8	Balance b/d	20,950.00	31/8	Balance c/d	36,450.00
	Journal 1	15,500.00			
		36,450.00			36,450.00

Delivery vehicles (accumulated depreciation)

Date	Details	Amount £	Date	Details	Amount £
2007			2007		
31/8	Balance c/d	20,125.00	31/8	Balance b/d	10,500.00
				Journal 3	9,625.00
		20,125.00			20,125.00

Delivery vehicles (cost)

Date	Details	Amount £	Date	Details	Amount £
2007			2007		
31/8	Balance b/d	38,500.00	31/8	Balance c/d	38,500.00

Depreciation charge

Date	Details	Amount £	Date	Details	Amount £
2007			2007		
31/8	Journal 3	20,314.60			

Disposals

Date	Details	Amount £	Date	Details	Amount £
2007			2007		
31/8	Journal 2	5,000.00	31/8	Journal 2	200.00
				Journal 2	1,000.00
				Loss on disposal (profit and loss account)	3,800.00
		5,000.00			5,000.00

Office and shop equipment (accumulated depreciation)

Date	Details	Amount £	Date	Details	Amount £
2007			2007		
31/8	Journal 2	1,000.00	31/8	Balance b/d	8,520.00
	Balance c/d	12,140.00		Journal 3	4,620.00
		13,140.00			13,140.00

Office and shop equipment (cost)

Date	Details	Amount £	Date	Details	Amount £
2007			2007		
31/8	Balance b/d	23,800.00	31/8	Balance c/d	28,100.00
	Journal 1	4,300.00			
		28,100.00			28,100.00

Sundry creditors

Date	Details	Amount £	Date	Details	Amount £
2007			2007		
			31/8/	Journal 1	23,210.75

Suspense

Date	Details	Amount £	Date	Details	Amount £
2007			2007		
31/8	Journal 2	200.00	31/8	Balance b/d	200.00

VAT

Date	Details	Amount £	Date	Details	Amount £
2007			2007		
31/8	Journal 1	3,410.75			

e) **Balances per main ledger accounts**

	Cost £	Accumulated depreciation £	Net book value per fixed asset register £
Butchery equipment	36,450.00	12,171.60	24,278.40
Office and shop equipment	23,100.00	12,140.00	10,960.00
Delivery vehicles	38,500.00	20,125.00	18,375.00

answers to chapter 8:
ACCRUALS AND PREPAYMENTS

1

Telephone account

	£		£
31 Mar Bank	845	31 Mar P&L	1,015
31 Mar Accrual	170		
	1,015		1,015

Accruals account

	£		£
		31 Mar Telephone	170

2

Electricity account

	£		£
30 June Balance b/d	2,300	30 June P&L	3,200
30 June Accruals	900		
	3,200		3,200

Accruals account

	£		£
21 July Bank	900	30 June Electricity	900

3

Heat and light account

	£		£
30 April Balance b/d	2,400	30 April P&L	2,880
30 April Balance c/d	480		
	2,880		2,880
		1 May Balance b/d	480

4

Advertising account

	£		£
31 March Bank	14,600	31 March P&L	15,800
31 March Balance c/d	1,200		
	15,800		15,800
30 April Bank	1,200	1 April Balance b/d	1,200

5

Insurance account

	£		£
31 May Bank	2,300	31 May Prepayment	250
		31 May P&L	2,050
	2,300		2,300
1 June Prepayments	250		

Prepayments account

	£		£
31 May Insurance	250	1 June Insurance	250

6

Rent account

	£		£
30 June Balance b/d	4,500	30 June Prepayment	400
		30 June P&L	4,100
	4,500		4,500
1 July Prepayment	400		

Prepayment account

	£		£
30 June Rent	400	1 July Rent	400

7 a)

Rental income account

	£		£
30 June Rental in advance	350	30 June Bank	5,600
30 June P&L	5,250		
	5,600		5,600
		1 July Rental in advance	350

Rental income received in advance account

	£		£
1 July Rental income	350	30 June Rental income	350

b)

Rental income account

	£		£
30 June P&L	5,250	30 June Bank	5,600
30 June Balance c/d	350		
	5,600		5,600
		1 July Balance b/d	350

8

Insurance account

	£		£
Balance b/f	282	Prepayment c/f	78
		P&L a/c	204
	282		282

Commission receivable

	£		£
P&L a/c	200	Balance b/f	150
		Sundry debtors	50
	200		200

Telephone

	£		£
Balance b/f	586	P&L a/c	738
Accrual c/f	152		
	738		738

Carriage expenses

	£		£
Balance b/d	154	P&L a/c	184
Accrual c/f	30		
	184		184

answers to chapter 9:
BAD AND DOUBTFUL DEBTS

1

Main ledger

Sales ledger control account

	£		£
Balance b/d	5,479	Bad debts expense	
		(321 + 124)	445
		Balance c/d	5,034
	5,479		5,479
Balance b/d	5,034		

Bad debt expense account

	£		£
Sales ledger control	445	P&L	445

Subsidiary ledger

G Simms & Co

	£		£
Balance b/d	321	Bad debts	321

L Fitzgerald

	£		£
Balance b/d	124	Bad debts	124

2

Main ledger

Sales ledger control account

	£		£
30 Sep Balance b/d	16,475	30 Sep Bad debts expense	
		(1,200 + 400 + 70)	1,670
		30 Sep VAT	210
		30 Sep Balance c/d	14,595
	16,475		16,475
1 Oct Balance b/d	14,595		

VAT account

	£		£
30 Sep Sales ledger control	210	30 Sep Balance b/d	2,451
30 Sep Balance c/d	2,241		
	2,451		2,451
		1 Oct Balance b/d	2,241

Bad debts expense account

	£		£
30 Sep Sales ledger control	1,670	30 Sep P&L	1,670

Subsidiary ledger

H Maguire

	£		£
30 Sep Balance b/d	1,410	30 Sep Bad debts	1,200
		30 Sep VAT	210
	1,410		1,410

J Palmer

	£		£
30 Sep Balance b/d	470	30 Sep Bad debts	470

(**Tutorial note:** VAT can only be reclaimed on bad debts if they are more than six months overdue.)

3

Main ledger

Sales ledger control account

	£			£
31 Dec 2007 Balance b/d	7,264	31 Dec 2007	Bad debts	
31 Dec 2007 Bad debts			expense	669
expense	488	31 Dec 2007	Bank	488
		31 Dec 2007	Balance c/d	6,595
	7,752			7,752

Bad debts expense account

	£			£
31 Dec 2007 Sales ledger		31 Dec 2007	Sales ledger	
control	669		control	488
		31 Dec 2007	P&L	181
	669			669

Subsidiary ledger

R Trevor

	£			£
		31 Dec 2007	Bad debt	
31 Dec 2007 Debt reinstated	488		recovered	488

E Ingham

	£		£
31 Dec 2007 Balance b/d	669	31 Dec 2007 Bad debts	669

4

Bad debts expense account

	£		£
31 Dec 2005 Provision	635	31 Dec 2005 P&L	635
31 Dec 2006 Provision	125	31 Dec 2006 P&L	125
31 Dec 2007 P&L	168	31 Dec 2007 Provision	168

Provision for doubtful debts account

	£		£
		31 Dec 2005 Bad debts	635
31 Dec 2006 Balance c/d	760	31 Dec 2006 Bad debts	125
	760		760
31 Dec 2006 Bad debts	168	1 Jan 2007 Balance b/d	760
31 Dec 2007 Balance c/d	592		
	760		760
		1 Jan 2008 Balance b/d	592

Working

Provision required each year:

		£
31 Dec 2005	£12,700 x 5%	635
31 Dec 2006	£15,200 x 5%	760
Increase		125
31 Dec 2006		760
31 Dec 2007	£14,800 x 4%	592
Decrease		168

5

Sales ledger control account

	£		£
b/d	218,940	Bad debt expenses	2,440
		c/d	216,500
	218,940		218,940

Provision for doubtful debts account

	£		£
		b/d	5,215
c/d	6,495	Doubtful debt expense	1,280
(£216,500 × 3%)			
	6,495		6,495

Bad and doubtful debt expense account

	£		£
SLCA	2,440		
Provision	1,280	P&L account	3,720
	3,720		3,720

Subsidiary ledger

Hendrick

	£		£
b/d	2,440	Bad debt expense	2,440

answers to chapter 10:
CONTROL ACCOUNT RECONCILIATIONS

1

Sales ledger control account

	£		£
Opening balance	4,268	Sales returns	995
Credit sales	15,487	Bad debt written off	210
Returned cheque	645	Cheques from debtors	13,486
		Discounts allowed	408
		Contra	150
	20,400	Closing balance	5,151
			20,400

2

Purchases ledger control account

	£		£
Cheques to creditors	10,379	Opening balance	3,299
Returns to suppliers	1,074	Credit purchases	12,376
Discounts received	302		
Contra	230		
Closing balance	3,690		
	15,675		15,675

3

Sales ledger control account

	£		£
Opening balance	12,634	Cheques from debtors	50,375
Credit sales	51,376	Sales returns	3,173
		Contra	630
		Discounts allowed	1,569
		Closing balance	8,263
	64,010		64,010

Purchases ledger control account

	£		£
Discounts received	1,245	Opening balance	10,553
Cheques to suppliers	35,795	Credit purchases	40,375
Purchases returns	2,003		
Contra	630		
Closing balance	11,255		
	50,928		50,928

4

	£
List of balances total	8,210
Contra	(123)
Credit note 2 x 320	(640)
Credit balance 2 x 60	(120)
Amended total	7,327

Sales ledger control account

	£		£
Balance b/d	6,237	Balance c/d	7,327
Sales day book undercast	1,000		
Discounts allowed	90		
	7,327		7,327

5

	£
List of balances total	1,850
Invoice 2 x 350	700
Creditors balance	(90)
Amended total	2,460

Purchases ledger control account

	£		£
Purchases returns 2 ? 288	576	Balance b/d	3,105
Contra	169	Cash payments book overcast	100
Balance c/d	2,460		
	3,205		3,205

6 a) and d)

Administration

Date	Details	Amount £	Date	Details	Amount £
31/1	PDB	1,298.02			

Cash

Date	Details	Amount £	Date	Details	Amount £
31/1	CB	33,026.73	31/1	CB	39,532.19

Despatch

Date	Details	Amount £	Date	Details	Amount £
31/1	PDB	2,817.29	31/1	PRDB	192.64
31/1	Journal	270.00			

Discounts allowed and received

Date	Details	Amount £	Date	Details	Amount £
31/1	CB	203.00	31/1	PRDB	192.50

Drawings

Date	Details	Amount £	Date	Details	Amount £
31/1	CB	2,000.00			

Interest received

Date	Details	Amount £	Date	Details	Amount £
			31/1	CB	103.00

Marketing

Date	Details	Amount £	Date	Details	Amount £
31/1	PDB	3,198.29	31/1	PRDB	32.00
31/1	Journal	742.13			

Motor vehicles

Date	Details	Amount £	Date	Details	Amount £
31/1	CB	15,000.00			

Purchase ledger control

Date	Details	Amount £	Date	Details	Amount £
31/1	PRDB	263.95	31/1	Balance b/d	19,190.62
31/1	CB	196.50	31/1	PDB	11,991.80
31/1	CB	15,439.50			
31/1	Balance c/d	15,282.65			
		31,182.42			31,182.42
31/1	Journal	582.45	31/1	Balance b/d	15,282.65
31/1	Balance c/d	15,842.20	31/1	Journal	872.00
			31/1	Journal	270.00
		16,424.65			16,424.65

Salaries

Date	Details	Amount £	Date	Details	Amount £
31/1	CB	7,092.87			

Sales

Date	Details	Amount £	Date	Details	Amount £
31/1	SRDB	200.00	31/1	SDB	20,189.73
31/1	Journal	1,225.54			
31/1	Journal	900.00			

Sales ledger control

Date	Details	Amount £	Date	Details	Amount £
31/1	Balance b/d	40,563.29	31/1	SRDB	235.00
31/1	SDB	23,722.93	31/1	CB	203.00
			31/1	CB	32,923.73
			31/1	Balance c/d	30,924.49
		64,286.22			64,286.22
31/1	Balance b/d	30,924.49	31/1	Journal	1,440.00
			31/1	Journal	582.45
			31/1	Journal	900.00
			31/1	Balance c/d	28,002.04
		30,924.49			30,924.49

VAT

Date	Details	Amount £	Date	Details	Amount £
31/1	PDB	1,786.01	31/1	SDB	3,533.20
31/1	SRDB	35.00	31/1	PRDB	39.31
31/1	Journal	214.46			
31/1	Journal	129.87			

Warehouse overheads

Date	Details	Amount £	Date	Details	Amount £
31/1	PDB	2,892.19			

b) **Sales ledger control account reconciliation**

	£
Balance per sales ledger control account	30,924.49
Less: overcast of January SDB invoice totals	(900.00)
Invoice total duplicated in SDB	(1,400.00)
Contra on account of Tremayne Holdings plc with Purchase Ledger	(582.45)
	28,002.04
Total sales ledger balances brought down	28,242.04
Less: posting of cash received £120.00 to wrong side (DR)	
of Nelson Ltd account	(240.00)
	28,002.04

Purchase ledger control account reconciliation

	£
Balance per purchase ledger control account	15,282.65
Add: undercast of January PDB invoice totals	270.00
Invoice total missing in PDB	872.00
Contra on account of Tremayne Holdings plc with Sales Ledger	(582.45)
	15,842.20
Total purchase ledger balances brought down	16,934.55
Less: duplicated invoice posted to Harrier Ltd purchase ledger account	(1,092.35)
	15,842.20

c) **Journal**

Date	Account names and narrative	Debit £	Credit £
31/1	Sales (1,440.00 × 40/47)	1,225.54	
	VAT (1,440.00 × 7/47)	214.46	
	Sales ledger control		1,440.00
	Purchase ledger control	582.45	
	Sales ledger control		582.45
	Sales ledger control		900.00
	Sales	900.00	
	Being correction of errors in sales ledger control account		
	Marketing (872.00 × 40/47)	742.13	
	VAT (872.00 × 7/47)	129.87	
	Purchase ledger control		872.00
	Purchase ledger control		270.00
	Despatch	270.00	
	Being correction of errors in purchase ledger control account		

Note. No journal is needed for item vi) as it affects only the memorandum accounts.

answers to chapter 11:
ERRORS AND THE SUSPENSE ACCOUNT

1

		Imbalance	No imbalance
a)	The payment of the telephone bill was posted to the cash payments book and then credited to the telephone account	X	
b)	The depreciation expense was debited to the provision for depreciation account and credited to the depreciation expense account		X
c)	The electricity account balance of £750 was taken to the trial balance as £570	X	
d)	The motor expenses were debited to the motor vehicles at cost account		X
e)	The discounts received in the cash payments book were not posted to the main ledger		X

2   A credit balance of £8,304

3

a) DR   Telephone account   £236
    CR   Electricity account   £236

Being correction of misposting of telephone expense

b) DR   Sales ledger control account   £180
    CR   Sales account   £180

Being correction of sales invoice entry in the sales day book

c) DR   Purchases ledger control account £38
    CR   Purchases returns account   £38

Being entry of credit note omitted from purchases returns day book

d) DR Bad debts expense account   £254
    CR Provision for doubtful debts   £254

    Being correction of error in increasing provision for doubtful debts

e) DR Purchases ledger control account   £400
    CR Sales ledger control account   £400

    Being correction of misposting of contra entry

4

Suspense account

	£		£
Sales ledger control	2,700	Balance	1,370
Sales ledger control	470	Wages – trial balance	1,800
	3,170		3,170

5

Suspense account

	£		£
Balance	3,100	Insurance (1,585 x 2)	3,170
Postage (62 – 26)	36		
Bank interest received – TB	34		
	3,170		3,170

6

DR	Accumulated depreciation	£10,500	
DR	Disposal	£15,000	
DR	Suspense	£ 4,000	
CR	Fixed asset at cost		£15,000
CR	Disposal account		£10,500
CR	Disposal account		£ 4,000

Suspense account

	£		£
Disposal account	4,000	Balance	4,000

7   a) and d)

Administration and marketing

Date	Details	Amount £	Date	Details	Amount £
1/4	Balance b/d	32,290.29	30/4	Balance c/d	40,381.95
30/4	Cash book	5,982.38			
30/4	PDB	2,109.28			
		40,381.95			40,381.95
30/4	Balance b/d	40,381.95			

Capital

Date	Details	Amount £	Date	Details	Amount £
30/4	Balance c/d	50,000.00	1/4	Balance b/d	50,000.00
		50,000.00			50,000.00
			30/4	Balance b/d	50,000.00

Cash

Date	Details	Amount £	Date	Details	Amount £
30/4	Cash book	61,947.68	1/4	Balance b/d	2,398.20
			30/4	Cash book	45,461.99
			30/4	Balance c/d	14,087.49
		61,947.68			61,947.68
30/4	Balance b/d	14,087.49			

Discounts allowed and received

Date	Details	Amount £	Date	Details	Amount £
1/4	Balance b/d	375.29	30/4	Cash book	636.00
30/4	Cash book	653.00	30/4	Balance c/d	392.29
		1,028.29			1,028.29
30/4	Balance b/d	392.29			

Drawings

Date	Details	Amount £	Date	Details	Amount £
1/4	Balance b/d	15,000.00			
30/4	Cash book	3,000.00	30/4	Balance c/d	18,000.00
		18,000.00			18,000.00
30/4	Balance b/d	18,000.00			

Factory labour

Date	Details	Amount £	Date	Details	Amount £
1/4	Balance b/d	43,529.18			
30/4	Cash book	7,209.86	30/4	Balance c/d	50,739.04
		50,739.04			50,739.04
30/4	Balance b/d	50,739.04	30/4	Journal	270.00
			30/4	Balance c/d	50,469.04
		50,739.04			50,739.04
30/4	Balance c/d	50,469.04			

Factory overheads

Date	Details	Amount £	Date	Details	Amount £
1/4	Balance b/d	28,254.38	30/4	Cash book	123.95
30/4	PDB	1,290.38	30/4	PRDB	139.25
			30/4	Balance c/d	29,281.56
		29,544.76			29,544.76
30/4	Balance b/d	29,281.56			

Fixed assets (NBV)

Date	Details	Amount £	Date	Details	Amount £
1/4	Balance b/d	32,100.10	30/4	Balance c/d	32,100.10
		32,100.10			32,100.10
30/4	Balance b/d	32,100.10			

Interest paid

Date	Details	Amount £	Date	Details	Amount £
1/4	Balance b/d	1,920.27	30/4	Balance c/d	2,150.27
30/4	Cash book	230.00			
		2,150.27			2,150.27
30/4	Balance b/d	2,150.27			

Loan

Date	Details	Amount £	Date	Details	Amount £
30/4	Balance c/d	15,000.00	1/4	Balance b/d	15,000.00
		15,000.00			15,000.00
			30/4	Balance b/d	15,000.00

Purchase ledger control

Date	Details	Amount £	Date	Details	Amount £
30/4	Cash book	636.00	1/4	Balance b/d	25,131.14
30/4	Cash book	29,039.75	30/4	PDB	14,948.21
30/4	PRDB	1,320.07			
30/4	Balance c/d	9,083.53			
		40,079.35			40,079.35
			30/4	Balance b/d	9,083.53
30/4	Balance c/d	9,263.53	30/4	Journal	180.00
		9,263.53			9,263.53
			30/4	Balance b/d	9,263.53

Raw materials

Date	Details	Amount £	Date	Details	Amount £
1/4	Balance b/d	80,265.35	30/4	PRDB	984.22
30/4	PDB	9,365.47			
			30/4	Balance c/d	88,646.60
		89,630.82			89,630.82
30/4	Balance b/d	88,646.60			

Sales

Date	Details	Amount £	Date	Details	Amount £
30/4	SRDB	2,673.36	1/4	Balance b/d	215,189.19
			30/4	SDB	35,864.86
30/4	Balance c/d	248,380.69			
		251,054.05			251,054.05
			30/4	Balance b/d	248,380.69

Sales ledger control

Date	Details	Amount £	Date	Details	Amount £
1/4	Balance b/d	67,585.12	30/4	Cash book	653.00
30/4	SDB	42,141.21	30/4	Cash book	61,823.73
			30/4	SRDB	3,141.19
			30/4	Balance c/d	44,108.41
		109,726.33			109,726.33
30/4	Balance b/d	44,108.41	30/4	Journal	1,191.38
			30/4	Balance c/d	42,917.03
		44,108.41			44,108.41
30/4	Balance b/d	42,917.03			

Stock

Date	Details	Amount £	Date	Details	Amount £
1/4	Balance b/d	10,198.19			
			30/4	Balance c/d	10,198.19
		10,198.19			10,198.19
30/4	Balance b/d	10,198.19			

Suspense

Date	Details	Amount £	Date	Details	Amount £
30/4	Journal	1,641.38	30/4	Balance	1,641.38

VAT

Date	Details	Amount £	Date	Details	Amount £
30/4	PDB	2,183.08	1/4	Balance b/d	2,158.26
30/4	SRDB	467.83	30/4	SDB	6,276.35
			30/4	PRDB	196.60
30/4	Balance c/d	5,980.30			
		8,631.21			8,631.21
			30/4	Balance b/d	5,980.30

b)

Trial balance

	£	£
Administration and marketing	40,381.95	
Capital		50,000.00
Cash	14,087.49	
Discount allowed and received	392.29	
Drawings	18,000.00	
Factory labour	50,739.04	
Factory overheads	29,281.56	
Fixed assets (NBV)	32,100.10	
Interest paid	2,150.27	
Loan		15,000.00
Purchase ledger control		9,083.53
Raw materials	88,646.60	
Sales		248,380.69
Sales ledger control	44,108.41	
Stock	10,198.19	
Suspense		1,641.38
VAT		5,980.30
	330,085.90	330,085.90

c) **Journal**

Date	Account names and narrative	Debit £	Credit £
30/4	Suspense	1,641.38	
	Factory labour		270.00
	Purchase ledger control		180.00
	Sales ledger control		1,191.38
	Being correction of errors in brought forward balances		

Note. Cash received only affects the memorandum accounts, not the double entry.

e)

Trial balance

	£	£
Administration and marketing	40,381.95	
Capital		50,000.00
Cash	14,087.49	
Discount allowed and received	392.29	
Drawings	18,000.00	
Factory labour	50,469.04	
Factory overheads	29,281.56	
Fixed assets (NBV)	32,100.10	
Interest paid	2,150.27	
Loan		15,000.00
Purchase ledger control		9,263.53
Raw materials	88,646.60	
Sales		248,380.69
Sales ledger control	42,917.03	
Stock	10,198.19	
Suspense		
VAT		5,980.30
	328,624.52	328,624.52

answers to chapter 12: STOCK

1 Stock No. 0434   Units

Quantity per stock record	266
Less: unrecorded returns to supplier	(20)
Quantity counted	246

Stock No. 0711

Quantity per stock record	78
Add: unrecorded delivery	30
	108
Add: unrecorded internal return	10
Quantity counted	118

Stock No. 0963

Quantity per stock record	118
Less: unrecorded materials requisition	(20)
	98
Quantity counted	93
Unresolved difference	5

In this case the quantity actually counted is less than the stock records. This could be due to a recording error. A goods received note or a return from the factory may have been recorded as 5 units too many or a return to a supplier or materials requisition may have been understated by 5 units. As the actual physical quantity is less than the stock records there is also the possibility that the 5 units have either been scrapped but that this has not been recorded, or that they have been stolen.

2 a)   Cost =   £24.60 + 0.50   =   £25.10

      NRV =   £25.80 – 1.00   =   £24.80

   b)   Valuation   125 units x £24.80   =   £3,100

3

Stock line	Quantity – units	Cost £	Selling price £	Selling costs £	Value per unit £	Total value £
A	180	12.50	20.40	0.50	12.50	2,250
B	240	10.90	12.60	1.80	10.80	2,592
C	300	15.40	22.70	1.20	15.40	4,620
D	80	16.50	17.80	1.50	16.30	1,304
E	130	10.60	18.00	1.00	10.60	1,378
						12,144

4 a) FIFO

Opening balance		80 units @ 8.20
Purchases		100 units @ 8.50
Sales	80 units @ 8.20	
	60 units @ 8.50	
	140 units	

Purchases		180 units @ 8.70
Sales	40 units @ 8.50	
	60 units @ 8.70	
	100 units	

Sales	70 units @ 8.70	
Closing stock	50 units @ 8.70	£435.00

b) LIFO

Opening balance		80 units @ 8.20
Purchases		100 units @ 8.50
Sales	100 units @ 8.50	
	40 units @ 8.20	
	140 units	

Purchases		180 units @ 8.70
Sales	100 units @ 8.70	
Sales	70 units @ 8.70	
Closing stock	40 units @ 8.20	£328
	10 units @ 8.70	£87
	50 units	£415

c)   AVCO

	Average cost £	Quantity	Value £
Opening balance	8.20	80	656
Purchases	8.50	100	850
	8.37	180	1,506
Sales	8.37	(140)	(1,172)
		40	334
Purchases	8.70	180	1,566
	8.64	220	1,900
Sales	8.64	(100)	(864)
Sales	8.64	(70)	(604)
	8.64	50	432

5   a)   Sales for October

(2 + 4 + 6) × £50 = £600

b)   Cost of goods sold for October

		£
Sale 13.10.X5: Cost =	2 × £30	60
Sale 18.10.X5: Cost =	4 × £30	120
Sale 30.10.X5: Cost =	4 × £30	120
	2 × £32	64
	12	364

c)   Closing stock

	£
10 at £32	320
10 at £31	310
	630

6   a)   FIFO

			£
Opening stock	200 @ 3.00		600.00
Purchases	200 @ 3.20		640.00
Sales		140 @ 3.00	(420.00)
Sales		60 @ 3.00	
		70 @ 3.20	
		130	(404.00)
Purchases	200 @ 3.40		680.00
Sales		130 @ 3.20	
		50 @ 3.40	
		180	(586.00)
Sales		120 @ 3.40	(408.00)
Purchases	200 @ 3.50		700.00
Sales		30 @ 3.40	
		130 @ 3.50	
		160	(557.00)
Closing stock		70 @ 3.50	245.00

b)   LIFO

Opening stock	200 @ 3.00			600.00
Purchases	200 @ 3.20			640.00
Sales		140	@ 3.20	(448.00)
Sales		60	@ 3.20	
		70	@ 3.00	
		130		(402.00)
Purchases	200 @ 3.40			680.00
Sales		180	@ 3.40	(612.00)
Sales		20	@ 3.40	
		100	@ 3.00	
		120		(368.00)
Purchases	200 @ 3.50			700.00
Sales		160	@ 3.50	(560.00)
Closing stock		30	@ 3.00	
		40	@ 3.50	
		70		230.00

c)   AVCO

	Average cost £	Quantity	Value £
Opening stock	3.00	200	600
Purchases	3.20	200	640
	3.10	400	1,240
Sales	3.10	(140)	(434)
Sales	3.10	(130)	(403)
Purchases	3.40	200	680
	3.28	330	1,083
Sales	3.28	(180)	(590)
Sales	3.28	(120)	(394)
Purchases	3.50	200	700
	3.47	230	799
Sales	3.47	(160)	(555)
	3.47	70	244

answers to chapter 13:
FROM TRIAL BALANCE TO FINAL ACCOUNTS – SOLE TRADER

1

	£
Opening capital	32,569
Net profit for the year	67,458
	100,027
Less: drawings (35,480 + 1,680)	37,160
Closing capital	62,867

2 Suspense account balance = 526,504 – 519,475 = £7,029 credit

3 Debit   Drawings   £560
    Credit   Purchases   £560

4 Rent   =   £3,600 + £1,200   =   £4,800
    Insurance   =   £4,250 - £850   =   £3,400

5 Depreciation charges

- machinery	=	£140,000 x 20%	=	£28,000
- motor vehicles	=	(£68,000 - 31,200) x 35%	=	£12,880
- fixtures and fittings	=	(£23,000 - 13,400) x 20%	=	£ 1,920

	Cost	Accumulated depreciation	Net book value
	£	£	£
Machinery	140,000	92,500	47,500
Motor vehicles	68,000	44,080	23,920
Fixtures and fittings	23,000	15,320	7,680
			79,100

6 a) **Draft initial trial balance as at 31 May**

	Debit £	Credit £
Bank		1,650
Capital		74,000
Creditors		40,800
Debtors	61,500	
Discount allowed	2,100	
Discount received		1,800
Drawings	30,000	
Fixtures and fittings at cost	24,500	
Electricity	2,300	
Insurance	3,000	
Miscellaneous expenses	1,200	
Motor expenses	3,400	
Motor vehicles at cost	48,000	
Purchases	245,000	
Provision for doubtful debts		1,000
Provision for depreciation		
- fixtures and fittings		6,100
- motor vehicles		22,000
Rent	4,200	
Sales		369,000
Stock	41,000	
Telephone	1,600	
VAT		4,100
Wages	52,000	
Suspense	650	
	520,450	520,450

b) **Journal entries – year end adjustments**

		Debit £	Credit £
i)	Stock – balance sheet	43,500	
	Stock – profit and loss account		43,500

Being the recording of the year end stock valuation.

ii)	Depreciation expense – fixtures and fittings £24,500 x 10%	2,450	
	Provision for depreciation – fixtures and fittings		2,450
	Depreciation expense – motor vehicles (£48,000 – £22,000) x 30%	7,800	
	Provision for depreciation – motor vehicles		7,800

Being provision of the depreciation charges for the year.

iii)	Bad debts expense	1,500	
	Debtors		1,500
	Bad debts expense ((£61,500 – £1,500) x 2%) – £1,000	200	
	Provision for doubtful debts		200

Being the writing off of a bad debt and the increase in provision for doubtful debts.

iv)	Electricity	650	
	Telephone	350	
	Accruals		1,000

Being the provision for accruals at the year end.

v)	Prepayments	1,500	
	Rent		800
	Insurance (£1,200 x 7/12)		700

Being the accounting for prepayments at the year end.

c) **Journal entries – correction of errors**

		Debit £	Credit £
i)	Miscellaneous expenses	300	
	Motor expenses		300

Being correction of error in posting miscellaneous expenses.

ii)	Discounts allowed (£425 x 2)	850	
	Suspense		850
	Suspense	200	
	Discounts received (£100 x 2)		200

Being correction of the posting errors for discounts allowed and received.

d) **Ledger accounts**

Stock – balance sheet

	£		£
31 May Journal	43,500		

Stock – profit and loss account

	£		£
		31 May Journal	43,500

Depreciation expense – fixtures and fittings

	£		£
31 May Journal	2,450		

Provision for depreciation – fixtures and fittings

	£			£
31 May Balance c/d	8,550	31 May Balance b/d		6,100
		31 May Journal		2,450
	8,550			8,550

Depreciation expense – motor vehicles

	£		£
31 May Journal	7,800		

Provision for depreciation – motor vehicles

	£			£
31 May Balance c/d	29,800	31 May Balance b/d		22,000
		31 May Journal		7,800
	29,800			29,800
		31 May Balance b/d		29,800

Bad debts expense

	£		£
31 May Journal	1,500	31 May Balance c/d	1,700
31 May Journal	200		
	1,700		1,700
31 May Balance b/d	1,700		

Debtors

		£			£
31 May	Balance b/d	61,500	31 May	Journal	1,500
			31 May	Balance c/d	60,000
		61,500			61,500
31 May	Balance b/d	60,000			

Provision for doubtful debts

		£			£
31 May	Balance c/d	1,200	31 May	Balance b/d	1,000
			31 May	Journal	200
		1,200			1,200
			31 May	Balance b/d	1,200

Electricity

		£			£
31 May	Balance b/d	2,300	31 May	Balance c/d	2,950
31 May	Journal	650			
		2,950			2,950
31 May	Balance b/d	2,950			

Telephone

		£			£
31 May	Balance b/d	1,600	31 May	Balance c/d	1,950
31 May	Journal	350			
		1,950			1,950
31 May	Balance b/d	1,950			

Accruals

		£			£
			31 May	Journal	1,000

Prepayments

		£			£
31 May	Journal	1,500			

Rent

		£			£
31 May	Balance b/d	4,200	31 May	Journal	800
			31 May	Balance c/d	3,400
		4,200			4,200
31 May	Balance b/d	3,400			

Insurance

		£			£
31 May	Balance b/d	3,000	31 May	Journal	700
			31 May	Balance c/d	2,300
		3,000			3,000
31 May	Balance b/d	2,300			

Miscellaneous expenses

		£			£
31 May	Balance b/d	1,200	31 May	Balance c/d	1,500
31 May	Journal	300			
		1,500			1,500
31 May	Balance b/d	1,500			

Motor expenses

		£			£
31 May	Balance b/d	3,400	31 May	Journal	300
			31 May	Balance c/d	3,100
		3,400			3,400
31 May	Balance b/d	3,100			

Discount allowed

		£			£
31 May	Balance b/d	2,100	31 May	Balance c/d	2,950
31 May	Journal	850			
		2,950			2,950
31 May	Balance b/d	2,950			

Discount received

		£			£
31 May	Balance c/d	2,000	31 May	Balance b/d	1,800
			31 May	Journal	200
		2,000			2,000
			31 May	Balance b/d	2,000

Suspense

		£			£
31 May	Balance b/d	650			
31 May	Journal	200			
		850			850

e) **Final trial balance at 31 May 2007**

	Debit £	Credit £
Bank		1,650
Capital		74,000
Creditors		40,800
Debtors	60,000	
Discount allowed	2,950	
Discount received		2,000
Drawings	30,000	
Fixtures and fittings at cost	24,500	
Electricity	2,950	
Insurance	2,300	
Miscellaneous expenses	1,500	
Motor expenses	3,100	
Motor vehicles at cost	48,000	
Purchases	245,000	
Provision for doubtful debts		1,200
Provision for depreciation – fixtures and fittings		8,550
– motor vehicles		29,800
Rent	3,400	
Sales		369,000
Stock	41,000	
Telephone	1,950	
VAT		4,100
Wages	52,000	
Stock – balance sheet	43,500	
Stock – profit and loss account		43,500
Depreciation expense – fixtures	2,450	
Depreciation expense – motor vehicles	7,800	
Bad debts expense	1,700	
Accruals		1,000
Prepayments	1,500	
	575,600	575,600

f) **Profit and loss account for the year ended 31 May 2007**

	£	£
Sales		369,000
Less: Cost of sales		
Opening stock	41,000	
Purchases	245,000	
	286,000	
Less: closing stock	(43,500)	
		242,500
Gross profit		126,500
Discount received		2,000
		128,500
Less: expenses		
Discount allowed	2,950	
Electricity	2,950	
Insurance	2,300	
Miscellaneous expenses	1,500	
Motor expenses	3,100	
Rent	3,400	
Telephone	1,950	
Wages	52,000	
Depreciation fixtures and fittings	2,450	
motor vehicles	7,800	
Bad debts	1,700	
		82,100
Net profit		46,400

Balance sheet as at 31 May 2007

	Cost £	Accumulated depreciation £	Net book value £
Fixed assets:			
Fixtures and fittings	24,500	8,550	15,950
Motor vehicles	48,000	29,800	18,200
	72,500	38,350	34,150
Current assets:			
Stock		43,500	
Debtors	60,000		
Less: provision	1,200		
		58,800	
Prepayments		1,500	
		103,800	
Current liabilities:			
Creditors	40,800		
Bank overdraft	1,650		
Accruals	1,000		
VAT	4,100		
		47,550	
Net current assets			56,250
			90,400
Opening capital			74,000
Net profit			46,400
			120,400
Less: drawings			30,000
			90,400

7 a) **Draft trial balance at 30 June 2007**

	£	£
Administration expenses	7,250	
Bank	3,280	
Capital		60,000
Carriage inwards	1,210	
Carriage outwards	1,530	
Creditors		20,200
Debtors	16,840	
Discount allowed	2,510	
Discount received		1,860
Drawings	14,600	
Machinery at cost	58,400	
Motor vehicles at cost	22,100	
Purchases	121,200	
Provision for doubtful debts		300
Provision for depreciation machinery		23,360
motor vehicles		9,680
Sales		167,400
Stock at 1 July 2006	15,400	
Selling expenses	5,800	
VAT		3,690
Wages	16,700	
Suspense		330
	286,820	286,820

b) **Journal entries**

	Debit £	Credit £

Errors

i)	Selling expenses	340	
	Bank		340

Being selling expenses omitted from the accounting records

ii)	Carriage inwards (£180 x 2)	360	
	Suspense		360

Being carriage entered on the credit side of the carriage inwards account

iii)	Suspense	690	
	Discount received		690

Being discounts allowed that were debited to the discounts received account

Year end adjustments

i) Stock – balance sheet   18,200
    Stock – profit and loss account   18,200

    Being closing stock valuation

ii) Bad debts expense   2,840
    Debtors   2,840

    Being write off of bad debt

    Provision for doubtful debts
    (£16,840 – 2,840) x 2% – 300   20
    Bad debts expense   20

    Being reduction in provision for doubtful debts

iii) Administration expenses   680
     Accruals   680

     Being accrued administration expenses

iv) Prepayments   440
    Administration expenses   440

    Being prepaid administration expenses

v) Depreciation expense – machinery
    (£58,400 x 20%)   11,680
    Provision for depreciation – machinery   11,680

    Depreciation expense – motor vehicles
    (£22,100 – 9,680) x 25%   3,105
    Provision for depreciation – motor vehicles   3,105

    Being depreciation charges for the year.

c) **Ledger accounts**

Selling expenses

		£			£
30 June	Balance b/d	5,800	30 June	Balance c/d	6,140
30 June	Journal	340			
		6,140			6,140
30 June	Balance b/d	6,140			

Bank

		£			£
30 June	Balance b/d	3,280	30 June	Journal	340
			30 June	Balance c/d	2,940
		3,280			3,280
30 June	Balance b/d	2,940			

Carriage inwards

		£			£
30 June	Balance b/d	1,210	30 June	Balance c/d	1,570
30 June	Journal	360			
		1,570			1,570
30 June	Balance b/d	1,570			

Discount received

		£			£
30 June	Balance c/d	2,550	30 June	Balance b/d	1,860
			30 June	Journal	690
		2,550			2,550
			30 June	Balance b/d	2,550

Suspense

		£			£
30 June	Journal	690	30 June	Balance b/d	330
			30 June	Journal	360
		690			690

Stock – balance sheet

		£		£
30 June	Journal	18,200		

Stock – profit and loss account

	£			£
	£	30 June	Journal	18,200

Bad debts expense

		£			£
30 June	Journal	2,840	30 June	Journal	20
			30 June	Balance c/d	2,820
		2,840			2,840
30 June	Balance b/d	2,820			

Debtors

		£			£
30 June	Balance b/d	16,840	30 June	Journal	2,840
			30 June	Balance c/d	14,000
		16,840			16,840
30 June	Balance b/d	14,000			

Provision for doubtful debts

		£			£
30 June	Journal	20	30 June	Balance b/d	300
30 June	Balance c/d	280			
		300			300

Administration expenses

		£			£
30 June	Balance b/d	7,250	30 June	Journal	440
30 June	Journal	680	30 June	Balance c/d	7,490
		7,930			7,930
30 June	Balance b/d	7,490			

Accruals

		£			£
			30 June	Journal	680

Prepayments

		£		£
30 June	Journal	440		

Depreciation expense – machinery

		£		£
30 June	Journal	11,680		

Provision for depreciation – machinery

		£			£
30 June	Balance c/d	35,040	30 June	Balance b/d	23,360
			30 June	Journal	11,680
		35,040			35,040
			30 June	Balance b/d	35,040

Depreciation expense – motor vehicles

		£			£
30 June	Journal	3,105			

Provision for depreciation – motor vehicles

		£			£
30 June	Balance c/d	12,785	30 June	Balance b/d	9,680
			30 June	Journal	3,105
		12,785			12,785
			30 June	Balance b/d	12,785

d) **Final trial balance as at 30 June 2007**

	£	£
Administration expenses	7,490	
Bank	2,940	
Capital		60,000
Carriage inwards	1,570	
Carriage outwards	1,530	
Creditors		20,200
Debtors	14,000	
Discount allowed	2,510	
Discount received		2,550
Drawings	14,600	
Machinery at cost	58,400	
Motor vehicles at cost	22,100	
Purchases	121,200	
Provision for doubtful debts		280
Provision for depreciation machinery		35,040
motor vehicles		12,785
Sales		167,400
Stock at 1 July 2006	15,400	
Selling expenses	6,140	
VAT		3,690
Wages	16,700	
Stock – balance sheet	18,200	
Stock – profit and loss a/c		18,200
Bad debts expense	2,820	
Accruals		680
Prepayments	440	
Depreciation – machinery	11,680	
Depreciation – motor vehicles	3,105	
	320,825	320,825

e) **Profit and loss account for the year ended 30 June 2007**

	£	£
Sales		167,400
Less: cost of sales		
Opening stock	15,400	
Carriage inwards	1,570	
Purchases	121,200	
	138,170	
Less: closing stock	(18,200)	
		(119,970)
Gross profit		47,430
Discount received		2,550
		49,980
Less: expenses		
Administration expenses	7,490	
Carriage outwards	1,530	
Discount allowed	2,510	
Selling expenses	6,140	
Wages	16,700	
Bad debts	2,820	
Depreciation machinery	11,680	
motor vehicles	3,105	
		(51,975)
Net loss		(1,995)

Balance sheet as at 30 June 2007

	Cost £	Accumulated depreciation £	Net book value £
Fixed assets:			
Machinery	58,400	35,040	23,360
Motor vehicles	22,100	12,785	9,315
	80,500	47,825	32,675
Current assets:			
Stock		18,200	
Debtors	14,000		
Less: provision	(280)		
		13,720	
Prepayments		440	
Bank		2,940	
		35,300	
Current liabilities:			
Creditors	20,200		
Accruals	680		
VAT	3,690		
		24,570	
Net current assets			10,730
			43,405
Capital			60,000
Net loss for the year			(1,995)
			58,005
Less: drawings			(14,600)
			43,405

8   a)   **Journal entries**

			£	£
i)	Debit	Bad debt expense (5% × 18,740)	937	
		Credit Provision for doubtful debts		937

Note. The bad debts written off figure (£830) has already been credited to the sales ledger control account.

			£	£
ii)	Debit	Drawings	500	
		Credit Purchases		500
iii))	Debit	Other debtors	3,500	
		Disposals		3,500
		Disposals	5,500	
		Credit Motor vehicles: cost		5,500
	Debit	Motor vehicles (acc. depn.)	2,400	
		Credit Motor vehicles: disposals		2,400
	Debit	Motor vehicles: disposals	400	
		Credit Profit and loss account		
		(profit on disposal)		400
iv)	Debit	Stock (balance sheet)	30,229	
		Credit Stock (profit and loss account)		30,229

b) **SANDRO VENUS**

Trading, profit and loss account for the year ended 31 March 2007

	£	£
Sales		187,325
Less: returns inwards		(1,437)
		185,888
Cost of sales		
Opening stock	27,931	
Purchases (W)	103,151	
	131,082	
Less: closing stock (Journal (iv))	(30,229)	
		(100,853)
Gross profit		85,035
Bank deposit interest		972
Profit on sale of vehicle (Journal (iii))		400
		86,407
Expenses		
Depreciation (6,094 + 1,375 + 2,780)	10,249	
Carriage outwards	657	
Rent, rates and insurance	7,721	
Bad debts (830 + 937) (Journal (i))	1,767	
Postage and stationery	524	
Wages and NIC	29,344	
Discounts allowed	373	
Bank charges	693	
Telephone	4,307	
Lighting and heating	3,755	
Motor expenses	4,762	
Net profit		64,152
		22,255

Working

Purchases

	£
Per trial balance	103,742
Plus carriage inwards	923
Less: drawings (Journal (ii))	(500)
Less: returns outwards	(1,014)
	103,151

c) **SANDRO VENUS**

Balance sheet as at 31 March 2007

	£	£
Fixed assets		
Motor vehicles		
(32,500 – 5,500 – (14,219 – 2,400)) (Journal (iii))		15,181
Office equipment (13,745 – 2,750)		10,995
Fixtures and fittings (27,800 – 5,560)		22,240
		48,416
Current assets		
Stock (Journal (d))	30,229	
Trade debtors (18,740 – 937) (Journal (i))	17,803	
Other debtors (Journal (iii))	3,500	
Prepayments	320	
Cash at bank and in hand (9,473 + 166)	9,639	
	61,491	
Current liabilities		
Trade creditors	17,725	
Accruals	1,131	
	18,856	
Net current assets		42,635
		91,051

Capital account

	£
Balance b/f	83,696
Profit for the year	22,255
	105,951
Drawings (14,400 + 500) (Journal (ii))	14,900
	91,051

9 Journal

	Debit £	Credit £
Sales	184,321	
Profit and loss account		184,321
Profit and loss account	91,201	
Purchases		91,201
Profit and loss account	16,422	
General expenses		16,422

answers to chapter 14: THE EXTENDED TRIAL BALANCE

This page is intentionally blank because the ETBs occupy an entire page.

1

Account name	Ledger balance DR £	Ledger balance CR £	Adjustments DR £	Adjustments CR £	Profit and loss account DR £	Profit and loss account CR £	Balance sheet DR £	Balance sheet CR £
Stock at 1 June 2006	1,600		2,100	2,100	1,600	2,100	2,100	
Motor vehicles at cost	23,800						23,800	
Computer at cost	2,400						2,400	
Fixtures and fittings at cost	12,800						12,800	
Provision for depreciation at 1 June 2006:								
Motor vehicles		12,140		3,498				15,638
Computer		600		600				1,200
Fixtures and fittings		2,560		2,560				5,120
Wages	16,400				16,400			
Telephone	900				900			
Electricity	1,200		400		1,600			
Advertising	400		100		500			
Stationery	600			100	500			
Motor expenses	1,700				1,700			
Miscellaneous expenses	300				300			
Insurance	1,000			300	700			
Sales		86,400				86,400		
Purchases	38,200				38,200			
Debtors	7,200						7,200	
Provision for doubtful debts at 1 June 2006		200		88				288
Bank (debit balance)	1,300						1,300	
Petty cash	100						100	
Creditors		3,180						3,180

Account name	Ledger balance DR £	Ledger balance CR £	Adjustments DR £	Adjustments CR £	Profit and loss account DR £	Profit and loss account CR £	Balance sheet DR £	Balance sheet CR £
VAT (credit balance)		960						960
Capital		25,000						25,000
Drawings	21,140						21,140	
Depreciation expense:								
Motor vehicles			3,498		3,498			
Computer			600		600			
Fixtures and fittings			2,560		2,560			
Accruals				400				400
Prepayments			300				300	
Bad debts expense			88		88			
Profit and loss					19,354			19,354
	131,040	131,040	9,646	9,646	88,500	88,500	71,140	71,140

Profit and loss account for the year ended 31 May 2007

	£	£
Sales		86,400
Less: cost of sales		
Opening stock	1,600	
Purchases	38,200	
	39,800	
Less: closing stock	(2,100)	
		37,700
Gross profit		48,700
Less: expenses		
Wages	16,400	
Telephone	900	
Electricity	1,600	
Advertising	500	
Stationery	500	
Motor expenses	1,700	
Miscellaneous expenses	300	
Insurance	700	
Depreciation – motor vehicles	3,498	
– computer	600	
– fixtures and fittings	2,560	
Bad debts	88	
		29,346
Net profit		19,354

Balance sheet as at 31 May 2007

	Cost £	Accumulated depreciation £	Net book value £
Fixed assets:			
Motor vehicles	23,800	15,638	8,162
Computer	2,400	1,200	1,200
Fixtures and fittings	12,800	5,120	7,680
	39,000	21,958	17,042
Current assets:			
Stock		2,100	
Debtors	7,200		
Less: provision for doubtful debts	288		
		6,912	
Prepayments		300	
Bank		1,300	
Petty cash		100	
		10,712	
Current liabilities:			
Creditors	3,180		
Accruals	400		
VAT	960		
		(4,540)	
Net current assets			6,172
			23,214
Capital			25,000
Net profit			19,354
			44,354
Less: drawings			21,140
			23,214

2

Account name	Ledger balance DR £	Ledger balance CR £	Adjustments DR £	Adjustments CR £	Profit and loss account DR £	Profit and loss account CR £	Balance sheet DR £	Balance sheet CR £
Capital		150,000						150,000
Creditors		40,400						40,400
Debtors	114,500			1,500			113,000	
Sales		687,000				687,000		
Stock at 1 July 2006	40,400		42,800	42,800	40,400	42,800	42,800	
Plant at cost	68,000						68,000	
Fixtures and fittings at cost	32,400						32,400	
Wages	98,700				98,700			
Sales returns	4,800			360	4,440			
Telephone	4,100		400		4,500			
Purchases	485,000				485,000			
Heat and light	3,400		1,010		4,410			
Advertising	8,200				8,200			
Purchases returns		3,000				3,000		
Selling costs	9,400				9,400			
Discount received		4,700		450		5,150		
Discount allowed	3,900				3,900			
Administrative expenses	14,800			700	14,100			
Miscellaneous expense	400				400			
Provision for depreciation at 1 July 2006:								
Plant and machinery		34,680		9,996				44,676
Fixtures and fittings		6,480		6,480				12,960

Account name	Ledger balance DR £	Ledger balance CR £	Adjustments DR £	Adjustments CR £	Profit and loss account DR £	Profit and loss account CR £	Balance sheet DR £	Balance sheet CR £
Provision for doubtful debts at 1 July 2006		2,000		260				2,260
Drawings	36,860						36,860	
Bank	6,400						6,400	
VAT (credit balance)		1,800						1,800
HMRC		1,400	450					1,400
Suspense account	200		360	1,010				
Depreciation expense:								
Plant and machinery			9,996		9,996			
Fixtures and fittings			6,480		6,480			
Bad debts expense			1,500 260		1,760			
Accruals				400				400
Prepayments			700				700	
Profit					46,264			46,264
	931,460	931,460	63,956	63,956	737,950	737,950	300,160	300,160

Profit and loss account for the year ended 30 June 2007

	£	£	£
Sales			687,000
Less: sales returns			(4,440)
			682,560
Less: cost of sales			
Opening stock		40,400	
Purchases	485,000		
Less: returns	(3,000)		
		482,000	
		522,400	
Less: closing stock		(42,800)	
			479,600
Gross profit			202,960
Discount received			5,150
			208,110
Less: expenses			
Wages		98,700	
Telephone		4,500	
Heat and light		4,410	
Advertising		8,200	
Selling costs		9,400	
Discount allowed		3,900	
Administrative expenses		14,100	
Miscellaneous expenses		400	
Depreciation plant and machinery		9,996	
fixtures and fittings		6,480	
Bad debts		1,760	
			161,846
Net profit			46,264

Balance sheet as at 30 June 2007

	Cost £	Accumulated depreciation £	Net book value £
Fixed assets:			
Plant	68,000	44,676	23,324
Fixtures and fittings	32,400	12,960	19,440
	100,400	57,636	42,764
Current assets:			
Stock		42,800	
Debtors	113,000		
Less:			
provision for doubtful debts	2,260		
		110,740	
Prepayments		700	
Bank		6,400	
		160,640	
Current liabilities:			
Creditors	40,400		
Accruals	400		
VAT	1,800		
HMRC	1,400		
		44,000	
Net current assets			116,640
			159,404
Capital			150,000
Net profit for the year			46,264
			196,264
Less: drawings			36,860
			159,404

3   a) – d)

Account	Trial balance Dr £	Trial balance Cr £	Adjustments Dr £	Adjustments Cr £	Profit and loss account Dr £	Profit and loss account Cr £	Balance sheet Dr £	Balance sheet Cr £
Administration costs	72,019.27		(b) 480.00	(b) 320.00	72,179.27			
Bank overdraft		8,290.12						8,290.12
Capital		50,000.00		(f) 10,000.00				60,000.00
Loan		100,000.00						100,000.00
Depreciation charge	12,000.00		(a) 15,000.00 (e) 1,000.00		28,000.00			
Drawings	36,000.00						36,000.00	
Fixed assets: Cost	120,287.00		(e) 4,000.00				124,287.00	
Fixed assets: Depreciation		36,209.28		(e) 1,000.00				37,209.28
Interest payable	12,182.26		(g) 650.00		12,832.26			
Interest receivable		21.00				21.00		
Labour	167,302.39		(e) 14,248.40		181,550.79			
Raw materials	104,293.38				104,293.38			
Stock as at 1/6/06	25,298.30				25,298.30			
Purchase ledger control		42,190.85						42,190.85
Sales		481,182.20				481,182.20		
Sales ledger control	156,293.00			(c) 6,092.35			150,200.65	
Suspense	17,156.05		(c) 6,092.35 (f) 10,000.00	(a) 15,000.00 (e) 14,248.40 (e) 4,000.00				
VAT		4,938.20						4,938.20
Accruals				(b) 480.00 (g) 650.00				1,130.00
Prepayments			(b) 320.00				320.00	
Closing stock			(h) 32,125.28	(h) 32,125.28		32,125.28	32,125.28	
Profit					89,174.48			89,174.48
	722,831.65	**722,831.65**	**83,916.03**	**83,916.03**	**513,328.48**	**513,328.48**	**342,932.93**	**342,932.93**

CLEGG & CO

Profit and loss account for year ended 31 May 2007

	£	£
Sales		481,182.20
Less: cost of sales		
opening stock	25,298.30	
purchases	104,293.38	
less: closing stock	(32,125.28)	
		(97,466.40)
		383,715.80
Interest receivable		21.00
Less: expenses		
administration costs	72,179.27	
depreciation charge	28,000.00	
interest payable	12,832.26	
Labour	181,550.79	
		(294,562.32)
Net profit		89,174.48

Balance sheet as at 31 May 2007

	£	£	£
Fixed assets	124,287.00	37,209.28	87,077.72
Current assets			
Stock		32,125.28	
Trade debtors		150,200.65	
Prepayments		320.00	
		182,645.93	
Current liabilities			
Trade creditors	42,190.85		
Bank overdraft	8,290.12		
VAT	4,938.20		
Accommodation	1,130.00		
		(56,549.17)	
			126,096.76
			213,174.48
Long-term liabilities			
Loan			(100,000.00)
Net assets			113,174.48

	£
Capital	60,000.00
Profit for the year	89,174.48
Drawings	(36,000.00)
	113,174.48

answers to chapter 15:
PARTNERSHIPS

1

Current account – Jim

	£		£
Drawings	58,000	Balance b/d	2,000
Balance c/d	4,000	Profit share (135,000 × 4/9)	60,000
	62,000		62,000
		Balance b/d	4,000

Current account – Rob

	£		£
Balance b/d	1,000	Profit share (135,000 × 3/9)	45,000
Drawings	40,000		
Balance c/d	4,000		
	45,000		45,000
		Balance b/d	4,000

Current account – Fiona

	£		£
Drawings	32,000	Balance b/d	3,500
Balance c/d	1,500	Profit share (135,000 × 2/9)	30,000
	33,500		33,500
		Balance b/d	1,500

2

Appropriation account

	£		£
Salary – Ken	8,000	Net profit b/d	39,950
Interest			
Josh (40,000 × 3%)	1,200		
Ken (25,000 × 3%)	750		
Balance c/d	30,000		
	39,950		39,950
		Balance b/d	30,000
Profit share			
Josh (30,000 × 2/3)	20,000		
Ken (30,000 × 1/3)	10,000		
	30,000		30,000

Current account – Josh

	£		£
Drawings	21,000	Balance b/d	1,300
Balance c/d	1,500	Profit share (1,200 + 20,000)	21,200
	22,500		22,500
		Balance b/d	1,500

Current account – Ken

	£		£
Drawings	17,400	Balance b/d	800
		Profit share	
Balance c/d	2,150	(8,000 + 750 + 10,000)	18,750
	19,550		19,550
		Balance b/d	2,150

Balance sheet extract at 30 June 2007

		£	£
Capital accounts	Josh		40,000
	Ken		25,000
			65,000
Current accounts	Josh	1,500	
	Ken	2,150	
			3,650
			68,650

3   a)   **Initial trial balance**

	£	£
Advertising	3,140	
Bank	1,400	
Capital Jo		25,000
Emily		15,000
Karen		10,000
Creditors		33,100
Current accounts Jo		1,000
Emily		540
Karen		230
Debtors	51,300	
Drawings Jo	12,000	
Emily	10,000	
Karen	10,000	
Electricity	3,860	
Fixtures and fittings at cost	12,500	
Fixtures and fittings – accumulated depreciation		5,200
Inland Revenue		680
Insurance	2,500	
Machinery at cost	38,000	
Machinery - accumulated depreciation		15,700
Provision for doubtful debts		1,250
Purchases	199,000	
Sales		306,000
Stock at 1 July 2006	23,400	
Sundry expenses	2,480	
Telephone	2,150	
VAT		1,230
Wages	43,200	
	414,930	414,930

b)   **Journal entries**

		Debit £	Credit £
i)	Stock – balance sheet	24,100	
	Stock – profit and loss account		24,100
	Being closing stock valuation		
ii)	Depreciation expense – machinery (38,000 x 20%)	7,600	
	Machinery – accumulated depreciation		7,600
	Depreciation expense - fixtures and fittings ((12,500 – 5,200) x 25%)	1,825	
	Fixtures and fittings – accumulated depreciation		1,825
	Being depreciation charges for the year		
iii)	Bad debts expense	1,300	
	Debtors		1,300
	Being write off of bad debt		
	Bad debts expense ((51,300 – 1,300) x 3%) – 1,250	250	
	Provision for doubtful debts		250
	Being increase in provision for doubtful debts		
iv)	Electricity	400	
	Accruals		400
	Being accrued expense at the year end		
	Prepayments	700	
	Insurance		700
	Being prepaid expense at the year end		

c)   **Ledger accounts**

Stock – balance sheet

	£		£
Journal	24,100		

Stock – profit and loss account

	£		£
		Journal	24,100

Depreciation expense – machinery

	£		£
Journal	7,600		

Machinery – accumulated depreciation

	£		£
		Balance b/d	15,700
Balance c/d	23,300	Journal	7,600
	23,300		23,300
		Balance b/d	23,300

Depreciation expense – fixtures and fittings

	£		£
Journal	1,825		

Fixtures and fittings – accumulated depreciation

	£		£
		Balance b/d	5,200
Balance c/d	7,025	Journal	1,825
	7,025		7,025
		Balance b/d	7,025

Bad debts expense

	£		£
Journal	1,300		
Journal	250	Balance c/d	1,550
	1,550		1,550
Balance b/d	1,550		

Debtors

	£		£
Balance b/d	51,300	Journal	1,300
		Balance c/d	50,000
	51,300		51,300
Balance b/d	50,000		

Provision for doubtful debts

	£		£
		Balance b/d	1,250
Balance c/d	1,500	Journal	250
	1,500		1,500
		Balance b/d	1,500

Electricity

	£		£
Balance b/d	3,860		
Journal	400	Balance c/d	4,260
	4,260		4,260
Balance b/d	4,260		

Accruals

	£		£
		Journal	400

Insurance

	£		£
Balance b/d	2,500	Journal	700
		Balance c/d	1,800
	2,500		2,500
Balance b/d	1,800		

Prepayments

	£		£
Journal	700		

d) **Final trial balance**

	£	£
Advertising	3,140	
Bank	1,400	
Capital Jo		25,000
Emily		15,000
Karen		10,000
Creditors		33,100
Current accounts Jo		1,000
Emily		540
Karen		230
Debtors	50,000	
Drawings Jo	12,000	
Emily	10,000	
Karen	10,000	
Electricity	4,260	
Fixtures and fittings at cost	12,500	
Fixtures and fittings – accumulated depreciation		7,025
Inland Revenue		680
Insurance	1,800	
Machinery at cost	38,000	
Machinery – accumulated depreciation		23,300
Provision for doubtful debts		1,500
Purchases	199,000	
Sales		306,000
Stock at 1 July 2006	23,400	
Sundry expenses	2,480	
Telephone	2,150	
VAT		1,230
Wages	43,200	
Stock – balance sheet	24,100	
Stock – profit and loss account		24,100
Depreciation expense – machinery	7,600	
Depreciation expense – fixtures and fittings	1,825	
Bad debts expense	1,550	
Accruals		400
Prepayments	700	
	449,105	449,105

e) **Profit and loss account for the year ended 30 June 2007**

	£	£
Sales		306,000
Less: cost of sales		
Opening stock	23,400	
Purchases	199,000	
	222,400	
Less: closing stock	24,100	
		198,300
Gross profit		107,700
Less: expenses		
Advertising	3,140	
Electricity	4,260	
Insurance	1,800	
Sundry expenses	2,480	
Telephone	2,150	
Wages	43,200	
Depreciation machinery	7,600	
fixtures and fittings	1,825	
Bad debts	1,550	
		68,005
Net profit		39,695

f) **Appropriation of profit**

	£
Net profit	39,695
Salary – Emily	(4,000)
Interest Jo (25,000 x 5%)	(1,250)
Emily (15,000 x 5%)	(750)
Karen (10,000 x 5%)	(500)
	33,195
Profit share (33,195/3)	
Jo	11,065
Emily	11,065
Karen	11,065
	33,195

Current account – Jo

	£		£
Drawings	12,000	Balance b/d	1,000
Balance c/d	1,315	Profit share (1,250 + 11,065)	12,315
	13,315		13,315
		Balance b/d	1,315

Current account – Emily

	£		£
Drawings	10,000	Balance b/d	540
		Profit share	
Balance c/d	6,355	(4,000 + 750 + 11,065)	15,815
	16,355		16,355
		Balance b/d	6,355

Current account – Karen

	£		£
Drawings	10,000	Balance b/d	230
Balance c/d	1,795	Profit share (500 + 11,065)	11,565
	11,795		11,795
		Balance b/d	1,795

g) **Balance sheet as at 30 June 2007**

		Cost £	Accumulated depreciation £	Net book value £
Fixed assets				
Machinery		38,000	23,300	14,700
Fixtures and fittings		12,500	7,025	5,475
		50,500	30,325	20,175
Current assets				
Stock			24,100	
Debtors		50,000		
Less: provision		1,500		
			48,500	
Prepayments			700	
Bank			1,400	
			74,700	
Current liabilities				
Creditors		33,100		
Accruals		400		
HM Revenue and Customs		680		
VAT		1,230		
			35,410	
Net current assets				39,290
				59,465
Capital accounts	Jo			25,000
	Emily			15,000
	Karen			10,000
				50,000
Current accounts	Jo	1,315		
	Emily	6,355		
	Karen	1,795		
				9,465
				59,465

4 a) **BESS, CHARLES AND GEORGE**

Profit and loss account for the year ended 31 March 2007

	£	£
Sales (W1)		559,821
Cost of sales (W2)		279,584
Gross profit		280,237
Less: expenses		
Salespersons' commission	6,659	
Carriage outwards	617	
Rent, rates and insurance	32,522	
Motor expenses	3,769	
Wages and NIC	48,317	
Lighting and heating	3,240	
Postage and stationery	705	
Depreciation charge (4,765 + 236 + 1,613)	6,614	
Telephone	2,926	
Sundries	868	
		106,237
Net profit		174,000

Workings

1   *Sales*

	£
Per trial balance	568,092
Less: returns inwards	8,271
	559,821

2   *Cost of sales*

	£
Opening stock	127,535
Purchases	302,117
	429,652
Carriage inwards	872
Returns outwards	(7,004)
	423,520
Less: closing stock	(143,936)
	279,584

b) **BESS, CHARLES AND GEORGE**

Appropriation account for the year ended 31 March 2007

	£	£
Net profit		174,000
Partners' salaries		
Bess	30,000	
Charles	25,000	
George	17,000	
		(72,000)
Interest on capital		
Bess: 5% x 60,000	3,000	
Charles: 5% x 40,000	2,000	
George: 5% x 20,000	1,000	
		(6,000)
		96,000
Balance of profits shared		
Bess: 5/12	40,000	
Charles: 4/12	32,000	
George: 3/12	24,000	
		96,000

c)

Current accounts

	B £	C £	G £		B £	C £	G £
Drawings	46,000	42,000	38,000	b/d	4,670	5,600	3,750
c/d	31,670	22,600	7,750	Salaries	30,000	25,000	17,000
				Interest	3,000	2,000	1,000
				Profit share	40,000	32,000	24,000
	77,670	64,600	45,750		77,670	64,600	45,750

BESS, CHARLES AND GEORGE

Balance sheet as at 31 March 2007

	£	£	£
Fixed assets			
Motor vehicles	37,412	18,651	18,761
Office equipment	2,363	1,285	1,078
Fixtures and fittings	8,575	3,754	4,821
	48,350	23,690	24,660
Current assets			
Stock		143,936	
Trade debtors		21,895	
Cash at bank		2,085	
Cash in hand		228	
		168,144	
Current liabilities			
Trade creditors	9,904		
Accounts	880		
		10,784	
			157,360
Net assets			182,020

		£	£
Capital accounts	B		60,000
	C		40,000
	G		20,000
			120,000
Current accounts	B	31,670	
	C	22,600	
	G	7,750	
			62,020
			182,020

5

Account name	Ledger balance DR £	Ledger balance CR £	Adjustments DR £	Adjustments CR £	Profit and loss account DR £	Profit and loss account CR £	Balance sheet DR £	Balance sheet CR £
Sales		483,400				483,400		
Stock at 1 May 2006	10,700		11,200	11,200	10,700	11,200	11,200	
Purchases	279,600				279,600			
Capital – Nigel Clark		60,000						60,000
– Julian Clark		50,000						50,000
Current – Nigel Clark		2,000						2,000
– Julian Clark		4,000						4,000
Drawings – Nigel Clark	30,000						30,000	
– Julian Clark	25,700						25,700	
Building at cost	80,000						80,000	
Motor vehicles at cost	28,600						28,600	
Provision for depreciation:								
Buildings		9,600		1,600				11,200
Motor vehicles		14,500		4,230				18,730
Wages	63,800				63,800			
Administration expenses	23,700		1,200		24,900			
Selling costs	42,100			800	41,300			
Debtors	60,400						60,400	
Bank (debit balance)	2,200						2,200	
Creditors		23,300						23,300
Accruals				1,200				1,200
Prepayments			800				800	
Depreciation – buildings			1,600		1,600			
– motor vehicles			4,230		4,230			
Profit – Julian					68,470			37,735
– Nigel								30,735
	646,800	646,800	19,030	19,030	494,600	494,600	238,900	238,900

Profit and loss account for the year ended 30 April 2007

	£	£
Sales		483,400
Less: cost of sales		
Opening stock	10,700	
Purchases	279,600	
	290,300	
Less: closing stock	(11,200)	
		279,100
Gross profit		204,300
Less: expenses		
Wages	63,800	
Administration expenses	24,900	
Selling costs	41,300	
Depreciation buildings	1,600	
motor vehicles	4,230	
		135,830
Net profit		68,470

Appropriation of profit

	£
Net profit	68,470
Julian – salary	(7,000)
	61,470
Profit share Julian	30,735
Nigel	30,735
	61,470

Balance sheet as at 30 April 2007

	Cost £	Accumulated depreciation £	Net book value £
Fixed assets			
Buildings	80,000	11,200	68,800
Motor vehicles	28,600	18,730	9,870
	108,600	29,930	78,670
Current assets			
Stock		11,200	
Debtors		60,400	
Prepayments		800	
Bank		2,200	
		74,600	
Current liabilities			
Creditors	23,300		
Accruals	1,200		
		24,500	
Net current assets			50,100
			128,770
Capital accounts			
Nigel Clark			60,000
Julian Clark			50,000
			110,000
Current accounts			
Nigel Clark (2,000 + 30,735 − 30,000)		2,735	
Julian Clark (4,000 + 37,735 − 25,700)		16,035	
			18,770
			128,770

6

Capital accounts

	Ian £	Max £	Len £		Ian £	Max £	Len £
				Bal b/d	85,000	60,000	
Goodwill	7,200	7,200	3,600	Goodwill	12,000	6,000	
Balance c/d	89,800	58,800	29,000	Bank			32,600
	97,000	66,000	32,600		97,000	66,000	32,600

7

Capital accounts

	Theo £	Deb £	Fran £		Theo £	Deb £	Fran £
				Balance b/d	84,000	62,000	37,000
				Current a/c		1,300	
Goodwill	36,000		18,000	Goodwill	27,000	18,000	9,000
Bank		10,000					
Loan		71,300					
Balance c/d	75,000		28,000				
	111,000	81,300	46,000		111,000	81,300	46,000

Current accounts

	Theo £	Deb £	Fran £		Theo £	Deb £	Fran £
Capital a/c		1,300		Balance b/d	4,500	1,300	6,200

8 **Appropriation account**

	1 October 2006 to 30 June 2007 £	1 July 2007 to 30 Sept 2007 £	Total £
Net profit 9/12 and 3/12 x £90,000	67,500	22,500	90,000
Salaries			
Will (9/12 x 10,000) and			
(3/12 x 12,000)	(7,500)	(3,000)	(10,500)
Clare (9/12 x 15,000) and			
(3/12 x 20,000)	(11,250)	(5,000)	(16,250)
Interest			
Will 9/12 and 3/12 x £2,400	(1,800)	(600)	(2,400)
Clare 9/12 and 3/12 x £1,500	(1,125)	(375)	(1,500)
Profit for distribution	45,825	13,525	59,350
Profit share			
Will (2/3 x 45,825) and			
(3/4 x 13,525)	(30,550)	(10,144)	(40,694)
Clare (1/3 x 45,825) and			
(1/4 x 13,525)	(15,275)	(3,381)	(18,656)
	–	–	–

Current accounts

	Will £	Clare £		Will £	Clare £
Balance b/d		3,000	Balance b/d	2,000	
Drawings	44,000	37,000	Salaries	10,500	16,250
Balance c/d	11,594		Interest	2,400	1,500
			Profit share	40,694	18,656
			Balance c/d		3,594
T	55,594	40,000		55,594	40,000

9   a)   Partners' capital accounts

Partners' capital accounts

	Mary £	Nelson £	Elizabeth £		Mary £	Nelson £	Elizabeth £
Goodwill (6:4)	–	54,000	36,000	Balance b/d			
Loan account				1.4.06	28,000	26,000	22,000
(bal. fig)	69,860	–	–	Cash		40,000	
Balance c/d				Goodwill			
31.3.07	–	39,000	13,000	(4:3:3)	36,000	27,000	27,000
	69,860	93,000	64,000	Current a/c	5,860		
					77,670	64,600	45,750

b)   **Mary, Nelson and Elizabeth**

Appropriation account for the year ended 31 March 2007

	£	£
Net profit		106,120
Less: partners' salaries		
Mary	18,000	
Nelson	16,000	
Elizabeth	13,000	
		47,000
Less: interest on capital		
Mary (£28,000 x 12%)	3,360	
Nelson (£26,000 x 12%)	3,120	
Elizabeth (£22,000 x 12%)	2,640	
		9,120
Net profit available for appropriation		50,000

	£	£
Balance of profits shared		
Mary 4/10	20,000	
Nelson 3/10	15,000	
Elizabeth 3/10	15,000	
		50,000

c)

Partners' capital accounts

	Mary £	Nelson £	Elizabeth £		Mary £	Nelson £	Elizabeth £
Drawings	38,000	30,000	29,000	Balance b/d			
Capital a/c	5,860	–	–	1.4.06	2,500	2,160	1,870
Balance c/d				Interest on			
31.3.07	–	6,280	3,510	capital	3,360	3,120	2,640
				Salaries	18,000	16,000	13,000
				Profit	20,000	15,000	15,000
	43,860	36,280	32,510		43,860	36,280	32,510

d)

Mary: loan account

	£		£
Balance c/f 31.3.07	69,860	Capital a/c	69,860
	69,860		

answers to chapter 16:
INCOMPLETE RECORDS

1   Increase in net assets = Capital introduced + profit – drawings

   £19,509 – 14,689 = 0 + profit – 9,670

   £4,820 + 9,670 = Profit

   Profit = £14,490

2   Increase in net assets = Capital introduced + profit – drawings

   £31,240 – 26,450 = 0 + profit – (£12,300 + 560)

   £4,790 = Profit – £12,860

   Profit = £4,790 + 12,860

   Profit = £17,650

3   Increase in net assets = Capital introduced + profit – drawings

   £28,575 – 23,695   = 0 + 17,370 – drawings

   £4,880 = 17,370 – drawings

   Drawings = £17,370 – 4,880

   Drawings = £12,490

4

<table>
<tr><td colspan="5" align="center">Cash account</td></tr>
<tr><td></td><td>£</td><td></td><td></td><td>£</td></tr>
<tr><td>Opening balance</td><td>100</td><td>Bankings</td><td></td><td>4,820</td></tr>
<tr><td>Sales</td><td>5,430</td><td>Drawings (bal fig)</td><td></td><td>610</td></tr>
<tr><td></td><td></td><td>Closing balance</td><td></td><td>100</td></tr>
<tr><td></td><td>5,530</td><td></td><td></td><td>5,530</td></tr>
</table>

Bank account

	£		£
Opening balance	368	Creditors	3,980
Bankings	4,820	Drawings (bal fig)	794
		Closing balance	414
	5,188		5,188

Total drawings	£
Cash	610
Bank	794
	1,404

5

Cash account

	£		£
Opening balance	250	Bankings	7,236
Sales (bal fig)	8,656	Wages	320
		Cleaning costs	50
		Drawings	1,050
		Closing balance	250
	8,906		8,906

6

Debtors account

	£		£
Opening balance	1,589	Bank	5,056
Sales (bal fig)	5,615	Discount allowed	127
		Closing balance	2,021
	7,204		7,204

7

Creditors account

	£		£
Bank	24,589	Opening balance	4,266
Discounts received	491	Purchases (bal fig)	25,925
Closing balance	5,111		
	30,191		30,191

8

	£	%
Sales (bal fig)	4,404	120
Cost of sales (640 + 3,600 – 570)	3,670	100
Gross profit	734	20

9

	£	£	%
Sales		5,200	130
Cost of sales			
Opening stock	300		
Purchases (bal fig)	4,200		
	4,500		
Less: closing stock	(500)		
Cost of sales (5,200 x 100/130)		4,000	100
Gross profit		1,200	30

10

	£	%
Sales (bal fig)	5,875	100
Cost of sales (670 + 5,010 - 980)	4,700	80
Gross profit	1,175	20

11 a) **Calculation of net profit**

For the year ended 31 October 2007

	£	£
Sales (W1)		133,590
Opening stock	12,200	
Purchases (W2)	78,080	
Closing stock	(13,750)	
Cost of sales		76,530
Gross profit		57,060
Rent received (W3)		2,750
		59,810
Expenses		
Rent and rates (W3)	6,700	
Postage and packing	2,200	
Motor expenses	5,050	
Admin expenses (W3)	5,390	
Wages	18,200	
Stock loss (£6,000 x 100/150 x 50%)	2,000	
Depreciation £(17,500 – 12,500)	5,000	
		44,540
Net profit		15,270

b) **Calculation of capital as at 31 October 2007**

	£
Opening capital (W4)	23,775
Profit	15,270
	39,045
Additional capital (investment income)	1,500
	40,545
Drawings (W5)	11,760
Closing capital	28,785

This figure can be confirmed by producing a balance sheet as at 31 October 2007, although this is not required by the question.

Balance sheet as at 31 October 2007

	£	£
Fixed assets		
Van		12,500
Current assets		
Stock	13,750	
Debtors	7,200	
Prepayments	200	
Insurance claim (50%)	2,000	
Rent receivable	250	
Bank	6,500	
	29,900	
Current liabilities		
Creditors	13,400	
Accruals	215	
	13,615	
		16,285
Net current assets		28,785
Closing capital		28,785

Workings

1   *Sales*

Cash book

Cash £		Bank £		Cash £		Bank £
86,390	Bankings	56,000	Bankings	56,000	Bal b/f	
	SLCA	46,000	Wages		1.11.05	3,250
	Investment		(350 × 52)	18,200	PLCA	78,000
	income	1,500	Drawings		Postage &	
	Rent	2,500	(220 × 52)	11,440	packaging	2,200
			Admin exps	750	Rent & rates	6,400
					Motor exps	5,050
					Admin exps	4,600
					Bal c/f	
					31.10.06	6,500
86,390		106,000		86,390		106,000

Note. As cash is banked daily, there will be no cash in hand b/fwd or c/fwd.

Sales ledger control account

2007		£	2007		£
1 Nov	Balance b/d	6,000	31 Oct	Bank	46,000
	Sales (bal fig)	47,200		Balance c/d	7,200
		53,200			53,200

Total sales = £(86,390 + 47,200) = £133,590

2   *Purchases*

Purchase ledger control account

2007		£	2007		£
	Bank	78,000	1 Nov	Balance b/d	9,000
31 Oct	Balance c/f	13,400		Purchases (bal fig)	82,400
		91,400			91,400

	£
Purchases per CC a/c	82,400
Less: stolen games £6,000 x 100/150	(4,000)
Less: Christmas presents £480 x 100/150	(320)
	78,080

3   *Expenses*

Rent and rates:	£(6,400 + 500 – 200) = £6,700
Admin expenses:	£(750 + 4,600 – 175 + 215) = £5,390
Rent received:	£(2,500 + 250) = £2,750

4   *Opening capital*

	£	£
Assets		
Van	17,500	
Stock	12,200	
Debtors	6,000	
Prepayments	500	
		36,200
Liabilities		
Creditors	9,000	
Accruals	175	
Bank overdraft	3,250	
		12,425
Net assets = capital		23,775

5   *Drawings*

	£
Cash (W1)	11,440
Christmas presents* 480 x 100/150	320
	11,760

*Note. Drawings from stock are at cost price. Selling price inclusive of VAT may also be used.

12 a)

		£
Opening stock		1,800
Payments: bank		18,450
cash		3,800
Creditors		1,400
Total purchases		25,450

b)

	£
Purchases (from i))	25,450
Closing stock	(2,200)
Total cost of sales	23,250

c)

	£
Cost of sales (from ii))	23,250
Total sales (x 2)	46,500

d)

	£	£
Sales (from iii))		46,500
Payments: materials	3,800	
general expenses	490	
bank account	27,000	
drawings (balance figure)	15,110	
		(46,400)
Float		100

e)

	£
Bank account	6,200
Cash account (from iv)	15,110
Total drawings	21,310

f)

	£	£
Sales (from iii))		46,500
Cost of sales (from ii))		(23,250)
Gross profit		23,250
General expenses (870 + 490)	1,360	
Depreciation (4,000 x 20%)	800	
		(2,160)
Net profit		21,090

13 Profit and loss account for the year ended 30 June 2007

	£	£
Sales (W2)		69,000
Less: cost of sales		
Opening stock	3,400	
Purchases (W3)	48,100	
	51,500	
Less: closing stock (bal fig)	(3,200)	
Cost of sales (69,000 x 70/100)		48,300
Gross profit		20,700
Less: expenses		
Electricity (1,400 – 120 + 150)	1,430	
Insurance (800 + 180 – 200)	780	
Telephone	1,300	
Wages	1,600	
Depreciation – motor vehicle (12,000 x 25%)	3,000	
– computer (2,000 x 20% x 6/12)	200	
		8,310
Net profit		12,390

Balance sheet as at 30 June 2007

	£	£	£
Motor vehicle (W4)			8,000
Computer (2,000 – 200)			1,800
			9,800
Stock (from P&L a/c)		3,200	
Debtors		6,300	
Prepayments		200	
Bank		4,700	
Cash		200	
		14,600	
Creditors	1,600		
Accruals	150		
		(1,750)	
			12,850
			22,650
Opening capital (W5)			23,360
Net profit for the year			1,239
			35,750
Less: drawings (10,700 + 2,400)			(13,100)
			22,650

Working 1

Cash account

	£		£
Opening balance	200	Bankings	62,800
Debtors (bal fig)	66,800	Wages	1,600
		Drawings	2,400
		Closing balance	200
	67,000		67,000

Working 2

Debtors account

	£		£
Opening balance	4,100	Cash (W1)	66,800
Sales (bal fig)	69,000	Closing balance	6,300
	73,100		73,100

Working 3

Creditors account

	£		£
Bank	48,600	Opening balance	2,100
Closing balance	1,600	Purchases (bal fig)	48,100
	50,200		50,200

Working 4

Motor vehicle

	£
Cost	12,000
Depreciation to June 2005	
(12,000 x 25% x 4/12)	(1,000)
Depreciation to June 2006	(3,000)
Net book value	8,000

Working 5

Opening capital

	£
Motor vehicle (W4)	11,000
Stock	3,400
Debtors	4,100
Prepayments	180
Bank	6,700
Cash	200
Creditors	(2,100)
Accruals	(120)
	23,360

PRACTICE SIMULATION 1

ANSWERS

Task 1

Balance on the cash book:

	£
1 June Balance b/d	(3,206.16)
Less: payments	(17,487.58)
	(20,693.74)
Add: receipts	26,241.70
	5,547.96

Tasks 1, 2, 4, 5, 7, and 11

Administration overheads

		£			£
31 May	Balance b/d	14,589.34	30 June	Balance c/d	15,729.34
30 June	Cash book	580.00			
30 June	Cash book	560.00			
		15,729.34			15,729.34

Bad debts expense

		£			£
30 June	Balance b/d	748.20	30 June	Balance c/d	850.70
30 June	Journal	102.50			
		850.70			850.70

Bank interest payable

		£			£
31 May	Balance b/d	495.68	30 June	Balance c/d	548.86
30 June	Cash book	53.18			
		548.86			548.86

438

Capital account – Keith Buxted

	£			£
		1 July	Balance b/d	38,500.00

Capital account – Fred Simons

	£			£
		1 July	Balance b/d	21,500.00

Current account – Keith Buxted

		£			£
30 June	Drawings	20,357.50	1 July	Balance b/d	3,821.35
30 June	Balance c/d	7,734.98	30 June	Profit share	24,271.13
		28,092.48			28,092.48

Current account – Fred Simons

		£			£
30 June	Drawings	19,703.00	1 July	Balance b/d	1,959.00
30 June	Balance c/d	6,891.56	30 June	Profit share	24,635.56
		28,092.48			26,594.56

Purchases ledger control

		£			£
30 June	Cash book	15,252.90	31 May	Balance b/d	9,102.36
30 June	Cash book – discounts	112.76	30 June	PDB	10,721.64
30 June	PRDB	824.38			
30 June	Balance c/d	3,633.96			
		19,824.00			19,824.00

Sales ledger control

		£			£
30 June	Balance b/d	56,310.82	30 June	Cash book	26,241.70
			30 June	Cash book – discount	267.74
			30 June	Bad debts	102.50
			30 June	Discounts – March	186.79
			30 June	Balance c/d	29,512.09
		56,310.82			56,310.82

Discount allowed

		£			£
31 May	Balance b/d	2,310.58	30 June	Balance c/d	2,765.11
30 June	Cash book	267.74			
30 June	Cash book – March	186.79			
		2,765.11			2,765.11

Discount received

		£			£
30 June	Balance c/d	1,044.20	31 May	Balance b/d	931.44
			30 June	Cash book	112.76
		1,044.20			
					1,044.20

Drawings account – Keith Buxted

		£			£
30 June	Balance b/d	20,357.50	30 June	Current a/c	20,357.50

Drawings account – Fred Simons

		£			£
30 June	Balance b/d	19,703.00	30 June	Current a/c	19,703.00

Fixtures and fittings – at cost

		£		£
30 June	Balance b/d	14,760.00		

Fixtures and fittings – depreciation expense

		£		£
30 June	Accumulated depreciation	2,952.00		

Fixtures and fittings – accumulated depreciation

		£			£
30 June	Balance c/d	8,632.50	1 July	Balance b/d	5,680.50
			30 June	Depreciation expense	2,952.00
		8,632.50			8,632.50

Motor vehicles at cost

		£		£
30 June	Balance b/d	76,200.00		

Motor vehicles – depreciation expense

		£		£
30 June	Accumulated depreciation	11,340.00		

Motor vehicles – accumulated depreciation

		£			£
30 June	Balance c/d	49,740.00	1 July	Balance b/d	38,400.00
			30 June	Depreciation expense	11,340.00
		49,740.00			49,740.00

Office equipment – at cost

		£		£
30 June	Balance b/d	10,845.50		

Office equipment – depreciation expense

		£		£
30 June	Accumulated depreciation	1,773.80		

Office equipment – accumulated depreciation

		£			£
30 June	Balance c/d	5,524.12	1 July	Balance b/d	3,750.32
			30 June	Depreciation expense	1,773.80
		5,524.12			5,524.12

Purchases

		£			£
31 May	Balance b/d	101,383.33	30 June	Balance c/d	110,508.13
30 June	PDB	9,124.80			
		110,508.13			110,508.13

Purchases returns

		£			£
30 June	Balance c/d	7,225.05	31 May	Balance b/d	6,523.45
			30 June	PRDB	701.60
		7,225.05			7,225.05

Sales

	£			£
		30 June	Balance b/d	290,446.12

Sales returns

		£		£
30 June	Balance b/d	15,365.66		

Selling overhead

		£			£
31 May	Balance b/d	9,254.67	30 June	Balance c/d	10,054.67
30 June	Cash book	800.00			
		10,054.67			10,054.67

Stock

		£		£
30 June	Balance b/d	10,256.38		

Suspense

	£			£
		30 June	Balance b/d	495.05

VAT

		£			£
30 June	Cash book	241.50	30 June	Balance b/d	2,105.47
30 June	PDB	1,596.84	30 June	PRDB	122.78
30 June	Balance c/d	389.91			
		2,228.25			2,228.25

Wages

		£		£
30 June	Balance b/d	73,840.56		

Task 2

Depreciation calculations

Motor vehicles

	£
Cost	76,200.00
Accumulated depreciation	38,400.00
NBV	37,800.00

Depreciation charge to 30 June 2007

$37,800.00 \times 30\% = £11,340.00$

Fixtures and fittings

Cost = 14,760.00

Depreciation charge to 30 June 2007

$14,760.00 \times 20\% = £2,952.00$

Office equipment

	£
Cost	10,845.50
Accumulated depreciation	3,750.32
NBV	7,095.18

Depreciation charge to 30 June 2007

$7,095.18 \times 25\% = £1,773.80$

Task 3

Sales ledger control account reconciliation

Sales ledger control

		£			£
30 June	Balance b/d	56,310.82	30 June Cash book		26,241.70
			30 June Cash book Discount		267.74
			30 June Bad debt		102.50
			30 June Discounts March		186.79
			30 June Balance c/d		29,512.09
		56,310.82			56,310.82

443

	£
Balance per amended control account	29,512.09

Balance per list of balances

	£
Jones Stores	4,628.49
Wax Wonders	7,321.18
Fantasy Isle Store	3,006.11
Treasures Untold	960.32
Candlistic Ltd	2,896.80
Fairtown Department Store	7,486.92
XTC Trading	3,212.27
Total debtor balances at 30 June 2007	29,512.09

Task 4

Journal entries

		DR £	CR £
Debit	Bad debts expense	102.50	
Credit	Sales ledger control		102.50

Being write off of a bad debt from Fantasy Isle Store

		DR £	CR £
Debit	Discount allowed	186.79	
Credit	Sales ledger control		186.79

Being March discounts allowed not posted to the main ledger.

Task 6

Purchases ledger control account reconciliation

	£
Balance on the purchases ledger control account	3,633.96

	£
Wax Suppliers	1,024.83
Endeavour Partners	201.60
Simply Six Ltd	521.86
Candlemania	406.21
J T Roberts	786.20
Jonathan Brown	331.30
F L Furle	100.00
Wax Wizards	261.96
	3,633.96

Tasks 7, 9 and 10

Account name	Ledger balance DR £	Ledger balance CR £	Adjustments DR £	Adjustments CR £	Profit and loss account DR £	Profit and loss account CR £	Balance sheet DR £	Balance sheet CR £
Administration overheads	15,729.34		2,050.00	543.33	17,236.01			
Bad debts expense	850.70			366.75	483.95			
Bank interest payable	548.86				548.86			
Capital – Keith		38,500.00						38,500.00
Capital – Fred		21,500.00						21,500.00
Current – Keith		3,821.35						3,821.35
Current – Fred		1,959.00						1,959.00
Purchases ledger control		3,633.96						3,633.96
Sales ledger control	29,512.09		366.75	366.75			29,512.09	
Discount allowed	2,765.11				2,765.11			
Discount received		1,044.20				1,044.20		
Drawings– Keith	20,357.50						20,357.50	
Drawings – Fred	19,703.00						19,703.00	
Fixtures and fittings – cost	14,760.00						14,760.00	
Fixtures and fittings – depr'n	2,952.00				2,952.00			
Fixtures – accumulated depr'n		8,632.50						8,632.50
Motor vehicles – cost	76,200.00						76,200.00	
Motor vehicles – depr'n	11,340.00				11,340.00			
Motor vehicles – acc depr'n		49,740.00						49,740.00
Office equipment – cost	10,845.50						10,845.50	
Office equipment – depr'n	1,773.80				1,773.80			
Office equipment – acc depr'n		5,524.12						5,524.12
Purchases	110,508.13			128.30	110,379.83			
Purchases returns		7,225.05				7,225.05		
Sales		290,446.12				290,446.12		
Sales returns	15,365.66				15,365.66			
Selling overheads	10,054.67				10,054.67			
Stock	10,256.38		7,188.15	7,188.15	10,256.38	7,188.15	7,188.15	
Suspense		495.05	128.30					
VAT		389.91						389.91
Wages	73,840.56				73,840.56			
Bank	5,547.96						5,547.96	
Accruals				2,050.00				2,050.00
Prepayments			543.33				543.33	
Profit for the year					48,906.69			48,906.69
	432,911.26	432,911.26	10,643.28	10,643.28	305,903.52	305,903.52	184,657.53	184,657.53

Task 8

Journal entries

	DR £	CR £
Suspense	366.75	
Sales ledger control	366.75	
Sales ledger control		366.75
Bad debts expense		366.75
	733.50	733.50

Being the accounting for a receipt from a debtor for a debt that had been previously written off.

	DR £	CR £
Suspense	128.30	
Purchases account		128.30

Being the owner's drawings of stock from the business.

Task 11

Appropriation account for the year ended 30 June 2007

	Total £	Keith £	Fred £
Net profit	48,906.69		
Salary – Fred	(12,500.00)		12,500.00
Profit available	36,406.69		
Keith (36,406.69 x 2/3)	(24,271.13)	24,271.13	
Fred (36,406.69 x 1/3)	(12,135.56)		12,135.56
	–	24,271.13	24,635.56

Task 12

Profit and loss account for the year ended 30 June 2007

	£	£
Sales		290,446.12
Less: sales returns		(15,365.66)
		275,080.46
Cost of sales		
Opening stock	10,256.38	
Purchases	110,379.83	
Less: purchases returns	(7,225.05)	
	113,411.16	
Less: closing stock	(7,188.15)	
		106,223.01
Gross profit		168,857.45

	£	£
Less: expenses		
Administration overheads	17,236.01	
Bad debts	483.95	
Bank interest	548.86	
Discount allowed	2,765.11	
Discount received	(1,044.20)	
Depreciation fixtures	2,952.00	
motor vehicles	11,340.00	
office equipment	1,773.80	
Selling overheads	10,054.67	
Wages	73,840.56	
		119,950.76
Net profit		48,906.69

Balance sheet as at 30 June 2007

	Cost £	Accumulated depreciation £	Net book value £
Fixed assets			
Fixtures and fittings	14,760.00	8,632.50	6,127.50
Motor vehicles	76,200.00	49,740.00	26,460.00
Office equipment	10,845.50	5,524.12	5,321.38
101,805.50	63,896.62	37,908.88	
Current assets			
Stock		7,188.15	
Debtors		29,512.09	
Prepayments		543.33	
Bank		5,547.96	
		42,791.53	
Current liabilities			
Creditors	3,633.96		
Accruals	2,050.00		
VAT	389.91		
		6,073.87	
Net current assets			36,717.66
			74,626.54
Capital accounts Keith Buxted			38,500.00
Fred Simons			21,500.00
			60,000.00
Current accounts Keith Buxted		7,734.98	
Fred Simons		6,891.56	
			14,626.54
			74,626.54

PRACTICE SIMULATION 2

ANSWERS

Task 1

PLANT REGISTER
TRUCKS AND CARS

	Acquisition date	Cost £	25% pa NBV Dep'n £	NBV £	Funding method	Disposal proceeds £	Disposal date
FE01 KJH	1 January 2002	50,000.00					
Truck							
31/12/02			12,500.00	37,500.00	Cash		
31/12/03			9,375.00	28,125.00			
31/12/04			7,031.25	21,093.75			
31/12/05			5,273.44	15,820.31			
31/12/06			3,955.08	11,865.23			
P983 GHA	1 January 2002	28,000.00					
Truck							
31/12/02			7,000.00	21,000.00	Cash		
31/12/03			5,250.00	15,750.00			
31/12/04			3,937.50	11,812.50			
31/12/05			2,953.13	8,859.37			
31/12/06			2,214.84	6,644.53			
FE02 GHJ	1 January 2002	20,000.00			Cash		
Car							
31/12/02			5,000.00	15,000.00			
31/12/03			3,750.00	11,250.00			
31/12/04			2,812.50	8,437.50			
31/12/05			2,109.38	6,328.12		5,000.00	30/12/X5
MB55 FER	30 December 2002				Credit and part exchange		
Car		21,737.50					
31/12/06			5,434.38	16,303.12			

WORKSHOP EQUIPMENT			20% pa NBV				
	Acquisition date	Cost	Dep'n	NBV	Funding method	Disposal proceeds	Disposal date
Service equipment	1 April 2002	40,000.00			Cash		
31/12/02			8,000.00	32,000.00			
31/12/03			6,400.00	25,600.00			
31/12/04			5,120.00	20,480.00			
31/12/05			4,096.00	16,384.00			
31/12/06			3,276.80	13,107.20			
Sundry equipment	14 April 2002	6,345.00			Cash		
31/12/02			1,269.00	5,076.00			
31/12/03			1,015.20	4,060.80			
31/12/04			812.16	3,248.64			
31/12/05			649.74	2,598.90		2,000.00	5 December 20X5

Tasks 1 to 3

Journal

Date 2006	Account names and narrative	Debit £	Credit £
	Journal 1		
31 Dec	Dr Trucks and cars: Cost (18500 + 3237.50)	21,737.50	
	Dr Transport supplies (160 + 16 + 200)	376.00	
	Dr VAT	37.80	
	Cr Sundry creditors		17,151.30
	Cr Disposals		5,000.00

Being the purchase of MB55 FER 30 December 2006, with FE02 GHJ being given in part exchange

Tutorial note. A road fund licence (being an annual expense) is not capitalised.

	Journal 2		
31 Dec	Dr Disposals	20,000.00	
	Cr Trucks and cars: Cost		20,000.00
	Dr Trucks and cars: Accumulated depreciation	13,671.88	
	Cr Disposals		13,671.88

Being the disposal of FE02 GHJ, given in part exchange for MB55 FER

	Journal 3		
31 Dec	Dr Disposals	6,345.00	
	Cr Workshop equipment: Cost		6,345.00
	Dr Workshop equipment: Accumulated depreciation	3,746.10	
	Cr Disposals		3,746.10
	Dr Sundry debtors	2,000.00	
	Cr Disposals		2,000.00

Being the disposal of workshop equipment

	Journal 4		
31 Dec	Dr Depreciation expense	17,881.10	
	Cr Trucks and cars: Accumulated depreciation		11,604.30
	Cr Office equipment: Accumulated depreciation		3,000.00
	Cr Workshop equipment: Accumulated depreciation		3,276.80

Being the depreciation charge for the year ended 31 December 2006

	Journal 5		
31 Dec	Dr Office equipment: Accumulated depreciation	500.00	
	Cr Office equipment: cost		500.00

Being the elimination of a fully depreciated printer scrapped in August 2006

Task 2

Calculation of depreciation charge on office equipment

	£
Cost at January 2006	22,000.00
Fully depreciated at 1 January 2006	(10,000.00)
Balance of undepreciated assets	12,000.00

Depreciation @ 25% on cost = £3,000.00

Task 3

MEMORANDUM

To: Matthew Brinton
From: Karim Persaud
Subject: Re: Various fixed asset matters   **Date:** 27 January 2007

The scrapping of a fully depreciated asset does not affect profit at all, but does need to be adjusted in the plant register and the ledger accounts, so that they agree with each other and with the physical existence of fixed assets. I have therefore drafted a journal to remove the £500 from the accounts, and I will update the plant register as well. So that this sort of thing does not get omitted in the future, I suggest that you send a memo re scrapping of old assets in the same way as you do with disposal of newer assets for some sort of consideration.

The new printer will not be included in fixed assets in 2007 as it is less than £100, and our policy is not to capitalise expenditure at less than £100, even if the asset will be used in the business for some years.

As far as the anticipated new truck is concerned, paying out £20,000 cash now will deplete the cash balance on your balance sheet, as the accounting entry will be:

DR	Fixed assets	£20,000	
CR	Cash		£20,000

There are a number of options open to you for funding the balance of £40,000.

Borrowing – approach the bank with a business plan setting out the benefits to the business of the truck, and agree the amount of the loan, the repayment period (this should not be longer than the expected useful life of the truck ie 7 years) and the interest rate. This will introduce a large credit balance on your balance sheet, rather than depleting your cash reserves.

DR	Cash	£40,000	
CR	Loan		£40,000

On drawing down the loan funds.

DR	Fixed assets	£40,000	
CR	Cash		£40,000

On paying the balance.

Hire purchase – regular payments are made over a period of time in respect of the asset. At the end of the period, the asset becomes the business's property. Suppose payments of £600 are made monthly for seven years, which includes about £125 interest per month.

Initially we would record:

DR	Fixed assets	£40,000	
CR	Hire purchase creditor		£40,000

Each month we would record:

DR	Hire purchase creditor	£475	
	Interest	£125	
CR	Cash		£600

In both these situations, the truck will be depreciated each year at 25% reducing balance ie £15,000 in the first year.

Leasing or hire – the truck will never become the property of the business, and so will not appear as a fixed asset and will not be depreciated. Instead, each month for 7 years a lease payment will be made, of perhaps £400. This will be treated as an operating lease and not a finance lease.

The monthly entry will be:

DR	Lease expense	£400	
CR	Cash		£400

Tutorial note. The printer was bought in January 2002 for £500. At 20% straight line depreciation (£100 pa), the 2006 depreciation calculation would result in an NBV of NIL (£500 – (5 × £100)). Hence the asset is fully depreciated as at 31 December 2006.

Tasks 4 to 8 and 11

MAIN LEDGER

Administration costs

Date	Details	Amount £	Date	Details	Amount £
2006			2006		
1 Dec	Balance b/d	12,875.65	31 Dec	Balance c/d	14,220.05
31 Dec	Petty cash book	56.40			
31 Dec	Bank	117.50			
		_____			_____
					14,220.05
					========
31 Dec	Balance b/d	14,220.05			

Bad debt expense

Date	Details	Amount £	Date	Details	Amount £
2006			2006		
1 Dec	Balance b/d	248.90	31 Dec	Balance c/d	248.90
		248.90			248.90
31 Dec	Balance b/d	248.90			

Bank control

Date	Details	Amount £	Date	Details	Amount £
2006			2006		
1 Dec	Balance b/d	37,764.55	31 Dec	Payments	32,205.80
31 Dec	Receipts	27,069.30			
		64,833.85			64,833.85
31 Dec	Balance b/d	32,628.05			

Capital

Date	Details	Amount £	Date	Details	Amount £
2006			2006		
31 Dec	Balance c/d	110,000.00	1 Dec	Balance b/d	110,000.00
		110,000.00			110,000.00
			31 Dec	Balance b/d	110,000.00

Depreciation expense

Date	Details	Amount £	Date	Details	Amount £
2006			2006		
31 Dec	Journal 4	17,881.10	31 Dec	Balance c/d	17,881.10
		17,881.10			17,881.10
31 Dec	Balance b/d	17,881.10			

Drawings

Date	Details	Amount £	Date	Details	Amount £
2006			2006		
1 Dec	Balance b/d	27,000.00	31 Dec	Balance c/d	29,580.00
31 Dec	Bank	2,455.00			
	Journal 6	125.00			
		29,580.00			29,580.00
31 Dec	Balance b/d	29,580.00			

Disposals

Date	Details	Amount £	Date	Details	Amount £
2006			2006		
31 Dec	Journal 2	20,000.00	31 Dec	Journal 1	5,000.00
31 Dec	Journal 3	6,345.00	31 Dec	Journal 2	13,671.88
			31 Dec	Journal 3	3,746.10
			31 Dec	Journal 3	2,000.00
			31 Dec	Balance c/d	1,927.02
		26,345.00			26,345.00
31 Dec	Balance b/d	1,927.02			

Office equipment: Cost

Date	Details	Amount £	Date	Details	Amount £
2006			2006		
1 Dec	Balance b/d	22,000.00	31 Dec	Journal 5	500.00
			31 Dec	Balance c/d	21,500.00
		22,000.00			22,000.00
31 Dec	Balance b/d	21,500.00			

Office equipment: Accumulated depreciation

Date	Details	Amount £	Date	Details	Amount £
2006			2006		
31 Dec	Journal 5	500.00	1 Dec	Balance b/d	19,000.00
31 Dec	Balance c/d	21,500.00	31 Dec	Journal 4	3,000.00
		22,000.00			22,000.00
			31 Dec	Balance b/d	21,500.00

Petty cash control

Date	Details	Amount £	Date	Details	Amount £
2006			2006		
1 Dec	Balance b/d	100.00	31 Dec	Payments	56.40
			31 Dec	Balance c/d	43.60
		100.00			100.00
31 Dec	Balance b/d	43.60			

Provision for doubtful debts

Date	Details	Amount £	Date	Details	Amount £
2006			*2006*		
31 Dec	Journal 4	2,000.00	1 Dec	Balance b/d	2,000.00
		2,000.00			2,000.00
			31 Dec	Balance b/d	2,000.00

Purchases ledger control account

Date	Details	Amount £	Date	Details	Amount £
2006			*2006*		
31 Dec	Bank	6,985.00	1 Dec	Balance b/d	8,860.00
31 Dec	Journal 6	27.00	31 Dec	Purchase day book	7,952.60
31 Dec	Balance c/d	9,800.00			
		16,812.60			16,812.60
			31 Dec	Balance b/d	9,800.60

Sales ledger control account

Date	Details	Amount £	Date	Details	Amount £
2006			*2006*		
1 Dec	Balance b/d	25,512.50	31 Dec	Bank	27,069.30
31 Dec	Sales day book	33,337.83	31 Dec	Journal – Lewin bad debt	419.50
			31 Dec	Balance c/d	31,361.53
		58,850.33			58,850.33
31 Dec	Balance b/d	31,361.53			

Sales: Transport

Date	Details	Amount £	Date	Details	Amount £
2006			2006		
31 Dec	Balance c/d	126,222.90	1 Dec	Balance b/d	105,395.55
			31 Dec	Sales day book	20,827.35
		126,222.90			126,222.90
			31 Dec	Balance b/d	126,222.90

Sales: Workshop

Date	Details	Amount £	Date	Details	Amount £
2006			2006		
31 Dec	Balance c/d	112,303.90	1 Dec	Balance b/d	104,758.60
			31 Dec	Sales day book	7,545.30
		112,303.90			112,303.90
			31 Dec	Balance b/d	112,303.90

Stock

Date	Details	Amount £	Date	Details	Amount £
2006			2006		
1 Dec	Balance b/d	4,356.05	31 Dec	Journal	352.46
			31 Dec	Journal 7	125.00
			31 Dec	Balance c/d	3,878.59
		4,356.05			4,356.05
31 Dec	Balance b/d	3,878.59			

Sundry creditors

Date	Details	Amount £	Date	Details	Amount £
2006			2006		
31 Dec	Balance c/d	17,151.30	31 Dec	Journal 1	17,151.30
		17,151.30			17,151.30
			31 Dec	Balance b/d	17,151.30

Sundry debtors

Date	Details	Amount £	Date	Details	Amount £
2006			2006		
31 Dec	Journal 3	2,000.00	31 Dec	Balance c/d	2,000.00
		2,000.00			2,000.00
31 Dec	Balance b/d	2,000.00			

Transport supplies

Date	Details	Amount £	Date	Details	Amount £
2006			2006		
1 Dec	Balance b/d	35,131.85	31 Dec	Balance c/d	39,010.50
31 Dec	Bank	308.85			
31 Dec	PDB	3,193.80			
31 Dec	Journal 1	376.00			
		39,010.50			39,010.50
31 Dec	Balance b/d	39,010.50			

Trucks and cars: Cost

Date	Details	Amount £	Date	Details	Amount £
2006			2006		
1 Dec	Balance b/d	98,000.00	31 Dec	Journal 2	20,000.00
31 Dec	Journal 1	21,737.50	31 Dec	Balance c/d	99,737.50
		119,737.50			119,737.50
31 Dec	Balance b/d	99,737.50			

Trucks and cars: Accumulated depreciation

Date	Details	Amount £	Date	Details	Amount £
2006			2006		
31 Dec	Journal 2	13,671.88	1 Dec	Balance b/d	66,992.20
31 Dec	Balance c/d	64,924.62	31 Dec	Journal 4	11,604.30
		78,596.50			78,596.50
			31 Dec	Balance b/d	64,924.62

VAT control

Date	Details	Amount £	Date	Details	Amount £
2006			2006		
31 Dec	Bank	2,957.80	1 Dec	Balance b/d	2,841.00
31 Dec	Purchases Day Book	1,180.40	31 Dec	Sales Day Book	4,965.18
31 Dec	Journal 1	37.80			
31 Dec	Balance c/d	3,630.18			
		7,806.18			7,806.18
			31 Dec	Balance b/d	3,630.18

Wages and salaries

Date	Details	Amount £	Date	Details	Amount £
2006			*2006*		
1 Dec	Bal b/d	109,685.30	31 Dec	Balance c/d	118,825.75
31 Dec	Bank	9,140.45			
		118,825.75			118,825.75
31 Dec	Balance b/d	118,825.75			

Workshop equipment: Cost

Date	Details	Amount £	Date	Details	Amount £
2006			*2006*		
1 Dec	Balance b/d	46,345.00	31 Dec	Journal 3	6,345.00
			31 Dec	Balance c/d	40,000.00
		46,345.00			46,345.00
31 Dec	Balance b/d	40,000.00			

Workshop equipment: Accumulated depreciation

Date	Details	Amount £	Date	Details	Amount £
2006			*2006*		
31 Dec	Journal 3	3,746.10	1 Dec	Balance b/d	27,362.10
31 Dec	Balance c/d	26,892.80	31 Dec	Journal 4	3,276.80
		30,638.90			30,638.90
			31 Dec	Balance b/d	26,892.80

Workshop purchases

Date	Details	Amount £	Date	Details	Amount £
2006			2006		
1 Dec	Balance b/d	26,189.65	31 Dec	Balance c/d	29,164.21
31 Dec	Journal	352.46			
31 Dec	Bank	241.20			
31 Dec	Purchases day book	2,380.90			29,164.21
		29,164.21			
31 Dec	Balance b/d	29,164.21			

Task 5

Sales ledger account balances at 31 December 2006

	£
ARC Ltd	706.98
Lewin Haulage	419.50
RetailHeaven	13,416.73
TRILOGISTIX	6,182.43
Wemble & Co	11,055.39
	31,781.03

Sales ledger control account:

Balance at 31 December 2006   31,361.53

Difference   419.50

The difference arises from a journal in the sales ledger control account in relation to a bad debt from Lewin for £419.50, which does not appear in the ledger account for Lewin Haulage.

Task 6

Purchases ledger account balances at 31 December 2006

	£
Bronwen & Co	1,546.32
Eddlestone Ltd	2,576.38
HighDry plc	1,963.72
Ormskirk Parts Ltd	975.29
Runcorn plc	1,552.06
Viscount Ltd	1,186.83
	9,800.60

Purchases ledger control account:

Balance at 31 December 2006	9,827.60
Difference	27.00

The difference arises from the fact that the purchases day book total column for December is overcast by £27.00 (there is a transposition error). Since this has been posted to the main ledger a correcting journal is required.

Journal

Date 2006	Account names and narrative	Debit £	Credit £
	Journal 6		
31 Dec	Dr Purchases ledger control account	27.00	
	Being the correction of an overcast in the Purchases Day Book for December 2006		

Tutorial note. As previous entries did not balance by £27.00, a one-sided entry is needed to complete the double entry.

Task 7

Workshop stock valuation schedule at 31 December 2006

Part number	FIFO cost £	NRV £	Valuation £
15674	21.23	58.00	21.23
43430	465.65	525.00	465.65
45446	801.28	789.65	789.65
46876	549.00	678.65	549.00
55564	1,158.45	1,500.00	1,158.45
68368	640.02	756.05	640.02
97531	254.59	482.70	254.59
Total			3,878.59

Stock ledger control account balance at 31 December 2006	4,003.59
Difference	125.00

The difference arises from the fact that the stock valuation schedule reflects £125.00 of stock removed by Matthew for his own use, while the stock account does not. An adjusting journal is required therefore.

Journal

Date 2006	Account names and narrative	Debit £	Credit £
	Journal 7		
31 Dec	Dr Purchases ledger control account	125.00	
	CR Stock		125.00
	Being reflection of £125 worth of stock removed for own use by Matthew Brinton 31 December 2006		

Tasks 8, 10 and 11

Brinton Longhaul Services year ended 31 December 2006

Account name	Trial balance DR £	Trial balance CR £	Adjustments DR £	Adjustments CR £	Profit and loss account DR £	Profit and loss account CR £	Balance sheet DR £	Balance sheet CR £
Administration costs	14,220.05		500.00	4,600.00	10,120.05			
Bad debt expense	248.90		2,419.50		2,668.40			
Bank control	32,628.05						32,628.05	
Capital		110,000.00						110,000.00
Depreciation expense	17,881.10				17,881.10			
Disposals	1,927.02				1,927.02			
Drawings	29,580.00						29,580.00	
Office equipment: acc dep'n		21,500.00						21,500.00
Office equipment: cost	21,500.00						21,500.00	
Petty cash control	43.60						43.60	
Provision for doubtful debts		2,000.00						2,000.00
Purchases ledger control		9,800.60						9,800.60
Sales ledger control	31,361.53						31,361.53	
Sales: transport		126,222.90				126,222.90		
Sales: workshop		112,303.90				112,303.90		
Stock	3,878.59						3,878.59	
Sundry creditors		17,151.30						17,151.30
Sundry debtors	2,000.00						2,000.00	
Transport supplies	39,010.50				39,010.50			
Trucks and cars: acc dep'n		64,924.62						64,924.62
Trucks and cars: cost	99,737.50						99,737.50	
VAT control		3,630.18						3,630.18
Wages and salaries	118,825.75				118,825.75			
Workshop equipment: acc dep'n		26,892.80						26,892.80
Workshop equipment: cost	40,000.00						40,000.00	
Workshop purchases	29,164.21				29,164.21			
Suspense	12,419.50			2,419.50			10,000.00	
Accruals				500.00				500.00
Prepayments			4,600.00				4,600.00	
Profit for the year					18,929.77			18,929.77
	494,426.30	494,426.30	7,519.50	7,519.50	238,526.80	238,526.80	275,329.27	275,329.27

Task 9

Withdrawal of £10,000

In order to discover what this item represents, I would look for supporting documentation, for example, a letter of authority or a withdrawal slip. The withdrawal is unlikely to be anything to do with the purchases ledger, because it has been reconciled.

It is possible that the withdrawal represents drawings by Matthew, or another transaction that directly involves him. If there were no supporting documentation, I should raise the matter as tactfully as I could with Matthew Brinton. The amount is material and it is extremely unlikely that he would not be able to identify it.

Journal

Date 2006	Account names and narrative	Debit £	Credit £
31 Dec	Dr Bad debts expense	2,419.50	
	Cr Suspense		2,419.50

Being the correction of single entries to the provision for doubtful debts and sales ledger control account on creation of £2,000 provision and writing off of £419.50 bad debt from Lewin Haulage.

Task 11

Profit and loss account

Date	Details	Amount £	Date	Details	Amount £
2006			2006		
31 Dec	Admin costs	10,120.05	31 Dec	Sales – transport	126,222.90
31 Dec	Bad debts	2,668.40	31 Dec	Sales – workshop	112,303.90
31 Dec	Depreciation	17,881.10			
31 Dec	Disposals	1,927.02			
31 Dec	Transport supplies	39,010.50			
31 Dec	Wages and salaries	118,825.75			
31 Dec	Workshop purchases	29,164.21			
31 Dec	Profit for the year	18,929.77			
		238,526.80			238,526.80

Task 12

BRINTON LONGHAUL SERVICES

Profit and loss account for the year ended 31 December 2006

	£	£
Sales		238,527
Less: cost of sales		
transport supplies	39,011	
workshop purchases	29,164	
		68,175
Gross profit		170,352
Expenses		
Wages and salaries	118,826	
Bad debts	2,668	
Admin costs	10,120	
Depreciation	17,881	
Loss on disposals	1,927	
		151,422
Net profit		18,930

Balance sheet at 31 December 2006

	£	£	£
Fixed assets			
Office equipment	21,500	21,500	0
Trucks and cars	99,738	64,925	34,813
Workshop equipment	40,000	26,893	13,107
	161,238	113,318	47,920
Current assets			
Stock		3,878	
Trade debtors		31,362	
Provision		(2,000)	
Sundry debtors		2,000	
Prepayments		4,600	
Suspense		10,000	
Cash at bank		32,628	
Cash in hand		44	
		82,512	
Current liabilities			
Trade creditors		9,801	
Sundry creditors		17,151	
VAT		3,630	
Accruals		500	
		31,082	
Net current assets			51,430
Net assets			99,350

	£
Capital b/f	110,000
Net profit for the year	18,930
Drawings	(29,580)
	99,350

Task 13

BRINTON TAXIS

Profit and loss account for the year ended 31 December 2006

	£	£
Sales		85,852
Purchases		(21,645)
Gross profit		64,207
Profit on disposal		1,995
Expenses		
Wages	15,742	
Depreciation	4,875	
Other expenses	1,865	
Loan interest	3,000	
		(25,482)
Net profit		40,720

Balance sheet at 31 December 2006

	£	£	£
Fixed assets	70,000	11,375	58,625
Current assets			
Stock			
Trade debtors		8,246	
Sundry debtors		1,000	
Prepayments		200	
Cash at bank		6,823	
Cash in hand		98	
		16,367	
Current liabilities			
Trade creditors		1,960	
Sundry creditors		300	
VAT		2,375	
Accruals		32	
		4,667	
Net current assets			11,700
			70,325
Bank Loan			(50,000)
Net assets			20,325

	£
Capital: Matthew	7,500
Capital: Cassandra	7,500
Current account: Matthew	721
Current account: Cassandra	4,604
	20,325

Appropriation account for year ended 31 December 2006

	£	£
Net profit		40,720
Salary		
Matthew	10,000	
Cassandra	25,000	
		35,000
Interest on capital		
Matthew	375	
Cassandra	375	
		750
Balance of net profit		4,970

	£
Share of profit	
Matthew 30	1,491
Cassandra 70	3,479
	4,970

Current accounts

Date	Details	Matthew £	Cassandra £	Date	Details	Matthew £	Cassandra £
2006				2006			
31 Dec	Brought down		800	31 Dec	Brought down	1,500	
31 Dec	Drawings	12,645	23,450	31 Dec	Share of profit	11,866	28,854
31 Dec	Carried down	721	4,604			13,366	28,854
		13,366	28,854				
				1 Jan	Brought down	721	4,604

Task 14

CASSANDRA'S COSMETICS

Profit and loss account for the year ended 31 December 2006

	£	£
Sales		14,490
Cost of sales		
Opening stock	2,875	
Purchases (10,455 – 5,585)	4,870	
Closing stock	(500)	
		(7,245)
Gross profit		7,245
Expenses		
Depreciation	2,250	
Net cost of stolen stock (5,585 – 2,000)	3,585	
Loan interest	270	
		(6,105)
Net profit		1,140

Balance sheet at 31 December 2006

	£	£	£
Fixed assets	10,000	4,500	5,500
Current assets			
Stock		500	
Trade debtors		3,820	
Sundry debtors – insurance		2,000	
Cash at bank		1,930	
Cash in hand		0	
		8250	
Trade creditors		(860)	
Net current assets			7,390
			12,890
Bank loan			(4,500)
Net assets			8,390

	£
Opening capital	9,650
Profit for the year	1,140
Drawings	(2,400)
	8,390

CASSANDRA'S COSMETICS

Opening balance sheet as at 1 January 2006

	£	£
Fixed assets (10,000 – (10,000 × 90% × 0.25))		7,750
Current assets		
Stock	2,875	
Debtors	1,975	
Cash at bank	2,430	
Petty cash	55	
	7,335	
Creditors	(935)	
		6,400
Bank loan		(4,500)
Opening capital		9,650

Total debtors account

Date	Details	Amount £	Date	Details	Amount £
2006			2006		
1 Jan	b/d	1,975	31 Dec	Cash	12,645
31 Dec	Sales	14,490	31 Dec	c/d	3,820
		16,465			16,465

Total creditors account

Date	Details	Amount £	Date	Details	Amount £
2006			2006		
31 Dec	Cash*	10,530	1 Jan	b/d	935
31 Dec	c/d	860	31 Dec	Purchases	10,455
		11,390			11,390

*Cash paid to suppliers: £7,535 cheques plus petty cash b/f £55 plus £5,340 less drawings (12 × £200) £2,400 = £10,530

Gross profit working

	£	%
Sales	14,490	100
Cost of sales	(7,245)	50
Gross profit	7,245	50

	£
Cost of stock stolen	
Opening stock	2,875
Purchases	10,455
	13,330
Less: closing stock	(500)
Cost of goods sold and stolen	12,830
Cost of sales	(7,245)
Cost of goods stolen	5,585

Task 15

MEMORANDUM

To: Matthew and Cassandra Brinton
From: Avril Baker
Date: 26 January 2007

RESPONSES TO YOUR FINANCIAL QUERIES

1 Sole traders and partnerships in the UK *are/are not bound by the Companies Act 1985.

2 The legislation by which partnerships are affected on points where they do not have a partnership agreement is **the Partnership Act 1890**.

3 If partners do not have a formal agreement as to how much salary they should receive and how profits should be split, the legislation states that **they should have no salary, and profits should be split equally**.

4 Accounting regulations which have a strong influence on the accounts of sole traders and partnerships are **Financial Reporting Standards (FRSs)** and **Statements of Standard Accounting Practice (SSAPs)**.

5 The selection of accounting policies is governed by **FRS 18**.

6 The basic accounting concepts that underlie the selection of accounting policies are **accruals** and **going concern**.

7 Definition of the accruals concept: **in computing profit, revenue earned must be matched against the expenditure incurred in earning it**.

8 Definition of the going concern concept: **the business will continue in operation for the foreseeable future, so assets should not be valued at their break-up value**.

---

9   When selecting accounting policies, according to the Statement of Principles the objective is to have information that is **relevant**, **reliable**, **understandable** and **comparable**.

10   An item is material in the context of a set of accounts when its omission or misstatement would **affect the impact of the accounts on the reader**.

11   The accounting regulation which states that depreciation should be charged on fixed assets is **FRS 15**.

12   If a fixed asset is most likely to wear out at an even rate, the most suitable depreciation method would be *straight line/~~reducing balance~~.

13   While the Companies Act allows the valuation of stock on the LIFO basis, this is prevented by **SSAP 9**.

14   Stocks should be valued at the lower of **cost** and **net realisable value**.

15   Under the FIFO basis, stock is deemed to comprise items bought *most recently/~~longest ago~~.

16   Assets acquired under leasing or hire purchase arrangements are governed by **SSAP 21**.

17   Value added tax should be *~~included~~/excluded from the sales figure in the profit and loss account. VAT owed to HM Revenue & Customs should be shown under **current liabilities** in the balance sheet. This is covered by **SSAP 5**.

AAT

PRACTICE EXAM 1

AMMAR

ANSWERS

SECTION 1

Task 1.1

Sales ledger control account

	£		£
Balance b/f	10,500	Bank	142,800
Sales day book	146,875	Discounts allowed	1,675
		Balance c/f	12,900
	157,375		157,375

Task 1.2

Rent

	£		£
Balance b/f – prepayment	750	Profit and loss account	6,000
Bank	6,250	Balance c/f (W)	1,000
	7,000		7,000

Working

£1,500 has been paid for the three months ending 31 December 2007.

Prepayment $= £1,500 \times 2/3 = £1,000$

Task 1.3

a) General expenses $= £4,700 \times 100/117.5 = £4,000$

b) VAT on general expenses $= £4,700 - £4,000 = £700$

OR $= £4,700 \times 17.5/117.5 = £700$

Task 1.4

VAT

	£		£
Bank	11,025	Balance b/f	2,200
Purchases day book	10,500	Sales day book	21,875
General expenses	700		
Balance c/f	1,850		
	24,075		24,075

Task 1.5

Payroll expenses

	£		£
Bank	22,000	Balance b/f – accrual	200
Balance c/f – accrual	320	Profit and loss a/c	22,120
	22,320		22,320

Task 1.6

a)

	£
Vehicle at cost	18,000
Depreciation at 31 Oct 2006	(4,500)
NBV at 31 Oct 2006	13,500

Depreciation for year ended 31 Oct 2007 = £13,500 x 25% = £3,375

b) Accumulated depreciation at 31 Oct 2007 = £4,500 + £3,375 = £7,875

Task 1.7

a) Closing trade debtors = £12,900

Provision required = £12,900 × 5% = £645

b) When goods are sold on credit to customers in general they are expected to pay the amounts due. However there may be some trade debts which you may be doubtful about whether or not they will be paid. For example if you cannot make contact with a trade debtor or have heard that a trade debtor may be going into liquidation. In these cases of doubt it is prudent to make a provision to reflect the fact that these debts may not be received. This is in contrast to a bad debt which is actually written out of the ledger accounts completely.

Task 1.8

AMMAR
Trial balance as at 31 October 2007

	Debit £	Credit £
Vehicle at cost	18,000	
Vehicle depreciation expense (Task 1.6)	3,375	
Vehicle accumulated depreciation (Task 1.6)		7,875
Opening stock	6,400	
Closing stock – balance sheet	7,200	
Closing stock – profit and loss account		7,200
Sales ledger control account	12,900	
Provision for doubtful debts (Task 1.7)		645
Bad debts expense (Task 1.7)	645	
Prepayment (Task 1.2)	1,000	
Accrual (Task 1.5)		320
Purchase ledger control account		6,300
VAT payable (Task 1.4)		1,850
Capital		26,650
Bank	2,525	
Drawings	30,000	
Rent Task 1.2)	6,000	
Payroll expenses (Task 1.5)	22,120	
General expenses (Task 1.3)	4,000	
Sales		125,000
Purchases	60,000	
Discounts allowed (Task 1.1)	1,675	
Total	175,840	175,840

Task 1.9

Would the errors below be detected by the trial balance?	Yes	No
a) A bank payment has been entered into the bank account but no other entries have been made.	✓	
b) A sales invoice for £420 + VAT has been entered as follows: DR Sales £420 CR Sales ledger control account £420		✓
c) Discounts received of £101 have been credited to discounts received as £110 and debited to the purchases ledger control account as £101.	✓	
d) Payroll expenses of £890 have been debited to payroll expenses and credited to the bank account. The correct amount should have been £980.		✓

Tutorial notes

1) This is a one-sided entry as only the credit in the bank account has been made therefore the credit entries on the trial balance will be higher than the debit entries

2) Although the VAT has been incorrectly excluded from the transaction the same amounts have been debited and credited in the ledger accounts, therefore this will not result in a difference in the trial balance

3) The credit entry in the ledger accounts is higher than the debit entry, therefore the credits in the trial balance will be higher than the debits.

4) Although the incorrect figure has been used it has been both debited and credited to the ledger accounts, therefore this will not result in a difference on the trial balance.

Task 1.10

Any two of:

- Cash
- A bank loan
- Leasing
- Hire purchase
- Part exchange

SECTION 2

Task 2.1

Journal

				Debit £	Credit £
a)	Debit		Administration expenses	820	
	Credit		Purchases		820
b)	i)	Debit	Equipment at cost	2,500	
		Credit	Suspense		2,500
	ii)	Debit	Depreciation expense	750	
		Credit	Equipment accumulated depreciation		750
c)	Debit		Suspense	1,500	
	Credit		Advertising expenses		1,500
	Debit		Suspense	1,500	
	Credit		Accruals		1,500
d)	Debit		Closing stock – balance sheet (W)	41,000	
	Credit		Closing stock – profit and loss account (W)		41,000

Working

Closing stock value

	£
From computerised stock system	43,500
Less: obsolete items at cost	(4,200)
Add: obsolete items at net realisable value	1,700
	41,000

Task 2.2

Workings	**GREAT GIFTS** **Profit and loss account for the year ended 30 September 2007**		
		£	£
	Sales		550,000
	Less: cost of sales		
	Opening stock	36,000	
290,820 – 820	Purchases	290,000	
		326,000	
Task 2.1	Less: closing stock	(41,000)	
			285,000
	Gross profit		265,000
	Less: expenses		
24,530 + 820	Administration expenses	25,350	
11,250 – 1,500	Advertising expense	9,750	
20,650 + 750	Depreciation expense	21,400	
	Payroll expenses	52,000	
	Rent	56,500	
			165,000
	Net profit		100,000

Task 2.3

Interest on capital	1 October 2006 to 31 March 2007 £	1 April 2006 to 30 Sept 07 £	Total £
Asma	750	–	750
Ben	750	750	1,500
Chris	750	750	1,500

Working

Interest on capital for six months = £30,000 × 5% × 6/12 = £750

Task 2.4

GREAT GIFTS
Appropriation account for the year ended 30 September 2007

	1 October 2006 to 31 March 2007	1 April 2007 to 30 September 2007	Total
	£	£	£
Net profit	50,000	50,000	100,000
Salaries			
Asma	(10,250)	–	(10,250)
Ben	(12,500)	(12,500)	(25,000)
Interest on capital			
Asma	(750)	–	(750)
Ben	(750)	(750)	(1,500)
Chris	(750)	(750)	(1,500)
Profit available for distribution	25,000	36,000	61,000
Profit share			
Asma (50%/0%)	(12,500)	–	(12,500)
Ben (25%/60%)	(6,250)	(21,600)	(27,850)
Chris (25%/40%)	(6,250)	(14,400)	(20,650)
Balance	–	–	–

Task 2.5

Goodwill account

	£		£
Asma (W1)	25,000	Ben (W2)	30,000
Ben (W1)	12,500	Chris (W2)	20,000
Chris (W2)	12,500		
	50,000		50,000

Workings

Goodwill in old profit share ratio

Asma = £50,000 × 50% = £25,000
Ben = £50,000 × 25% = £12,500
Chris = £50,000 × 25% = £12,500

Goodwill in new profit share ratio

Ben = £50,000 × 60% = £30,000
Chris = £50,000 × 40% = £20,000

Task 2.6

a)
Debit	Capital – Asma	Credit	Trade creditors	
Debit	Loan – Asma	Credit	Capital – Asma	
Debit	Capital – Asma	Credit	Loan – Asma	✓
Debit	Bank	Credit	Capital – Asma	

b)
Tangible fixed assets
Intangible fixed assets   ✓
Current assets

Task 2.7

There are a number of reasons why the computerised stock records may sometimes disagree with the amount of physical stock held. These include:

- goods have been received but not yet updated on the computerised system

- goods have been returned to suppliers but not yet updated on the computerised system

- goods have been returned from customers but not yet updated on the computerised system

- goods may have been stolen or otherwise disposed of

(Note that only three reasons were required.)

The value for closing stock is deducted from the purchases and opening stock total in order to find the figure for cost of sales in the profit and loss account. Therefore if there is an error in the stock records and the closing stock value is incorrect then this will affect cost of sales and therefore both gross profit and net profit. If the stock value is too high then cost of sales will be smaller than it should be and a greater profit will be recorded. If the stock value is lower than the correct figure then cost of sales will be too high and a smaller profit will be reported.

AAT

PRACTICE EXAM 2

MARK GOSS

ANSWERS

SECTION 1

Task 1.1

Capital account

	£		£
Balance c/f	11,000	Bank	5,000
		Vehicle	6,000
	11,000		11,000

Tutorial note. The Chief Assessor noted that a common mistake was to omit the vehicle from capital. Remember that any asset can be introduced as capital – not just cash.

Task 1.2

Sales ledger control account

	£		£
Credit sales	29,200	Bank	25,800
		Balance c/f	3,400
	29,200		29,200

Tutorial note. The main problem with this task is making sure that you enter the opening and closing balances on the correct side. The closing debtors are an asset of the business and as such are brought down on the debit side. This means that they are carried down from the credit side.

Task 1.3

Purchases ledger control account

	£		£
Bank	8,840	Purchases	11,200
Discounts received	1,165		
Balance c/f	1,195		
	11,200		11,200

Tutorial note. See above for the importance of putting the opening and closing balances on the correct side. The closing balance is a liability of the business and as such will be brought down as a credit balance – therefore entered as a debit entry above the line.

486

Chief Assessor's comment, Tasks 1.1 to 1.3 In practice the balances would be carried down and brought down. The model answers show the balance carried forward. Students would not be penalised for showing balances carried down and brought down, and this could be helpful in preparing the trial balance. However, as this was not required, it is not shown in the model answer.

Task 1.4

Cost of vehicle introduced $= £6,000$

Depreciation $= £6,000 \times 25\% = £1,500$

Task 1.5

Rent account

	£		£
Bank	4,500	Prepayment	900
		Rent for the year	3,600
	4,500		4,500

Tutorial note. The prepayment is given as £900. This is an asset of the business and will be brought down as a debit balance in the prepayment account – it is therefore entered as a credit entry in the rent ledger account.

Task 1.6

	£
General expenses per bank	1,750
Accrual (working)	90
	1,840

Working

Three months' electricity $= £135$

Accrual (2 months) $= 135 \times 2/3 = £90$

Task 1.7

Journal entry

	Debit £	Credit £
Bad debt expense	290	
Sales ledger control account		290

Narrative
Being the writing off of an irrecoverable bad debt for Unready Limited.

Tutorial note. Because the debt is irrecoverable the £290 is written out of the sales ledger control account (and the £290 that is in the ledger account of Unready Limited in the subsidiary (sales) ledger will also be removed and the account closed). Had the debt only been doubtful with a possibility of being paid then a bad debt provision would have been made for the amount. The debit to the bad debt expense account is written off to the profit and loss account reflecting the fact that the business has lost £290.

Task 1.8

MARK GOSS
Trial balance as at 31 March 2007

	Debit £	Credit £
Capital		11,000
Vehicle at cost	6,000	
Sales		29,200
Sales ledger control account	3,400	290
Purchases	11,200	
Purchases ledger control account		1,195
Discounts received		1,165
Vehicle accumulated depreciation		1,500
Depreciation expense	1,500	
Rent	3,600	
Prepayment	900	
General expenses	1,840	
Accrual		90
Bad debt expense	290	
Travel expenses	2,100	
Equipment rental payments	1,000	
Drawings	12,000	
Bank	610	
Total	44,440	44,440

Tutorial note. The Chief Assessor noted that many candidates produced very few entries in the trial balance and many were on the wrong side. Even though you are not asked to produce a complete set of written up accounts you must remember that and item such as 'equipment rental payments' that are a credit in the bank account must be a debit in some other account – namely the 'equipment rentals account'. There will also typically be a prepayment and an accruals account, a depreciation expense and provision account, and don't forget the balance on the bank account.

Task 1.9

a) The purpose of depreciation is to spread the cost less residual value of a fixed asset over its useful life to the business. This is an application of the accruals/matching concept.

b) 25% straight line method ☐

25% reducing balance method ☐

20% straight line method ☑

20% reducing balance method ☐

Task 1.10

Any two from:

- Comparability
- Relevance
- Reliability
- Understandability

Tutorial note. You are asked for two objectives, not concepts or policies or any other item. This was simply a matter of learning the detail of FRS 18 – make sure you do that.

SECTION 2

Tasks 2.1 and 2.2

NR Copiers – Extended trial balance as at 31 March 2007

	Ledger balances		Adjustments		Profit and loss account		Balance Sheet	
	Debit	Credit	Debit	Credit	Debit	Credit	Debit	Credit
	£	£	£	£	£	£	£	£
Administration expenses	70,400		1,500		71,900			
Bank	34,505						34,505	
Capital account – Neru		40,000						40,000
Capital account – Rob		40,000						40,000
Cash	120		50				170	
Closing stock	24,000	24,000				24,000	24,000	
Current account – Neru	30,100						30,100	
Current account – Rob	20,700						20,700	
Depreciation charge for the year	10,500				10,500			
Opening stock	19,000				19,000			
Provision for doubtful debts		500		300				800
Purchases	158,500				158,500			
Purchases ledger control account		25,000						25,000
Rent	11,000				11,000			
Sales		359,000	5,000			354,000		
Sales ledger control account	30,700						30,700	
Selling expenses	55,650			50	55,600			
VAT		8,175						8,175
Vehicles at cost	56,000			12,000			44,000	
Vehicles accumulated depreciation		24,500	5,250					19,250
Accrual				1,500				1,500
Provision for doubtful debt adjustment			300		300			
Disposal of fixed asset			12,000	5,250				
				5,000	1,750			
Profit for the year					49,450			49,450
Total	521,175	521,175	24,100	24,100	378,000	378,000	184,175	184,175

Workings

1) Administration expenses – accrue £1,500

   Debit   Administration expenses
   Credit   Accruals

2) The £50 was correctly credited to the bank account. The error was to debit selling expenses rather than cash (the transaction was probably money paid into petty cash or some sort of cash float). The correcting journal is:

   Debit   Cash
   Credit   Selling expenses

3) The provision needs to be increased by £300 (from £500 to £800)

   Debit   Provision for doubtful debts adjustment
   Credit   Provision for doubtful debts

4) First remove the cost and accumulated depreciation of the car from the relevant accounts

Dr	Vehicle accumulated depreciation	£5,250	
Cr	Disposal of fixed assets		£5,250
Dr	Disposal of fixed assets	£12,000	
Cr	Vehicles at cost		£12,000

   Then, remove the £5,000 sales proceeds from the sales account and put it in the disposal account:

Dr	Sales	£5,000	
Cr	Disposal of fixed asset		£5,000

Task 2.3

Current accounts

	Neru £	Rob £		Neru £	Rob £
31 March 2007			**31 March 2007**		
Balance b/f	30,100	20,700	Profit share	24,725	24,725
Balance c/f	–	4,025	Balance c/f	5,375	–
	30,100	24,725		30,100	24,725

Working

Profit share £49,450 x 50% = £24,725

Task 2.4

Workings

NR Copiers Balance Sheet as at 31 March 2007

	Cost £	Depreciation £	Net book value £
Fixed assets			
Vehicles	44,000	19,250	24,750
Current assets			
Stock		24,000	
Debtors		29,900	
Bank		34,505	
Cash		170	
		88,575	
Current liabilities			
Creditors	25,000		
VAT	8,175		
Accruals	1,500		
		(34,675)	
Net current assets			53,900
Net assets			78,650

30,700 – 800

	Neru £	Rob £	Total £
Financed by			
Capital accounts	40,000	40,000	80,000
Current accounts	(5,375)	4,025	(1,350)
Total	34,625	44,025	78,650

Task 2.5

Capital accounts

	Neru £	Rob £	Kim £		Neru £	Rob £	Kim £
Goodwill eliminated	67,500	52,500	30,000	Balances b/f	40,000	40,000	
Balances c/f	47,500	62,500	50,000	Bank:			
				cash introduced			80,000
				Goodwill introduced	75,000	75,000	
	115,000	115,000	80,000		115,000	115,000	80,000

Working

The goodwill of the partnership is not carried in the books of account. When a new partner is admitted, the goodwill is reintroduced into the accounts by debiting a goodwill account and crediting the old partners in their old profit sharing ratio. The goodwill is then removed immediately by crediting the goodwill account and debiting the new partners in the new ratios.

Introduction of goodwill in old profit sharing ratios:

£150,000 x 50% = £75,000 each

Elimination of goodwill in new profit sharing ratios:

Neru £150,000 × 45% = £67,500
Rob   £150,000 × 35% = £52,500
Kim   £150,000 × 20% = £30,000

Tutorial note. In practice dates would have to be shown in the accounts.

Task 2.6

Even though my friend knows Kim, the information requested is confidential and should not be given to anyone without the permission of the partners, and such permission should be obtained in writing to avoid any misunderstanding in the future. My friend should ask Kim directly.

Task 2.7

a) **Cost structure**

	£	£
Sales price	140	1,260
Cost of sales	100	900
Gross profit	40	360

Sales price = cost + 40% mark-up on cost = £900 × 140% = £1,260

b) **Cost structure**

	£	£
Sales price	100	1,500
Cost of sales	60	900
Gross profit	40	600

Gross profit is 40% × sales price. Therefore cost = 60% × sales price

Therefore sales price = £900/60% = £1,500

AAT

PRACTICE EXAM 3

ACE CARS

ANSWERS

SECTION 1

Task 1.1

	£
Credit sales (net of VAT)	46,000
Cash sales (net of VAT)	212,000
Total sales (net of VAT)	258,000

Task 1.2

		£
a)	Credit sales (net of VAT)	46,000
	VAT (46,000 x 17.5%)	8,050
	Credit sales inc VAT	54,050

Alternatively

Credit sales including VAT = £46,000 x 1.175 = £54,050

b) **Sales ledger control account**

Sales ledger control account

	£		£
Balance b/f	4,120	Bank (balancing figure)	52,460
Credit sales	54,050	Balance c/f	5,710
	58,170		58,170

Chief Assessor's comment. All students should go into the exam being prepared to construct a sales or purchases ledger control account from incomplete records.

Task 1.3

		£
a)	Cash sales (net of VAT)	212,000
	VAT (212,000 x 17.5%)	37,100
	Cash sales inc VAT	249,100

Alternatively

Cash sales including VAT = £212,000 x 1.175 = £249,100

b)

Bank account

	£		£
Balance b/f	5,630	Payroll expenses	48,000
Sales ledger control a/c	52,460	Administration expenses	6,400
Cash sales	249,100	Vehicle running expenses	184,475
	307,190	Drawings – Alex	19,800
		Drawings – Charles	22,000
		VAT	17,300
		Balance c/f	9,215
			307,190

Task 1.4

	£
Vehicle running expenses (inc VAT)	184,475
VAT (184,475/117.5 x 17.5) (W)	27,475
Vehicle running expenses (net of VAT) (184,475/117.5 x 100) (W)	157,000

Working

VAT percentages

	%
Net	100.0
VAT	17.5
Inc VAT (gross)	117.5

Therefore if given the VAT inclusive figure (gross figure) divide it by 117.5 and multiply it by 17.5 to give the VAT amount , or 100 to give the net figure

Chief Assessor's comment. The Chief Assessor makes two references to the difficulties that some students have with VAT calculations.

'....the tasks which included adjusting for VAT often caused problems due to what seemed like a fundamental lack of understanding of what was meant by terms such as 'net of VAT' or 'including VAT', together with an inability to calculate the figures correctly.'

'This task required students to extract a net figure from the gross by deducting the VAT.........Students should practise this so that they can confidently find the gross, net or VAT from any figure.'

Task 1.5

a) **Depreciation charge for the year ended 30 September 2006**

	£
Cost	60,000
Accumulated depreciation 30 Sept 2005	(16,770)
NBV 30 Sept 2005	43,230

Depreciation for year ended 30 Sept 2006 = £43,230 x 30% = £12,969

b) **Accumulated depreciation as at 30 September 2006**

	£
Depreciation for the year	12,969
Accumulated depreciation at 30 Sept 2005	16,770
Accumulated depreciation at 30 Sept 2006	29,739

Task 1.6

Administration expenses

	£
Paid through Bank	6,400
Add accrual for accountancy fees	675
Adjusted administration expenses	7,075

Task 1.7

Payroll expenses

	£
Paid through Bank	48,000
Add accrual	950
Less Alex's drawings	(2,200)
Adjusted payroll expenses	46,750

Task 1.8

Current accounts

	Alex	Charlie		Alex	Charlie
	£	£		£	£
Drawings	19,800	22,000	Balance b/f	5,590	3,190
Correction to payroll	2,200		Balance c/f	16,410	18,810
	22,000	22,000			
	22,000	22,000		22,000	22,000

Notes

1) It is coincidence that the totals for both partners are the same.

2) The double entry for the misposting of Alex's drawings is:

	Debit £	Credit £
DR Current account (Task 1.8)	2,200	
CR Payroll expenses (Task 1.7)		2,200

Task 1.9

ACE CARS
Trial balance as at 30 September 2006

	£	£
Accrual for administration expenses (accountancy fee)		675
Accrual for payroll expenses		950
Administration expenses	7,075	
Bank	9,215	
Capital account – Alex		20,000
Capital account – Charlie		20,000
Current account – Alex	16,410	
Current account – Charlie	18,810	
Depreciation expense	12,969	
Payroll expense	46,750	
Sales		258,000
Sales ledger control account	5,710	
VAT		4,575
Vehicles – cost	60,000	
Vehicles – accumulated depreciation		29,739
Vehicle running expenses	157,000	
Total	333,939	333,939

Task 1.10

a) Fixed asset register

b) Any four from

Date of purchase	Net book value
Description	Date of disposal
Location of assets	Disposal proceeds
Rate of depreciation	Method of finance
Method of depreciation	Expected lifetime
Depreciation charges for each period	Expected residual value
Accumulated depreciation at the end of each period	

c) (**Note** – the fixed asset register serves two main functions

- To provide information for writing up the books of accounts
- To provide information to control the assets)

Any two from

- The information assists in the main calculations of depreciation for the year, accumulated depreciation, NBV

- It contains information about the cost and therefore balance sheet value of the assets

- It contains the relevant information for calculations when an asset is disposed of

- It shows if there is any outstanding finance on an asset that should be shown in the accounts

- It is a list of assets that should be physically verified, and gives their normal location

Task 1.11

a) One of the partners of Ace Cars
b) Over £500

Chief Assessor's comment. The Chief Assessor makes the important point that you have to answer the question in the context of the specific question rather than any general rules. You might think that £50,000 is in a general sense a good figure to start capitalising assets, but in this question it was clear that the capitalisation figure was under £50,000 'because the vehicle costs were shown' (ie capitalised). Students need to answer this type of question in the context which is given.

SECTION 2

Task 2.1

	£
Total from listing of balances	2,990
Adjustment for a) – add	83 (W1)
Adjustment for b) – subtract (175 – 157)	(18)
Adjustment for c) – subtract	(50) (W2)
Adjustment for d) – subtract	(30) (W3)
Revised total to agree with sales ledger control account	2,975

Workings

1) If a balance is omitted from the list, you simply have to add it to the list – no changes are needed to the actual accounting records.

2) The incorrect entry made was:

Customer account			
	£		£
Balance b/f	X		
Credit note	25		

The correct entry should have been:

Customer account			
	£		£
Balance b/f	X	Credit note	25

To correct this you have to both:

- Remove the incorrect debit ie reduce the listing total by £25; and

- Put in the correct credit ie reduce the listing total by another £25 (remember that the listing total is the total of Debits)

The effect is to reduce the list of balances by 2 x £25 = £50

3) The discount should have been accounted for as follows.

Customer account

	£		£
Balance b/f	X	Credit allowed	30

This entry has been omitted. When it is made it is a credit entry and it will reduce the list of balances by £30.

Task 2.2

MEMO

To: Rita Bunn   **Subject:**   Sales ledger reconciliation
From: Accounting Technician   **Date:**   6 December 2006

Thank you for asking me about the sales ledger reconciliation.

The sales ledger is the collection of accounts that keep track of our credit sales to customers by recording invoices for sales and any payments that the customer makes, plus any credit notes and discounts that apply. It is sometimes referred to as the 'debtors ledger' or the 'subsidiary sales ledger'. The sales ledger is not part of the double entry.

The double entry is made through the sales ledger control account by posting the totals of invoices, payments, credit notes etc for a period. The purpose of the control account is to control and act as a check on the entries made in the sales ledger.

The total invoices etc for a period that are posted to the control account should be the same as the total of the individual invoices etc that are posted to the sales ledger. If they are, then the balance on the control account should be the same as the sum of the individual balances in the sales ledger. If the balances do not agree then errors must have been made in the accounting entries.

This comparison of the two balances provide a very good control or check on the accuracy of the accounting entries.

Task 2.3

JOURNAL

		DR	CR
		£	£
a)	Prepayments – paid for period after year end	900	
	Rent		900
b)	Provision for doubtful debts account (W1)	31	
	Adjustment to provision for doubtful debts		31
c)	Loan interest (W2)	15	
	Accruals		15
d)	Closing stock (balance sheet) (4,238 – 138)	4,100	
	Closing stock (profit and loss a/c)		4,100
e)	Sales (W3)	275	
	Fixed asset disposals		275
	Fixed asset disposals (W4)	500	
	Equipment at cost		500
	Equipment accumulated depreciation (W4)	300	
	Fixed asset disposals		300

Workings

		£
1)	Adjusted provision for doubtful debts £2,975 x 0.04	119
	Existing provision for doubtful debts	150
	Reduction in provision	31
2)	Loan interest – charge to profit and loss £2,500 x 0.072	180
	Loan interest currently charged in accounts	165
	Accrual	15

3) The correct entry should have been to debit the bank and credit the fixed asset disposal account, not credit the sales account.

4) The fixed asset disposal account will be:

Fixed asset disposal account

	£		£
Equipment at acost	500	Equipment accumulateds dep'n	300
Profit on disposal	75	Bank (sales proceeds)	275)
	575		575

Accumulated depreciation

Full year's depreciation for 2003, 2004 and 2005 = 3 x (£500 x 20%) = 3 x £100 = £300

Chief Assessor's comment. Although the disposal of a fixed asset is nearly always included in the exam, many students still do not know the correct entries. Make sure you do.

503

Tasks 2.4 and 2.5

IMPACT
Extended trial balance as at 30 September 2006

	Ledger balances		Adjustments		Profit and loss account		Balance sheet	
	Dr	Cr	Dr	Cr	Dr	Cr	Dr	Cr
Bank		1,100						1,100
Capital		7,500						7,500
Cash	150						150	
Depreciation expense	900				900			
Drawings	15,000						15,000	
Equipment at cost	5,000			500			4,500	
Equipment accumulated depreciation		1,900	300					1,600
General expenses	3,700				3,700			
Loans		2,500						2,500
Loan interest	165		15		180			
Opening stock	3,320				3,320			
Provision for doubtful debts		150	31					119
Purchases	24,700				24,700			
Rent	4,500		275	900	3,600			
Sales		47,260		900		46,985		
Sales ledger control a/c	2,975						2,975	
Accruals				15				15
Prepayments			900				900	
Closing stock – BS			4,100				4,100	
Closing stock – P and L				4,100		4,100		
Adjustment to provision for doubtful debts				31		31		
Disposal of fixed assets			500	300		75		
				275				
Net profit for the year					14,791			14,791
Total	60,410	60,410	6,121	6,121	51,191	51,191	27,625	27,625

Task 2.6

IMPACT
Profit and loss account for the year ended 30 September 2006

	£	£
Sales		46,985
Opening stock	3,320	
Purchases	24,700	
Closing stock	(4,100)	
Cost of goods sold		(23,920)
Gross profit		23,065
Depreciation	900	
General expenses	3,700	
Loan interest	180	
Rent	3,600	
Adjustment to provision for doubtful debts	(31)	
Profit on disposal of fixed assets	(75)	
		(8,274)
Net profit		14,791

Task 2.7

a) Any two from

  Cash
  Stock
  Debtors
  Prepayments

  (**Note.** Bank might normally be a current asset, but in this case the business is overdrawn so the bank balance is a credit balance and is not an asset.)

b) Capital

  Drawings are a debit balance but that does not make them an asset – they reduce the value of the capital.

AAT

PRACTICE EXAM 4

EBONY GEE

ANSWERS

SECTION 1

Task 1.1

Rent

	£		£
Balance b/d (prepayment)	1,100	Profit and loss account	4,800
Cash	4,900	Balance c/d (prepayment)	1,200
	6,000		6,000

Rent for year ending 31 March 2007 = £4,800

Tutorial note. Take care with the opening and closing prepayments. A prepayment is an asset and is therefore brought down as a debit balance.

Task 1.2

Selling expenses

	£		£
Cash	2,395	Balance b/d (accrual)	205
Balance c/d (accrual) (W)	260	Profit and loss account	2,450
	2,655		2,655

Selling expenses for year ending 31 March 200 = £2,450

Working

Closing accrual = 2/3 x £390
             = £260

Tutorial note. Make sure that if you calculate any figure that you show your workings and cross reference these workings to your answer. The examiner's comments constantly complain about the lack of workings and how credit cannot be given for incorrect answers if the workings are not shown.

Task 1.3

Capital

	£		£
Balance c/d	15,157	Balance b/d	5,157
		Capital introduced	10,000
	15,157		15,157

Task 1.4

a) Net book value

	£
Cost	1,200
Depreciation to 31 March 2005 (1,200 x 35%)	(420)
NBV at 31 March 2005	780
Depreciation to 31 March 2006 (780 x 35%)	(273)
Net book value at 31 March 2006	507

Tutorial note. Read the accounting policy carefully. There is a full year of depreciation in the year of acquisition but none in the year of disposal so only two years' depreciation needs to be deducted.

b)

Disposals

	£		£
Equipment at cost	1,200	Acc depn (420 + 273)	693
		Part exchange allowance	300
	1,200	Loss on disposal	207
			1,200

Task 1.5

a) **Cost of equipment purchased**

	£
Bank	1,700
Part exchange allowance	300
	2,000

Tutorial note. It is important to appreciate the double entry for a part exchange allowance:

Debit   Fixed assets at cost
Credit   Disposals

Not only is the part exchange allowance effectively the proceeds for the old asset but also part of the cost of the new asset which therefore must be added to the cash cost of any new fixed assets.

b) **Revised total equipment cost**

	£
Opening balance	3,100
Less: disposal at cost	(1,200)
Add: new equipment (part a))	2,000
	3,900

c) **Depreciation charge for year ended 31 March 2007**

	£
Opening accumulated depreciation	1,593
Less: accumulated depreciation on asset disposed of (Task 1.4)	(693)
Revised accumulated depreciation	900
Cost of equipment (part b)	3,900
Less: accumulated depreciation	(900)
Net book value	3,000
Depreciation charge 35% x 3,000	1,050

Chief Assessor's comment: In many cases the answers to this part of the task were very muddled. You must remember that the accounting policy is reducing balance depreciation therefore the charge for the year must be based upon net book value and not cost. When there have been acquisitions and disposals, you have to calculate the net book value of the assets remaining at the year end. You deduct the accumulated depreciation (adjusted for any disposals) from the cost (adjusted for any acquisitions and disposals).

d) **Accumulated depreciation at 31 March 2007**

	£
Revised opening accumulated depreciation (part c))	900
Charge for the year (part c))	1,050
	1,950

Task 1.6

	£
Stock for sale	1,980
Stock in transit	120
Closing stock	2,100

Tutorial note. According to SSAP 9 stock must be valued at the lower of cost and net realisable value. In this instance cost is lower than net realisable value. However that was not all that was being tested in this task. The other principle being tested here was "cut-off" at the stock take. The items that had been sold already must not be included in the stock figure as they are already included in sales. However the stock in transit has been purchased but is not included in the stock that was counted and therefore must be added in.

Task 1.7

<table>
<tr><th colspan="3">Ebony Gee
Trial balance as at 31 March 2007</th></tr>
<tr><th></th><th>DR
£</th><th>CR
£</th></tr>
<tr><td>Rent (Task 1.1)</td><td>4,800</td><td></td></tr>
<tr><td>Prepayment (Task 1.1)</td><td>1,200</td><td></td></tr>
<tr><td>Selling expenses (Task 1.2)</td><td>2,450</td><td></td></tr>
<tr><td>Accrual (Task 1.2)</td><td></td><td>260</td></tr>
<tr><td>Purchases</td><td>26,300</td><td></td></tr>
<tr><td>Postage and packing expenses</td><td>4,200</td><td></td></tr>
<tr><td>Payroll expenses</td><td>18,000</td><td></td></tr>
<tr><td>Office expenses</td><td>3,600</td><td></td></tr>
<tr><td>Equipment at cost (Task 1.5)</td><td>3,900</td><td></td></tr>
<tr><td>Accumulated depreciation (Task 1.5)</td><td></td><td>1,950</td></tr>
<tr><td>Drawings</td><td>6,000</td><td></td></tr>
<tr><td>Sales</td><td></td><td>55,000</td></tr>
<tr><td>Capital</td><td></td><td>15,157</td></tr>
<tr><td>Bank</td><td></td><td>1,090</td></tr>
<tr><td>Closing stock (Task 1.6) – balance sheet</td><td>2,100</td><td></td></tr>
<tr><td>Closing stock (Task 1.6) – profit and loss account</td><td></td><td>2,100</td></tr>
<tr><td>Opening stock</td><td>1,750</td><td></td></tr>
<tr><td>Depreciation expense</td><td>1,050</td><td></td></tr>
<tr><td>Loss on disposal</td><td>207</td><td></td></tr>
<tr><td></td><td>75,557</td><td>75,557</td></tr>
</table>

Tutorial note. You need a careful and logical approach to this task to ensure that you get a correct trial balance. Work carefully through all the information given in the initial case study listing any balances that are relevant. Make sure that you use the closing figures for accruals, prepayments and bank rather than the opening figures. Then work through each of the tasks you have completed, listing any further balances that have been calculated or revised. Take care with the closing bank balance as this is in fact an overdraft balance and therefore must be on the credit side of the trial balance.

Chief Assessor's comments. The Chief Assessor commented that when candidates had a trial balance that did not actually balance, credit was given for the use of a suspense account in order to make it balance.

Task 1.8

From: accounting.technician@harper.co.uk
To: paul.chin@harper.co.uk
Date: 14 June 2007
Subject: Depreciation

When fixed assets are purchased by the business the intention is that they will be used throughout their useful lives to make profits within the business. Therefore they are a long term asset of the business. As such their cost is taken to the balance sheet as a fixed asset rather than being charged immediately to the profit and loss account.

However these fixed assets are being used every year and as such some of their cost is being used up by the business in the process of making sales and profits. The using up of this cost is reflected by the annual depreciation charge to the profit and loss account based upon the cost or net book value of the fixed assets. Depreciation is the method of spreading the cost of the fixed assets over their useful life to the business.

The accruals concept says that charges should be made to the profit and loss account for expenses **incurred** during a period rather than those that are actually paid for during the period.

The annual depreciation charge is an example of the accruals concept in that it is charging some of the cost of the fixed assets used within the business during the period to the profit and loss account even though these assets were purchased and paid for in earlier periods.

Tutorial note: It is important that you understand that the purpose of depreciation is to charge the cost of the fixed assets to the profit and loss account over their useful lives. The purpose of depreciation is not to show the market value or other realisable value of the fixed assets in the balance sheet.

Task 1.9

Going concern

Tutorial note. The going concern assumption underlies the preparation of financial statements for a business. It is an assumption that the business will continue for the foreseeable future. However if a business makes continued losses year in year out then this may not be a valid assumption as the business may have to be ended.

SECTION 2

Task 2.1

JOURNAL

		DR £	CR £
a)	Rent	7,500	
	General expenses		7,500
b)	Suspense	80,000	
	Capital – Pat		80,000

Tutorial note. In this instance only one entry has been made – to the bank account. Therefore the other entry, credit to Pat's capital account, must be journalled, leaving the final debit to go to the suspense account.

c)	Wages	2,300	
	Suspense		2,300

Tutorial note. The credit entry to the accruals account is correct, however the other side of the entry should have been a debit to the wages account. Instead the wages account was also credited with £1,150. In order to remove this credit and add in a debit of £1,150 the wages account must be debited with £2,300 and the other side of the entry is to the suspense account.

d)	Depreciation expense	9,000	
	Equipment accumulated depreciation		9,000
e)	VAT	420	
	Suspense	420	
	Purchases		420
	Purchases ledger control account		420

Tutorial note. The easiest way to deal with this problem is to firstly correct each individual posting:

■ VAT has not been posted at all, therefore a debit to the VAT account

■ Purchases have been debited with the gross rather than net amount so this needs to be reduced to £2,400 by crediting purchases with £420

■ Purchases ledger control account has been credited with the net rather than the gross amount therefore this needs to be increased to £2,820 by crediting purchases ledger control with £420.

Finally, the remaining amount to make the journal balance is a debit of £420 which must go to the suspense account.

Alternatively, you can write what should have been posted next to what was posted and the differences will be clear.

	Incorrect posting		Correct posting	
	DR	CR	DR	CR
	£	£	£	£
Purchases	2,820		2,400	
Purchases ledger control account		2,400		2,820
VAT			420	

The journal corrects these differences and the balancing figure goes to the suspense account.

Task 2.2

JADON
Profit and loss account for the year ended 30 April 2007

	£	£
Sales		365,000
Opening stock	1,900	
Purchases (124,920 – 420)	124,500	
Closing stock	(2,200)	
Cost of goods sold		124,200
Gross profit		240,800
Wages (51,238 + 2,300)	53,538	
Rent (22,500 + 7,500)	30,000	
General expenses (19,500 – 7,500)	12,000	
Depreciation (vehicles and equipment) (14,062 + 9,000)	23,062	
		118,600
Net profit		122,200

Tutorial note. You need to make sure that you include the journal adjustments made in Task 2.1 where relevant in the profit and loss account figures.

Chief Assessor's comment. Even though a workings column was given many candidates did not use it. If a figure is incorrect the marker cannot give any credit if there are no workings to show how that figure was derived.

Task 2.3

Capital accounts

	Ade £	Jon £	Pat £		Ade £	Jon £	Pat £
Goodwill eliminated	60,000	60,000	30,000	Balance b/d as at 1 May 2006	30,000	35,000	
Balance c/d	45,000	50,000	50,000	Goodwill introduced	75,000	75,000	
				Bank			80,000
	105,000	110,000	80,000		105,000	110,000	80,000

Working – Goodwill

			£
Goodwill introduced	DR	Goodwill	150,000
	CR	Ade	75,000
		Jon	75,000
Goodwill eliminated	DR	Ade 40%	60,000
		Jon 40%	60,000
		Pat 20%	30,000
	CR	Goodwill	150,000

Task 2.4

Interest on capital

	1 May 2006 to 31 January 2007 £	1 February 2007 to 30 April 2007 £	Total £
Ade	1,350	675	2,025
Jon	1,575	750	2,325
Pat	–	750	750

Working – interest on capital

Ade	£30,000 x 6% x 9/12 = £1,350
	£45,000 x 6% x 3/12 = £675
Jon	£35,000 x 6% x 9/12 = £1,575
	£50,000 x 6% x 3/12 = £750
Pat	£50,000 x 6% x 3/12 = £750

Tutorial note. You must read the information given carefully and appreciate that you have to time apportion the interest according to the capital balance for each month of the year.

Task 2.5

JADON
Appropriation account for the year ended 30 April 2007

Interest on capital

	1 May 2006 to 31 January 2007 £	1 February 2007 to 30 April 2007 £	Total £
Net profit			
(122,200 x 9/12)	91,650		
(122,200 x 3/12)		30,550	122,200
Salaries:			
Ade			
(10,900 x 9/12)	(8,175)		
(10,900 x 3/12)		(2,725)	(10,900)
Jon			
(15,000 x 9/12)	(11,250)		
(15,000 x 3/12)		(3,750)	(15,000)
Pat		(6,600)	(6,600)
Interest on capital:			
Ade (task 2.4)	(1,350)	(675)	(2,025)
Jon (task 2.4)	(1,575)	(750)	(2,325)
Pat (task 2.4)		(750)	(750)
Profit available for distribution	69,300	15,300	84,600
Profit share:			
Ade			
(50% x 69,300)	(34,650)		
(40% x 15,300)		(6,120)	(40,770)
Jon			
(50% x 69,300)	(34,650)		
(40% x 15,300)		(6,120)	(40,770)
Pat			
(20% x 15,300)		(3,060)	(3,060)
Balance	–	–	–

Task 2.6

Capital accounts

	Ade £	Jon £	Pat £		Ade £	Jon £	Pat £
Drawings	60,000	60,000	7,500	Balance b/d as			
Balance c/d	495	1,195	2,910	at 1 May 2006	6,800	3,100	
				Salaries	10,900	15,000	6,600
				Int on capital			
	60,495	61,195	10,410	(Task 2.4)	2,025	2,325	750
				Profit share			
				(Task 2.5)	40,770	40,770	3,060
					60,495	61,195	10,410

Task 2.7

a) Capital
b) Assets

Tutorial note. The partners' current account balances would be listed in the balance sheet just below their capital account balances, forming a part of the total capital.

Task 2.8

The suspense account

Tutorial note. Once the journal entries to correct the errors have been put through, the balance on the suspense account should be zero. Therefore after putting through the journal entries the suspense account should be checked to make sure that it does have a zero balance. If there is still a balance on the suspense account this means that there are more errors/omissions which should be discovered and amended before the financial statements are prepared.

AAT

PRACTICE EXAM 5

PL TRADING

ANSWERS

SECTION 1

Task 1.1

Purchases ledger control account

	£		£
Cash paid	251,870	b/d	36,800
Discounts received	**2,130**	Purchases day book	258,500
c/f	41,300		
	295,300		295,300

Task 1.2

a)

Rent

	£		£
Cash paid	15,000	b/d	1,000
		Rent for year ended	
		31 October 2007	**12,000**
		c/d (3,000 x 2/3)	2,000
	15,000		15,000

b)   Matching, or accruals

Task 1.3

a)   General expenses = £27,824 x 40/47
           = £23,680

b)   VAT on general expenses = £27,824 x 7/47
                     = £4,144

Task 1.4

VAT

	£		£
Input tax on purchases	38,500	b/d	5,300
Input tax on general expenses	4,144	Output tax	63,175
Cash paid	20,575		
c/d	5,256		
	68,475		68,475

Task 1.5

a) Depreciation on vehicles = £40,000 x 25%
= £10,000

b) Updated accumulated depreciation = £15,000 + £10,000
= £25,000

Task 1.6

	£	%
Sales value of closing stock	22,750	140
Cost = closing stock for TB	16,250	100
Mark-up	6,500	40

Task 1.7

	£
Purchases figure from PDB	220,000
Less: Pat's drawings	(1,200)
Adjusted purchases figures for TB	218,800

Current accounts

	Pat £	Lee £		Pat £	Lee £
Drawings	30,000	24,000	31 October 2006		
Stock drawings	1,200		Balance b/d	750	1,050
			Interest 40,000 x 5%	2,000	
			Interest 32,000 x 5%		1,600
			Balance c/d	28,450	21,350
	31,200	24,000		31,200	24,000

b)   Total figure for interest on capital: £3,600 DR on TB.

Task 1.9

PL Trading Trial Balance as at 31 October 2007		
	DR £	CR £
Trade debtors	68,400	
Trade creditors (purchases ledger control account)		41,300
Capital – Pat		40,000
Capital – Lee		32,000
Bank	22,206	
Discounts received		2,130
Payroll expenses	38,500	
Rent	12,000	
General expenses	23,680	
VAT		5,256
Depreciation charge	10,000	
Vehicles at cost	40,000	
Vehicles accumulated depreciation		25,000
Opening stock	17,700	
Closing stock – balance sheet	16,250	
Closing stock – profit and loss account		16,250
Purchases	218,800	
Sales		361,000
Current account – Pat	28,450	
Current account – Lee	21,350	
Interest on capital	3,600	
Prepayment	2,000	
Total	522,936	522,936

for closing stock must be included in the final account so that the cost of stock held at the f the period, and therefore to be used in the subsequent period, is not deducted from the t for the year but is carried forward as a current asset on the balance sheet. SSAP 9 *Stocks and g-term contracts* states that closing stock should be valued at the lower of its cost (that is cost to ring the stock into its current condition, including delivery cost) and its net realisable value (the amount that can be obtained for the stock, less selling costs). When the stock cost is determined either on an actual basis, or on the bases of FIFO (first in first out) or AVCO (average cost), then SSAP 9 is being applied.

b)   Profit would be overstated.

SECTION 2

Task 2.1

a)

Sam James – Trial Balance as at 30 September 2007				
	Ledger balances			
	DR £	CR £	DR £	CR £
Administration expenses	8,700			
Bank	3,532			
Capital account		20,000		
Cash	250			
Closing stock – balance sheet	4,890			
Closing stock – profit and loss account		4,890		
Drawings	24,000			
Equipment at cost	15,800			
Equipment accumulated depreciation		12,496		826
Opening stock	4,250			
Purchases	89,440		790	
Purchases ledger control account		8,700		
Rent	8,000			790
Sales		146,520		400
Sales ledger control account	5,600			
Vehicles at cost	22,000		3,500	12,000
Vehicles accumulated depreciation		5,856	5,856	3,375
Wages	12,000			
Depreciation charge			3,375	
			826	
Loss on disposal			2,644	
Bad debt expense			400	
			104	
Doubtful debt provision				104
TOTAL	198,462	198,462		

525

	£
nt at cost	15,800
ent accumulated depreciation	(12,496)
	3,304 @ 25% = £826 depreciation

Disposal account

	£		£
Cost	12,000	Acc. depreciation	
		(12,000 – 6,144)	5,856
		Vehicles cost	3,500
		Loan on disposal	2,644
	12,000		12,000

d) Depreciation on new vehicle = £(10,000 + 3,500) x 25%
= £3,375

e) Provision for doubtful debts = £(5,600 – 400) x 2%
= £104

Task 2.2

SAM JAMES
Profit and loss account for year ended 30 September 2007

	£	£
Sales		147,310
Less: cost of sales		
opening stock	4,250	
purchases	90,230	
less: closing stock	(4,890)	
		(89,590)
Gross profit		57,720
Less: expenses		
administration expenses	8,700	
rent	8,000	
wages	12,000	
depreciation charge	4,201	
loss on disposal	2,644	
bad and doubtful debt expense	504	
		(36,049)
Net profit		21,671

Task 2.3

SAM JAMES
Balance sheet at 30 September 2007

	Cost £	Account depreciation £	£
Fixed assets			
Equipment	15,800	13,322	2,478
Vehicles	13,500	3,375	10,125
	29,300	16,697	12,603
Current assets			
Stock		4,890	
Trade debtors		5,200	
(Less: provision for doubtful debts)		(104)	
Cash at bank		3,532	
Cash in hand		250	
		13,768	
Current liabilities			
Trade creditors		(8,700)	
			5,068
			17,671

	£
Capital account	20,000
Drawings	(24,000)
Profit for the year	21,671
	17,671

Task 2.4

a)   Administration expenses are treated as revenue items and are written off immediately in the profit and loss account of the year in which they are incurred. Equipment is treated as capital expenditure which is shown on the balance sheet of the enterprise, less accumulated depreciation. Each year an amount of depreciation is calculated for each item, and this is charged to the profit and loss account. The effect of this treatment is that the cost of capital items is written off to the profit and loss account over the number of years in which the item is used in the business.

b)   Information would be needed on the exact nature of each item, its cost (small amounts of capital expenditure are usually treated as revenue expenditure), the number of years which Sam believes the items will be used for, and the estimated price it will fetch at the end of its useful life when it is sold.

c)   This information could be obtained from Sam James and from the invoices he received when he paid for the items.

d)   Administration expenses
     Equipment at cost
     Equipment accumulated depreciation
     Depreciation charge

527